ISLAM'S BLACK SLAVES

ISLAM'S
BLACK SLAVES

THE OTHER BLACK DIASPORA

RONALD SEGAL

FARRAR, STRAUS AND GIROUX

NEW YORK

Farrar, Straus and Giroux
19 Union Square West, New York 10003

Distributed in Canada by Douglas & McIntyre Ltd.
Printed in the United States of America
First edition, 2001

Library of Congress Cataloging-in-Publication Data
Segal, Ronald, 1932–
    Islam's Black slaves: the other Black diaspora/Ronald Segal. — 1st ed.
        p.   cm.
    Includes index.
    ISBN 0-374-22774-8 (hardcover)
        1. Slavery and Islam — History.   2. Slavery — Islamic countries — History.
    3. African diaspora.   I. Title.
    HT919.S45 2001
    306.3'62'0917671 — dc21

                                                    00-062256

Designed by Jonathan D. Lippincott

Permissions appear on page 261–62.

*For Martha, Daniel, Benedict, and Charlotte —
in descending chronological order, my grandchildren*

CONTENTS

Preface   ix

ONE: Contrasts   3

TWO: Out of Arabia   13

THREE: Imperial Islam   23

FOUR: The Practice of Slavery   35

FIVE: The Farther Reaches   67

China   67

India   71

Spain   76

SIX: Into Black Africa   89

SEVEN: The Ottoman Empire   103

EIGHT: The "Heretic" State: Iran   119

NINE: The Libyan Connection   129

TEN: The Terrible Century   145

East Africa   145

The Sudanic States and Sahara   162

ELEVEN: Colonial Translations   177

Northern Nigeria   178

French Soudan   180

Mauritania   183

Somalia   187

Zanzibar and the Kenyan Coast   190

TWELVE: Survivals of Slavery   199

Mauritania   204

Sudan   213

EPILOGUE: America's Black Muslim Backlash   225

Notes   243

Index   263

PREFACE

My previous book, *The Black Diaspora: Five Centuries of the Black Experience Outside Africa*, dealt with the emergence, development, and character of the black communities engendered by the Atlantic slave trade. As I wrote in the Preface: "The subject of the book excludes the substantial trade in slaves for the Islamic world. The story of what happened to those blacks, I decided early on, would have to be told in another book. The subject I had marked off for myself was enough."

At the time, I had not the slightest intention of undertaking that other book. I had no connections with the Islamic world the way I had—in environment, culture, language, and political commitment—a base camp from which to explore the subject of *The Black Diaspora*.

Some reviewers, generous in their comments on that book, nonetheless expressed regret that I had not dealt with the Islamic trade in black slaves. Prodded to explore the subject, I initially found more difficulties than encouragement. For *The Black Diaspora*, the problem had been the very profusion of material; for this book, it was one of apparent paucity. In Islam slavery was never the moral, political, and economic issue that it was in the West, where it engendered a multitude of tracts and books in denunciation or defense of the institution, and promoted racial attitudes that profoundly affected the development of Western societies.

As I persisted, however, the material on slavery in Islam proved to be richer, and the research more rewarding. There are revealing accounts, if sometimes scarcely more than asides, on aspects of the Islamic trade and the character of slavery at particular times in particular places. By the light of recent scholarship, it is possible to move beyond mere groping in the dark. Now and then, one reference led to another, in a trail of discovery. The search for clues quickly became an adventure, and I hope that the reader will share at least some of the excitement that the writing of this book has given me.

The use of Arabic words presents a problem. Various marks, whose character or positioning relate mainly to pronunciation and stresses, were not part of my equipment. I decided that it would be more dangerous to attempt acquiring a little knowledge than to accept and admit my own ignorance in such matters. I have accordingly taken the prudent path of copying the marks as I find them, except for names of cities and dynasties that are widely known in their Anglicized forms. For any inconsistencies and errors, I apologize.

Another problem is presented by the use of the word "Sudan"—blacks—both for the northern belt of black Africa and for the particular country of that name. I thought of distinguishing the first by using the French "Soudan," but this presented a different problem, of inconsistent spellings in quoted passages. In the end I decided to use, as far as possible, "the Sudan," with the adjective "Sudanic," for the northern belt; "Sudan," without a preceding "the," and "Sudanese," for the country and its inhabitants. I hope the context will indicate which area is meant.

This is not a book about Islam, though Islam is crucial to the subject. I am an essential humanist, but I am also so awed by the cosmos as not to exclude any possibility of how or why it was created, except the particular divinity projected by one or other of the established religions. But I am no more dismissive of the human achievements we owe to Islam than I am of those we owe to Judaism, of whose heritage and history I am partly a product. It is rational to recognize what the developing culture of a particular religion has done for human progress, as well as all that it has impeded.

Christian societies were responsible for an engagement to slavery in its most hideous, dehumanizing form. Yet it was Christians who led the campaign to abolish the slave trade and then slavery itself. Islam has been, by specific spiritual precept and in common practice, relatively humane in its treatment of slaves and its readiness to free them, even though individual Muslims have been among the most ferocious slavers in history. It is necessary to record this as a warning against demonizing either religion, along with its collective adherents.

Nor is this a book about what is coming to be called the "new slavery," applied to a form of captivity such as bonded labor through debt or through the survival of feudal practices, especially repugnant in its entrapment and exploitation of children. This captivity exists within certain Islamic societies—in Pakistan, for instance—and elsewhere too, as in India. But it is not slavery in the strict sense of the term, as the legal ownership of one person by another.

Islam's Black Slaves is designed as a companion volume to *The Black Diaspora*, which set out to tell the story of blacks in the western hemisphere, from the Atlantic slave trade to the black peoples and communities, with their creative heritage, that exist today. Accordingly, it does not deal just with the nature and experience of black slavery in Islam—a phenomenon deplorably not yet at an end—but with the paradox of a black diaspora whose very existence is denied, though it survives in substantial numbers, and whose creative achievements have been no less real for the failure or refusal to recognize them.

Without the help and patience of Mike Christian and Paul James, I would have continued avoiding or soon abandoned the use of a computer, and I would still be writing this book. I owe an enormous debt to the various scholars whose names and works are cited in the notes; especially to Christopher Fyfe, who read drafts of the book, to provide invaluable comments and suggestions; and to Basil Davidson, that eminent and influential historian of Africa, who guided me in some of my research. To my American publishers, I must pay more than a ceremonial tribute. Without the support of Roger Straus, *Islam's Black Slaves* would simply never have reached beyond the contemplative stage. John Glusman, my editor, has given the same lucid and constructive attention to this book as he did to its predecessor. His assistant, Aodaoin O'Floinn, has always cheerfully responded to any request for help. Peggy Miller has been, as before, all that one expects from a dear friend.

ISLAM'S BLACK SLAVES

ONE

CONTRASTS

Both Christianity and Islam asserted the unique value of the individual human being, as created by God for His special purposes. Yet, for their own special purposes, Christian and Muslim societies long sanctioned the capture, sale, ownership, and use of men, women, and children from black Africa. We can never know the extent of the human cost. It is certain that many millions lost their lives in the warfare and raiding that provided the captives for slavery. Millions more died in the process of collection, initial transport, and storage.

The statistics connected with the West's so-called Atlantic Trade, of the slaves who were loaded onto boats and of the survivors who landed in the Americas, have been comprehensively researched. Total numbers are now widely accepted as subject to no more than relatively minor adjustment in the light of new evidence. Much, too, is known of mortality rates—from overwork, undernourishment, and brutal discipline—in the slave-labor force. The Atlantic Trade and the plantation economies it fed became such a highly developed and organized business that ledgers recording the details were commonly kept.

The Islamic Trade was conducted on a different scale and with a different impact. Unlike the Atlantic Trade, which began late and grew intensively, it had begun some eight centuries earlier and, except at certain periods, it involved lower average annual volumes. The social and cultural importance of slavery itself was greater than its economic one. Certainly, bankers and merchants, as individual investors or in partnership enterprises, were prominently engaged, but only sparse records of their related accountancy survive. There were also numerous small-scale dealers, with stocks of a few slaves each, who were likely to have kept any accounts in their heads.

Crucially informing the difference between the two trades was the economic system involved in each. Historians dispute the degree to which the Atlantic Trade promoted the development of Western capitalism and its industrial revolution, primarily in the eighteenth century. But there can be no doubt of the connection between them. The evidence is plentiful that some of the huge profits engendered by the trade were invested in the development of industry, and also that much industry developed in order to supply the trade goods required for the procurement of slaves in black Africa. Not least, from the predominant use to which slaves were put, there developed a view of slaves as essentially units of labor in a productive process that disregarded or denied their personality.

Slavery in Islam was very different. A system of plantation labor, much like that which would emerge in the Americas, developed early on, but with such dire consequences that subsequent engagements were relatively rare and reduced. Moreover, the need for agricultural labor, in an Islam with large peasant populations, was nowhere near as acute as in the Americas, where in some West European colonies, conquest had led to the virtual extermination of the indigenous peoples from new diseases and forced labor.

Slaves in Islam were directed mainly at the service sector—concubines and cooks, porters and soldiers—with slavery itself primarily a form of consumption rather than a factor of production. The most telling evidence of this is found in the gender ratio. The Atlantic Trade shipped overall roughly two males for every female. Among black slaves traded in Islam across the centuries, there were roughly two females to every male.

The difference between the two trades was related to the very nature of the state in Islam, as distinct from that in Western Christendom. Indeed, the term "Christendom"—though still useful as a defining difference—effectively became an anachronism for states whose religious allegiances increasingly gave place to national preoccupations and the secular employment of power. In Islam the state itself was essentially an extension of the religion, without legitimacy or corresponding allegiance beyond this. Even in the one arguable exception of Iran, whose historical Persian identity confronted Arab linguistic and political dominance, the independence it successfully asserted was based on a rival view of the legitimate succession to leadership of the entire Islamic community.

To a degree unmatched by the various states of Western Christendom, for all the conflict between Protestant and Catholic, the nature of society in Islam was informed by reference to the divine will, as communicated in the Koran. And the Koran dealt in some detail with slaves. That pretensions to piety might coexist with disregard for the spirit and even the letter of such details did not preclude their overall influence. Slaves were to be regarded and treated as people, not simply as possessions.

This is not to romanticize their condition. A slave was a slave for all that. Owners were endowed with such power over their slaves that few can have failed to abuse it, more often in trivial but still humiliating, and sometimes in brutal, ways. Even masters persuaded of their own piety and benevolence sexually exploited their concubines, without a thought of whether this constituted a violation of their humanity. In the provision of eunuchs, indeed, Islamic slavery was scarcely more compassionate than its Western counterpart; and those who purchased them were the accomplices of those who provided them. Yet the treatment of slaves in Islam was overall more benign, in part because the values and attitudes promoted by religion inhibited the very development of a Western-style capitalism, with its effective subjugation of people to the priority of profit. So crucial was the religious dynamic to Islamic society that those who served the faith, by scholarship or soldiering, enjoyed greater prestige than those who grew rich by economic enterprise. While trade was accepted as necessary and useful, enrichment by speculation, or by any other pursuits construed to be in conflict with the welfare of the community, was not only regarded with suspicion but might be severely penalized.

Since enrichment brought such obvious rewards, from the purchase of pleasures to the means of exercising or extending power, there were inevitably those more attracted to amassing riches than to devout self-denials whose rewards in another world required death as well as delay. In the business of this world, the advantages of enterprise were widely recognized. But the conditions for related capital accumulation on a socially transforming scale were largely absent.

It was no accident that in the Ottoman Empire, for instance, charitable foundations were a prime source of investment capital but spent most of their income on building mosques, establishing or subsidizing schools, and contributing to social welfare; that wealth so often went into the purchase of property rather than into productive assets; and that foreign goods were permitted to compete so damagingly with domestic production because their relative cheapness served the needs of the poor in the community.

Of some significance, too, was the absence of primogeniture as the principle of inheritance. The distribution of estates among the family members of the deceased, in conformity with Koranic precepts, might well have been both fair and compassionate. In contrast to the practice of primogeniture in the West, however, it did little to secure the concentration of wealth and its related investment. Moreover, Muslims tended to respect the prohibition of usury in the Old Testament, while in the West, Jews, often barred from other forms of economic enterprise, and increasingly Christians, tended to ignore it. In short, far from pursuing the development of an economic system that promoted the depersonalization of slave labor, Islamic influence was responsible for impeding it.

Such influence also successfully confronted the emergence of racism as a form of institutionalized discrimination, because the Koran expressly condemned racism along with tribalism and nationalism. In the West, economic enterprise and the advance of the secular state promoted each other, to mock such spiritual messages as that the meek should inherit the earth. The slave system was so incompatible not only with the teachings of Christianity but with the decent sensibilities of the less devout that they required some rationalization to sustain them. The Bible was scrutinized to find support, however specious, for a divine curse on blacks; and science was perverted to support a biological case for their enslavement.

Christianity did come to play a crucial part in the opposition led by

Britain, first to the slave trade and then to slavery itself. Most of the leading abolitionists took the teachings of their religion seriously. Yet it is doubtful that they would have succeeded without support from industrial capitalists. The workshop of the world had outgrown the value of slave-labor colonies whose land, exploited to relative impoverishment, now produced high-cost sugar, while other slave-labor colonies produced an abundance of low-cost sugar from still richly productive land.

The cry for "free trade" was also one for a level competitiveness of "free labor" that would enable Britain to sustain her industrial leadership and extend its scope to new markets, including an Africa rescued from pillage for the achievement of such prosperity as would afford a much greater demand for British goods. By the time this combination of moral and economic campaigns captured the state, so that British financial, diplomatic, and naval power came to be deployed in their cause, the days of the Atlantic slave trade and then of slavery itself in the West were numbered.

Yet racism vigorously survived the end of slavery. If old habits die hard, racism would already have been old enough to take an unconscionable time dying. But there were reasons why it thrived rather than declined. The colonial powers, engaged in extending their rule across most of the world, found a pretext in the concept of "the white man's burden," with its corresponding presumption of the cultural and even biological inferiority of blacks and others of color.

Within the metropolitan societies, there were many whites at the lower social levels who found comfort or consolation in asserting their racial superiority to blacks. In the late nineteenth century and for much of the twentieth, white workers, particularly in the United States with its large black population, found in racism a cause with which to confront the competition for jobs from blacks now free to sell their labor. Racial segregation, written into law or so secured by custom as to have hardly less force, took elaborate form.

Neither law nor custom had precluded miscegenation during slavery, even in the South of the United States. But with the notable exception of Brazil—where the lack of sufficient white immigrants had long allowed a selective merging by mulattos into a pragmatic whiteness—those descended from such unions were no less barred than were blacks from social assimilation with whites. And they remained so under the reinvigorated regime of racism after slavery.

White supremacy bred among those discriminated against an imitative high value on lightness of complexion and a corresponding disparagement of dark features. Yet the very exclusiveness of white supremacy guarded the frontier against all but a few furtive crossings. It was this that essentially promoted and secured the existence of a vast black diaspora, increasingly conscious of its peculiar identity, its collective past, and its cultural heritage. Relevantly, in a movement that might have emerged somewhat tentatively but developed an assertive assurance, leadership came from among the "colored" as well as the black. Decisively from the 1960s, the term "Negro," rejected for its historical associations with racial disparagement, gave place to "black" as the term used even by many of light complexion.

It is not inconsistent both to deplore the causes and conditions that created a black diaspora and to exult in its achievements; the expression of its identity and experience, in every artistic form, especially music, and in that passion for freedom which belongs to a people born in slavery and released into racial victimization. Nor is that victimization by any means at an end.

In many "host" countries of their settlement, and for all that some of them have attained the higher reaches of society, blacks are, in undeniable disproportion, numbered among the poor, the unemployed, the ill-educated, the imprisoned, and even—where such barbarism still survives—the judicially killed. In similar disproportion, blacks inhabit functionally segregated areas of shantytowns or inner-city decay. And those blacks whose material success has enabled them to live in sleek and guarded apartment complexes or suburbs can scarcely doubt that racism, albeit in an attentuated functional form, is alive and well and evident in the very ghettos they have escaped.

Racism in any form is all the more painful and cruelly ironic when associated with a culture that asserts, as its peculiar contribution to civilized development, its devotion to the rational, the democratic, the liberty and equality of the individual. The United States took its constitutional form from these values and remains the most fervent in ceaselessly expounding them. However, it is difficult to review the record of racism and its residual influence without wondering at the extent of institutionalized hypocrisy. And the same may be said, in varying degrees, of other states whose professedly civilized ideals have hosted the parasite that deforms them.

Such hypocrisy has a price that not only its immediate victims pay. The nationalisms of Western Europe, in their imperial rivalries, ended up killing or maiming multitudes of their own young men in a First World War whose moral purpose was widely taken for granted at the time, though the assumption that there was such a purpose at all seems widely incomprehensible now. A generation later, a racism toward Jews and blacks, so common and casual that much of popular fiction and even literature of the highest order carried its taint, reached its culmination in Nazi Germany and the Holocaust.

Alongside that, the history of Islam emerges with some credit. Certainly, it continued to encompass slavery, long after slaves had been freed throughout Christendom. But while slavery was practiced in Christendom and Islam alike, the freeing of individual slaves by their owners was much more frequent and widespread in Islam. This was of particular relevance to the social assimilation of blacks. As slaves, they were subject to no special racial discrimination in law; and once freed, they enjoyed in law equal rights as citizens

If color prejudice might have affected market prices, the treatment accorded by individual masters, and the pace or extent of social advancement by many of the free, this fell far short of the elaborate discriminations of racism in the West. Indeed, there were black slaves in Islam who rose to positions of power without parallel among their counterparts in the West; even a few who, by becoming rulers, were automatically free. To be sure, still today it is easy enough to find in parts of Islam a significant correlation between blackness and poverty. But given the likely numbers of black slaves that the Islamic trade involved over the centuries, this is more indicative of a marginal prejudice, whose consequences have perpetuated themselves, than of a historical racism. The comparative smallness of a black diaspora in Islam is evidence not of the small numbers carried by the trade, but of the degree to which large numbers were absorbed by the wider population.

The difference between Islam and Christendom in the experience of the black diaspora is clear today. Despite the prominent part played by individual Christians, including members of the clergy, in opposing slavery and subsequently racist practices, the established Churches long tended to reflect dominant social attitudes, sometimes to the extent of having separate sectors for black and white in their congregations. And while dissenting denominations, such as the Methodists and Baptists, took a socially less supine position, they were wary of provoking their white adherents too far, and were reluctant to cede white organizational control. All this, together with enforced or functioning residential segregation, led blacks to found churches and even sects of their own.

Given the extent of residual as well as historical racism, it is scarcely surprising that separatist development should persist. Across the West, from Britain to Brazil, among blacks who still profess some sort of Christianity, most do so in virtually all-black congregations; belong to virtually all-black sects; or are increasingly turning to others, such as Pentecostalism, which have black origins, elements of black culture in their worship, and no record of white organizational dominance. Furthermore, Islam itself has come to exercise a growing attraction among blacks, most notably in the United States, where the Islamic message of a universal community beyond race and united in faith has been—not altogether consistently—combined with a militant political black separatist movement.

Paradoxically, however, in Western societies so long deformed by racism and an ultimate totalitarianism of money, there exist, too, a constitutional secularism and democracy that allow a much larger measure of freedom to proselytize, dissent, and denounce than may be found in most Islamic societies, and especially those "fundamentalist" ones governed by religious law. Such repressiveness has little to do with the spirit or even letter of the faith as communicated by the Prophet. Islam's ideal community is one of unity, justice, and compassion, with specific guidance in the Koran to tolerance. Yet too much of Islam's history has involved coercive regimes that have had a great deal less to do with promoting unity, justice, and compassion than with serving and securing the interest of corrupt, avaricious rulers, their courts, or associated elites.

Nor need one look very far to find the counterparts of these regimes in Islam today: exploiting a nationalism whose initial development was a response to Western imperial conquest; and even, in Mauritania and Sudan, pursuing policies with a distinct racist component. Such regimes, so remote from the values they expound in their allegiance to Islam, feed on their own form of institutional hypocrisy.

In this developing contradiction, the state, represented by whatever dynasty or despot, political party or conspiracy of colonels came to command it, has effectively prevailed even while lacking the legitimacy that only acceptance of its religious merit and corresponding authority can bestow. Without such legitimacy, neither its regime nor even the state itself has the right to allegiance. 'Abū Bakr, the first *Khalīfa* (Caliph), or successor to the Prophet as Commander of the Faithful, declared on his own election: "Obey me as long as I obey God and His Prophet. But if I disobey them, then no obedience is incumbent upon you."[1]

For those in search of signs by which to recognize the righteousness of disobedience to established state authorities, there is one preeminently available. The advance of Western political and economic power has come to represent for many Muslims a rebuke and retribution for the religious shortcomings of their own societies. The spread of fundamentalism has been a clear response to this and to the mortifying awareness of historical decline. As Elie Kedourie writes:

> In all countries which had been non-Muslim and which were conquered for Islam, the preacher of the Friday sermon holds a wooden sword in his hand. The Friday sermon is the ruler's prerogative which he delegates to the preacher, and the sword in his hand is a striking symbol and reminder for the congregation of the power and sway of Islam. In the modern world there has come to be a progressive disjunction between the symbol and what it is meant to symbolize, while the reminder points up the bitter contrast between past glories and present humiliation.[2]

The history of Islam is not only about glories, however. It involves an investment in slavery that had millions of black victims. There is a conscious and articulate black diaspora in the West that confronts the historical record of slavery and racism there. That Islam has no comparably conscious and articulate black diaspora to confront it with the reminders of slavery does not make that record any more immune to examination and judgment. Islam owes such an examination and judgment not only to itself but also to its victims. They have the right, most precious of all for the voiceless, to be heard.

TWO

OUT OF ARABIA

The history of Islam, like that of other great religions, is replete with contradictions between precept and practice. The vision and values communicated by the Prophet were all too soon confronted by the dynamic of conquest and the discriminating distribution of the spoils. Yet the vision and the values survived, to be invoked by successive movements of protest and the summons to purifying reform. Their enduring force was manifest as well in modifying both public and private conduct. All this was exemplified in the experience of Islam's black slaves, and to explore that experience, it is necessary to explore the development of Islam itself from its very beginnings.

In the sixth century of the Christian Era, Arabia was prosperous, with a resurgence in the caravan trade from the south of the peninsula, itself rich in frankincense and having commercial links with Africa and even the East. Northward to Syria, there moved a variety of spices, perfumes, and silks, along with slaves.

Until recently it was the conventional view of historians that Mecca had risen to particular prominence from the trade, for several reasons. It was situated at the crossroads of major caravan routes in Arabia, had developed an important slave market, had local access to silver, and could draw on less valuable but nonetheless exportable local produce such as leather and certain foodstuffs. Mecca had, moreover, a unique advantage over competing Arabian commercial centers. It was the site of the Ka'ba, a religious shrine that accommodated many tribal deities and drew worshippers from far and wide in annual pilgrimage, to promote as well the ascendancy of a concurrent Meccan trade fair.

If the benefits accrued mainly to the locally dominant Quraysh tribe, prosperity also attracted numerous new settlers—merchants, exiles, refugees, adventurers—many of them detribalized and cosmopolitan in outlook, whose arrival brought new social tensions and ideas. It was a setting congenial to the emergence of a prophet whose revolutionary teachings would change human history.

In Mecca, around the year 571 of the Christian Era, a Qurayshi child was born after the death of his father. His mother, who named him Muḥammad, died when he was about six years old, and the orphan could hardly have had a secure and untroubled life in the remaining years of childhood, in adolescence, and in early manhood. At last, however, he found employment in the business house of Khadijah, the Qurayshi widow of a wealthy merchant, and married her when she was forty years old and he was twenty-five. For the first time free of economic pressures and encouraged by a wife whose commercial interests did not preclude a concern with higher values, Muḥammad took to meditating in the seclusion of a small cave on a hill outside the city. And it was there, in 610, that he heard the archangel Gabriel commanding him to speak in the name of the Lord, his creator.

Muḥammad obeyed, calling upon all to accept the one God, who would reward obedience to His commandments with the delights of paradise, but punish disobedience with the horrors of hell. It was a call—communicated first in secrecy and then, from 613, through public preaching—that increasingly attracted followers, especially from among the slaves and the poor, with its concern for their plight. The initial ridicule with which the Quraysh aristocracy had greeted his efforts turned to persecution. A number of converts, first in 615 and again in 617, fled to Ethiopia, where the Christian ruler, or *negus*, resisted all pressures to surrender them.

The Prophet continued to preach in Mecca and communicate the revelations with which he was visited. Aware, however, of the increasing danger from Quraysh hostility, he came to be convinced of the need for a base of support beyond the city. He already had followers in Medina, an agricultural oasis where two local tribes were in conflict. In 622, a delegation of seventy-five followers, drawn from both tribes, invited him to settle in Medina, pledging that there he would be obeyed and protected. Muḥammad found the proposal the more appealing because Medina had a large number of Jews who would, he supposed, prove receptive to his teachings. Together with his followers in Mecca, he left the city, in what came to be known as the *hijra*, or migration, and established in Medina the first *umma*, or community of Muslims. So crucial to the development of the new faith would this event subsequently be deemed that the year 622 was designated as the first in the Islamic Era.

The Jews of Medina proved to be a disappointment. They might well have believed that the past had provided them with enough prophets already. In rejecting the summons from yet another, however, they set themselves against one who now wielded political as well as religious authority, and this soon developed a military dimension. In 624, the Muslims of Medina dispatched a force to intercept a caravan on its way from Syria to Mecca. The Meccans, forewarned, dispatched a force to defend it. In the ensuing engagement, three hundred Muslims defeated the thousand men sent against them. Their success was widely seen as a sign of divine intervention in favor of the new faith, and the Prophet, his prestige much enhanced, turned to deal with the local Jews, who were accused of having aligned themselves with the enemy. Some six hundred of their men were killed and the remainder expelled from Medina. Their date plantations were given to the Muslims who had accompanied the Prophet from Mecca.

By 630, the military power of the new faith was such as to capture Mecca itself, and in the following year, the Prophet concluded treaties with Jewish and Christian leaders from oases in the south, which afforded their communities the protection of Islam in return for the payment of a special tax, the *jizyah*. Increasingly, tribal deputations from far and wide arrived to declare their allegiance to the Prophet and their adherence to his teachings. By the time of the Prophet's death in 632, Islam had become the virtual state religion across a large part of Arabia, but with a message directed at all humanity.

One modern scholar, Patricia Crone, in her bold book *Meccan Trade and the Rise of Islam,* has persuasively challenged or qualified some elements of this conventional account.[1] There is no historical evidence, she argues, beyond the repetition of subsequent stories that cite one another for confirmation, that Mecca was a pre-Islamic object of pilgrimage at all, let alone one that attracted multitudes to a concurrent trade fair: "A famous list of pre-Islamic fairs enumerates some sixteen fairs as having been of major importance in Arabia before Islam. Not one of the several versions of this list mentions Mecca."[2]

Nor is there evidence that Mecca was a commercial center of the long-distance trade. In fact, geography is in conflict with any such development before the arrival of Islam. According to Crone: "Mecca was not located on the incense route, still less at the crossroads of all the major routes in Arabia . . . The site was barren, devoid of a fertile hinterland except for Ta'if, ill-equipped for maritime trade, and much too far away for a caravan trade with Syria of a kind that the sources describe."[3] There was no silver mined in the Meccan area, and whatever was mined in the south of the peninsula would only have reached Mecca by way of an unaccountable detour. Certainly, pre-Islamic Arabs owned slaves, some of them from East Africa and collectively called "Ethiopians," but Yemen was a far more likely center for their distribution than Mecca would have been.

In short, the only reliable evidence for a pre-Islamic Meccan trade was for one in typically pastoral products—leather goods, animals, coarser and cheaper cloth, and cheese and clarified butter—scarcely the sustenance of a great commercial hub. There were, to be sure, individual Qurayshi merchants who traded elsewhere in Arabia—Muhammad himself is reported to have traveled as a trader in leather—and certain ones were even settled in Syria. Among them were some who might well have grown rich in the process, but this would hardly have made Mecca into a cosmopolitan center for foreign merchants, exiles, refugees, and adventurers.

From this revised view of Mecca, Crone proceeds to a wider revision of the context and content of Muhammad's message. If this was not a time of peculiar social excitement in Mecca, it was one of tribal unrest across Arabia from unprecedented foreign intrusions. The Byzantine

Empire had extended its sphere of influence from the Syrian desert, where it had client kings, along the west of the peninsula, to Yemen, which its Ethiopian allies had recently ruled, while the Sassanid Persian Empire, which had colonies throughout eastern Arabia, now commanded Oman and Yemen.

What Muḥammad provided, in Crone's view, was the exclusive claim to divinity of a particular Arab god—shared with the Jews as the god of their common ancestor, Abraham, and, by derivation from the Jews, shared with the Christians as well—who mandated all who believed in him to confront unbelievers wherever they might be found. And it was this unifying summons, an instrument against foreign interventions, that attracted so many followers. As she states: "Muḥammad was a prophet with a political mission, not, as is so often asserted, a prophet who merely happened to become involved with politics."[4]

Muḥammad had his first success in Medina, where his solution to the endemic feuding of tribal society was that of a divinely mandated state structure. And Crone adds: "It was Muḥammad's state, not his supposed blueprint for social reform, which had such a powerful effect on the rest of Arabia."[5] Furthermore, it was military conquest, by followers of the new faith, that initially accounted for the spread of the message to so many millions.

And yet the message itself clearly had such power and relevance, for these and many millions more beyond the compass of conquest, that it came to inform one of the great and lasting world religions. Alexander the Great had been a conqueror with an inclusive political summons, but there is no corresponding religion still practiced today that hallows his name.

The Prophet's revelations and teachings are contained in the *Qu'rān*, or Koran, which he dictated to scribes, and the authorized version of which was proclaimed by 'Uthmān during his Caliphate, or leadership of Islam (644–56). Its authority is held to be absolute, as the word of God transmitted by His Prophet. Supplementing this is the *sunnah*, or collection of the Prophet's sayings and acts, each of which is known as a *ḥadīth*. Since the Koran itself commands obedience to the Prophet and equates it with obedience to God, every *ḥadīth* might be supposed to possess and convey divine authority as well. But a distinction is drawn between the ḥadīth of the Prophet in his prophetic capacity and others concerned with his personal and social judgments or conduct, as husband and father, neighbor and friend, political and military leader. It is essentially a distinction between what is binding as law and what is, however potently, guidance.[6]

The Koran itself lays down the five basic obligations of the faith: ṣalāt (ritual prayer); zakāt (almsgiving); ḥajj (pilgrimage); the fast of Ramadan; and, above all, shahādah, or the requirement to acknowledge and propagate the existence of a single God, Allah, and to recognize Muḥammad as His chosen Prophet. It also provides a code of religious, social, and political laws, on a multitude of subjects, including the required treatment—markedly enlightened and compassionate for the times—of slaves and orphans, the poor and the oppressed.

The Koran recognizes differences of culture and color, but does so with no suggestion that one is superior to another. In one passage (30:22), such differences are identified merely as the products of God's will and illustrations of His wonders:

> *And of His signs*
> *is the creation of the heavens and earth*
> *and the variety of your tongues and hues.*[7]

Furthermore, the Koran values piety as supreme over any such differences, including that of gender (49:13):

> *O mankind, We have created you*
> *male and female, and appointed you*
> *races and tribes, that you may know*
> *one another. Surely the noblest*
> *among you in the sight of God is*
> *the most godfearing of you.*[8]

In the last year of his life, the Prophet visited Mecca, now his religious capital, on the annual pilgrimage. The sermon he gave there contained an emphatic reference to the requirements of a unity that had displaced the old divisions: "O ye men! harken unto my words and take ye them to heart! Know ye that every Moslem is a brother to every other

Moslem, and that ye are now one brotherhood. It is not legitimate for any of you, therefore, to appropriate unto himself anything that belongs to his brother unless it is willingly given him by that brother."[9]

Large claims have been made for the peculiar inclusiveness of Islam. It has even been asserted that "Humanism" is a constituent of the "world-view" provided by Koranic ideas of the divine being and by the corresponding principles that govern "man's response to divinity." These principles include the doctrine that all humans are born innocent; that "they are free to determine their individual destinies . . . [and] to order their lives in accordance with the best dictates of their own consciences"; and that "they are equal before God and the law since no discrimination is legitimate that bases itself upon race, color, language, inherited culture, religion, or inherited social position."[10]

All of this is difficult to sustain. There is an essential contradiction between Humanism, which puts humanity, and Islam, which puts God at the center of its moral system. Certainly, however, the Islamic doctrine that all humans are born innocent is substantially closer to the spirit of Humanism than is the Christian preoccupation with original sin. And despite the attendant threats of divine punishment for disobedience, close to the spirit of Humanism, too, is the Koranic injunction against the use of force to advance the faith, strengthened by an express appeal to religious and even moral tolerance. Mark Huband explains:

> The rejection of force is raised in the Koran in several different contexts: "Whoso doeth that through aggression and injustice, We shall cast him into the fire, and that is ever easy for Allah" (sura 4, verse 30); "Fight in the way of Allah against those who fight against you, but begin not hostilities. Lo! Allah loveth not aggressors" (sura 2, verse 190); "I do not worship that which you worship, and neither do you worship that which I worship. And I will not worship that which you have ever worshipped, and neither will you [ever] worship that which I worship. Unto you, your moral law, and unto me, mine" (sura 109, verses 1–6).[11]

In fact, virtually from the very outset, only the adherents of stipulated religions, regarded as sufficiently related to the beliefs of Islam, were effectively allowed the freedom to determine their individual destinies in accordance with the best dictates of their own consciences. Other non-Muslims, held to be infidels or unbelievers, were free only to choose between readily accepting the summons to Islam or being compelled by force of arms to do so. The principle of *jihad*, or holy war, righteous only in the cause of self-defense, soon came to require no more reason than the advancement of the faith.

Nor, for all the relative benevolence that marked the Koranic treatment of slavery and even recommended the freeing of slaves as an act of piety pleasing to God, could acceptance of the practice itself be justified as compatible with Humanism. In effect, these incompatibilities promoted conquest, compulsion, and enslavement as consistent with the divine design.

Muḥammad died in 632, and the unity that the Prophet had achieved in a large part of Arabia began to fragment as some tribes proceeded to reassert their independence and even proclaim prophets of their own. A group of leading Muslims met and elected as Caliph, or Commander of the Faithful, Muḥammad's father-in-law and early close companion, 'Abū Bakr. As Ira Lapidus states: "He was successor to the Prophet, but not himself a Prophet. He was rather to be a shaykh or chief, who led the collectivity, arbitrated disputes, and followed the precedents set by Muḥammad."[12]

With the principle of such a successor to the Prophet, and his own selection ratified by the Muslim community at large, 'Abū Bakr set out to enforce his authority against refractory tribes. In a series of battles, his forces subdued the secessionists, and a reunited Islam started a career of conquest that would, by the middle of the eighth century, extend its rule westward across North Africa to the bulk of the Iberian peninsula and eastward to Samarkand and the Indus River.

It was during the Caliphate of 'Abū Bakr's successor, 'Umar (634–44), that certain principles for the government of the expanding empire developed. The conquerors were to constitute a military elite, accommodated on the outskirts of existing cities or in new garrison cities, such as Basra in Iraq and Fusṭāṭ in Egypt. They were to avoid becoming landowners or peasants in conflict with the subject peoples and were instead to be provided with a share of the taxes raised from the peasantry and the urban communities. Zoroastrians as well as Jews and Christians were permitted to practice their religion in peace, with a tax as the price of the protection they enjoyed. Beyond the pressure on others to accept Islam, it was a system designed to leave the subjugated societies largely undisturbed.

Predictably, however, the performance came to fall far short of the prescriptions. Few of the conquerors failed to be affected by the experience of power, and in particular by their discovery of the sumptuous style in which the rulers and rich in some of the conquered territories had been living. Mecca had not prepared them for the splendors of Alexandria, Damascus, and the capital of Persia, Ctesiphon.

When the Arab general 'Amr ibn al-'Ās, in his conquest of Egypt, reached Alexandria, his report to the Caliph 'Umar clearly communicated his wonder: "I have taken a city of which I can only say that it contains 4,000 palaces, 4,000 baths, 400 theatres, 1,200 greengrocers and 40,000 Jews."[13]

The new rulers soon enough acquired tastes, and the means for satisfying them, of which the Prophet would scarcely have approved. The succession of the Umayyad dynasty to the Caliphate, with the accompanying removal of the capital to Damascus, reflected the distance Islam had traveled from the initial austerities of the desert.

It was the genesis of this succession, indeed, that produced the great schism still at the heart of Islam today. In 656, 'Alī, the Prophet's son-in-law, became the fourth Caliph and was acknowledged as such by virtually the entire Muslim world. A party of disaffection emerged against him, however, formidably led by Mu'āwiyah, his distant cousin, who was governor of Syria. In the fighting that followed, 'Alī was killed in 661, and Mu'āwiyah instituted the Umayyad Caliphate. This was accepted by the orthodox, or *Sunni* majority of Muslims, but was rejected by the *Shi'a*, or separatist strain, initially centered in Iraq, which regarded such a succession as illegitimate; the only legitimate Caliph, by divine right, was al-Ḥasan, the son of the martyred 'Alī and of the Prophet's only child, his daughter, Fāṭima.

Al-Ḥasan proved all too captivated by the new delights that conquest had brought. By the time he died, at the age of forty-five, he had contracted and dissolved one hundred marriages, so that he came to be called "the great divorcer." Astute at least in recognizing his weaknesses, he accepted Mu'āwiyah's offer of suitable financial support as the price of abandoning all claim to the command of the faithful. The belief survived, however, as the core of the Shiʻa sect, that the only legitimate line of succession was that of the Prophet's direct descendants. Moreover, the issue of such descent ceased to be the sole source of rival claims to the title of Caliph. For some time during the Middle Ages, there would be no fewer than three Caliphates: the ʻAbbasid in Baghdad (750–1258); the Fatimid, with its capital at Cairo (909–1171); and the Umayyad (929–1031), in Islamic Spain with its capital at Qurṭubah (Cordoba), and only the Fatimid Caliphate claimed descent from ʻAlī.

Mounting numbers of the conquered, freely or in response to sometimes formidable pressures, adhered to Islam. As Muslims, however recent their conversion, they were supposedly equal to all other members of a united community. Instead, they frequently found themselves treated by their Arab conquerors as second-class citizens and made to pay a form of tribute in the land tax to which as Muslims they were meant to be immune. Such effectively ethnic discrimination was in conflict not only with religious doctrine but with the forces of demography and sexual selection. In the event, increasing intermarriage served to submerge the original distinctions, and increasing numbers of the conquered, having adopted the religion and language of the conquerors, took to assuming the identity of Arabs themselves.

What survived was a class structure in which adherence to Islam was no protection against poverty and oppression. Taxes on the peasantry came to reach half the value of production, and many peasants simply abandoned the land to search for sustenance in the swelling cities. Yet there was wealth in abundance, generated not only by a corresponding expansion in trade from the enormous integrated market that the conquests of Islam had created but by the pillage accompanying such conquests and extending beyond them. Included in the pillage, and at particular times or in particular places its primary component, were slaves from black Africa, whose increasing numbers were required in the pursuit of conspicuous consumption, the performance of manifold menial tasks, and the maintenance of order. In the development of that high civilization attained by imperial Islam, the part played by slaves was no less important for being subsequently submerged.

THREE

IMPERIAL ISLAM

When Islam conquered the Persian Sassanid Empire and much of the Byzantine one, including Syria and Egypt, in the seventh century, it acquired immense quantities of gold. This acquisition involved seizing hoards and ornaments in the Sassanid treasuries and palaces; stripping churches and monasteries in the former Byzantine provinces, either directly or by taxes, payable in gold, imposed on the clergy; and looting gold from Pharaonic tombs in Egypt, where the state encouraged the search and sanctioned the seizure, in return for a fifth of the finds.

In addition, supplies of newly minted gold, mainly from Africa, arrived along the trade routes that the empire had inherited or developed. One of these routes, dating back to Pharaonic times, reached from the mines of Nubia to Aswan; another, far to the south, led from a dimly known land called "golden Sofala" to merchant cities along the east coast of Africa and the shore of the Red Sea. The major source, which provided a seemingly ceaseless supply, lay south of the Sahara, in the area known as *Bilad as-Sudan*, or "Land of the Blacks." Caravans with Berber camel drivers made their long and difficult way between settlements at the northern edge of the desert and the collection points for gold in the region of the Senegal and Niger rivers. Much of this gold eventually went to the commercial and banking centers, where coins were minted for circulation throughout Islam and beyond.

Islam inherited from the Sassanid Empire the widespread circulation of a silver coinage and began minting its own related *dirhem* during the last decade of the seventh century. Supplies of the metal were abundant, from mines in southern Spain and the Moroccan Atlas Mountains as well as Armenia, northern Persia, and central Asia, while copper and tin, also abundant, were used for the minting of small change. But it was the gold standard that eventually prevailed, and the gold dinar accordingly became the predominant measure of money.[1]

This profusion of money fueled a prodigious economic growth, whose prime beneficiaries were those with the power to tax or otherwise direct it to their personal advantage. An exuberance of consumption involved the purchase of slaves, in numbers sometimes explicable more for the display of status than for the command of services. The huge retinues of rulers, with harems that might contain thousands of concubines, were testimony to the extent of the riches required to afford them, and given the effective identity of the public purse with the ruler's personal resources, such riches were phenomenal indeed. According to Maurice Lombard:

> In Spain, on the death of 'Abd al-Rahman III in 961, the Treasury contained 5,000,000 dinars, or 250 hundredweight of minted gold. Under his successor, al-Hakam II (961–976), the total moneys paid into the Public Treasury (*Khizanat al-mal*) amounted to 40,000,000 dinars. In Egypt, on the death of the powerful eleventh-century Minister, al-Afdal, his treasury was found to contain 6,000,000 dinars, representing 300 hundredweight of minted gold. At Baghdad under Hārūn al-Rashīd (786–809), the Public Treasury (*bayt al-mal*) received annually 7,500 hundredweight of minted gold, that is 150,000,000 dinars.[2]

At the market price of gold in the closing years of the twentieth century, the annual revenues of the Public Treasury in Baghdad twelve hundred years ago would have been equivalent to well over $1 billion. Even today, this would represent a considerable sum. It would have been immensely greater in the relative purchasing power it represented at the time. A few centuries later, when inflation had somewhat eroded the purchasing power of the precious metals and a gold dinar was roughly equivalent to thirty-six silver dirhems, a skilled laborer earned on average five dirhems a day.[3] An immigrant to Palestine from the West was able to open a shop in Jerusalem on a loan of five dinars. His notable success involved a profit of one dinar in the first two months of the enterprise.[4]

Inflation—though mainly moderate, occasionally sharp—promoted investment as an alternative to the accumulation of idle and depreciating liquid capital. Those with the skill and the means to manipulate money thrived mightily. There were merchants who not only operated as wholesalers on a large scale but financed trading expeditions by ship or caravan; and there were bankers who exchanged currencies and provided credit at often high rates of return. With a cultural unity stretching from Morocco and Spain in the west to Persia and beyond to the east, long-distance traders in Islam were able to journey with relative ease from North Africa and the Middle East to China or, effectively, from the Atlantic to the Pacific oceans.[5] Trade promoted investment in industry: the manufacture of silk, wool, linen, cotton textiles; pottery and glass; a variety of metalwork, from gold and silver ornaments to copper kitchen utensils; and leather goods, from shoes and bottles to furniture and parchment for books. Slaves as well as waged free laborers were employed in the multiplicity of workshops.

Accompanying this economic growth was an urban expansion prodigious in extent and pace. The single comparable instance was that of Ch'ang-an, the capital of China's T'ang dynasty (618–907), which came to have almost two million inhabitants within its urban area, a million of them within the city walls;[6] but there the growth was rather more protracted. In 762, Baghdad had no more than a few hundred inhabitants. By the year 800, its estimated population was little short of two million. During the ninth and tenth centuries, Baghdad measured some nine by ten kilometers, much larger than imperial Rome had been, and roughly equal to the area that Paris would eventually cover only by the close of the nineteenth century. Samarkand had a population of half a million by the late ninth century; and Cairo, founded in 972, rapidly reached a population of similar size.[7]

Conditions in contemporary Christian Europe precluded any even remotely comparable urban development. Only in the fourteenth century, as economic recovery gathered force, would there be four Italian towns—Milan, Venice, Naples, and Florence—with populations exceeding fifty thousand and perhaps reaching a hundred thousand. In the Low Countries, the largest town, Ghent, would have little more than fifty-six thousand inhabitants. A figure of eighty thousand for Paris would be "perfectly plausible." Cologne, by far the largest town in Germany, would have barely forty thousand. And London, the largest town in England, would have between thirty-five and forty-five thousand inhabitants.[8]

The great merchants and bankers of Islam—some of them Jews and Christians—were, by any economic measure, members of an upper, as distinct from a ruling, class. They lived in sumptuous town houses— some of them owned large landed estates as well—with numerous retainers and slaves. Often, they were men of high culture who employed or subsidized artists and scientists. Not least, they were prime private sources of public philanthropy, providing alms for the poor of the community and funds for places of worship, schools, hostels, and such civic amenities as fountains.

Below them stretched a complex middle class that encompassed considerable disparities in status and income. There were civil servants of various grades and functions. There were physicians and apothecaries, lawyers and clerics, teachers and scholars, writers and musicians. The successful became rich, and not always by restricting themselves to their professional pursuits. In the thirteenth century, for instance, there was a veritable rage among physicians for investing in sugar factories,[9] which might well have used black slaves in their labor force. Renowned musicians and poets could be munificently rewarded, while others survived only by finding supplementary forms of employment. There were merchants with large businesses, who disparaged as "beggars" those with small ones.[10] The "beggarly" shopkeepers included some who made a safe enough living, but also some who barely survived. Others, succumbing to the pressures of debt, simply disappeared into the swollen mass of the urban poor.

The enormous numbers of free workers, skilled and unskilled, contract and casual, did not enjoy much respect for the dignity of labor. The loss of independence in being employed by someone else was regarded as demeaning. Nor did the payment for labor compensate for this disparagement. Even a master mason, under contract for the building of a synagogue in 1040, was paid a lump sum that amounted to roughly four dirhems a day, though this payment was accompanied by a lunch (on working days only) that was worth three-quarters of a dirhem. (The value of the lunch itself suggests that the wage was hardly handsome.) Each of the master mason's helpers got two and three-quarter dirhems a day, but without lunch. Moreover, workers had to pay their poll tax out of their own wages; and since many, probably most, had no such lump sum available, employers would often pay the tax themselves and dock the wage accordingly. In one instance, a packer needed the equivalent of 12 working days to earn enough for his poll tax; in another, a substitute overseer needed the equivalent of no fewer than 132.[11]

Since taxes tended to increase along with prices, and inflation generally outstripped rises in wages, differentials within the working class are likely to have been mainly gradations of poverty. There were also, however, many who were poorer still and for whom the modern term "underclass" would be apt. They were the urban unemployed, who survived on the help of relatives often almost as poor as themselves, by doing odd jobs for food or a few copper coins, by pilfering, or by begging. Many were refugees from the countryside, where conditions were scarcely better.

There, the urban rich bought up large tracts of land for investment or prestige, from minor landowners ruined by taxes and debt, and evicted the peasants employed on them. Slaves and hired workers from among the landless would have supplied any necessary labor. Subsistence farmers were taxed regardless of their capacity to pay. Many abandoned their villages in an attempt to escape taxes or the debts they had contracted. A modern archaeological survey of the agricultural district nearest Baghdad revealed a decline of 37 percent in the area under cultivation between the middle and the end of the ninth century.[12]

In form, slaves were at the bottom of the social scale, inferior to all who at least had their freedom. In force, their status depended on various factors, including their attributes and functions, their corresponding market values, the social and personal character of their owners. Some labored in the harshest conditions on large-scale construction schemes or estate agriculture. Some were pampered favorites of kings or highly prized artists in the homes of great merchants. Some were nurses, house-maids, cooks, or porters. Some became generals. In their own differences, they reflected the social system, its mobilities and rigidities.

It was a system whose very concentrations of wealth and power seemed oppressively at odds with the doctrines of Islam. The disaffection this provoked often took religious shape. Messianism, for instance, based on the belief in the Mahdi, a spiritual and temporal leader inspired and guided by God to purge Islam, infused or influenced revolt. As early as the eighth and ninth centuries, such revolts, led by self-proclaimed prophets who gathered large followings, broke out among the peasantry in various parts of the Islamic world from Mesopotamia (Iraq) to Armenia and Azerbaijan.

Other rural revolts seem to have resulted simply from intolerable hardships. One such revolt was by the "Zotts" or "Djatts," Indians deported from the Lower Indus to the swamps of Lower Mesopotamia, where, in conditions of extreme poverty, they bred water buffalo. They were joined in their uprising by groups of runaway slaves, but were defeated and deported yet again to various parts of the empire. Black slaves, working in mines and plantations, rebelled in 770, to little effect. Then, in 883, black slaves in Lower Mesopotamia rose up, joined by disaffected peasants. This time, the rebels pillaged cities, to threaten Baghdad itself.

Nor was it only the rural disaffected who rose in rage or despair. When, after the death of Hārūn al-Rashīd, his two sons disputed the succession, an uprising of the poor that came to be known as the "Revolt of the Naked" controlled Baghdad for a while. And in the reign of Al-Ma'mūn (813–33), Coptic workers in the small textile-manufacturing towns of the Egyptian Delta rose in revolt, only to be defeated and subsequently sold as slaves in Syria and Mesopotamia. Then, in tenth-century Egypt, increasing discontent and dissent gave rise to the development and spread of the militant, mainly clandestine Qarmat movement.

Among the many religious strains involved in this movement, Islam's Shi'a sect, with its faith in a purifying Mahdi, was dominant. Yet at least as important as the religious component was the essentially social one, based on labor grievances increasingly manifested by strikes and revolts. Indeed, Qarmatism came to encompass Jews, Christians, and heretics of one sort or another. The secret writings in which the doctrines and activities of the movement were wrapped reveal a particular concern with working conditions and a particular emphasis on the dignity of labor.

This spirit spurred the development of independent trade guilds, which soon came into conflict with authority and suffered intermittent persecution. They protected themselves by forming an association that bore some resemblance to the much later and different Masonic movement elsewhere, as Lombard explains, "with initiation rites, secret oaths, elected leaders known as 'masters,' councils composed of these leaders, and a doctrine with both mystical and social elements."[13]

From 969 to 1171 the Fatimid dynasty ruled the Maghrib, Egypt, parts of Syria, and beyond. Asserting its descent from Fāṭima, daughter of the Prophet, and 'Alī, her husband, the Fatimid dynasty associated itself with the Isma'īlī strain of Shi'a; declared itself a succession of *imams*, or leaders of Islam; and accordingly assumed the title of Caliph, in conflict with the increasingly hollow Caliphate in Baghdad. Its real power derived from Berber tribal forces, along with regiments of Turkish and of Sudanese black military slaves.[14]

The trade guilds came to be officially recognized by the Fatimid state. The success enjoyed by the Guild of the Teachers and Students of the University of al-Azhar, itself inaugurated in 972, only two years after the founding of Cairo, was an influential symbol of the new tolerance. Yet the underlying distortions remained. Cairo became the richest city in Islam, its wealth based on tribute from the provinces and the taxation of Egypt's extensive transit trade. A Persian missionary traveler, visiting the country in 1046–49, expressed his awe: "I could neither limit nor estimate its wealth and nowhere else have I seen such prosperity as I saw there." He described the palace of the Caliphate as housing thirty thousand people, of whom twelve thousand were servants, with a thousand horse and foot guards.[15] Such was the appetite of the state for revenue—not only to sustain the Caliphate in the style to which it quickly grew accustomed but also to meet the costs of the military force securing it—that the Egyptian peasantry and the artisans in the provincial towns were subjected to increasingly oppressive taxation.

At any sign of impending food shortages, courtiers, state officials, and leading merchants bought up supplies, thus aggravating the rise in prices. During the eleventh century, these shortages and related waves of speculation became more serious and frequent. While expenditures on the extravagance of rule only increased, poorly paid soldiers pillaged the countryside and the suburbs, and crowds took advantage of Muslim festivals to plunder the closed bazaars. The army itself was prey to the ethnic conflict of Berbers, Turks, and Sudanese blacks in its ranks. The last six Fatimid Caliphs, none of whom chose his successor, ruled in name only. The real power was exercised by a military vizier with enough force at his disposal to seize and sustain his dominance.[16] In 1171, Ṣalāḥuddīn, renowned in the Christian West as Saladin, conquered Egypt. A Sunni Muslim, he promptly stripped the Egyptian guilds there of the rights they had enjoyed.

Meanwhile, the empire centered on the Caliphate in Baghdad was in terminal decline, as a result of spreading disaffection within and the emergence of expansionary forces without. In the eleventh century, Saljuq Turkish tribesmen from central Asia captured the capital; however, once having overwhelmed the followers of the Prophet, they proceeded to become followers themselves and to impose the rule of Islam across western Asia. In the thirteenth century, a still more menacing enemy gathered and struck. Mongol warriors swept through eastern Islam, sacking such cities as Bukhara and Samarkand, and slaughtering or carrying away into captivity many of their inhabitants. In 1258, the Mongols attacked and captured Baghdad, slaughtering much of its population, including the Caliph, his family, and officials, and turning a large part of the city into smoldering ruins.

Islam had won over the Saljuq Turks with its message. Half a century after the fall of Baghdad, it won over the Mongols, when their seventh Khan proclaimed Islam the state religion. In the West, Christianity accompanied its own message with the sword. In 1095, Pope Urban II responded to appeals for help from the Byzantine emperor, whose Asian domains had been all but completely devoured by the Saljuq Turks. Urban called on Christendom to conquer the land of the Holy Sepulcher from "the wicked race"[17]—a telling phrase, similar to "the accursed race" that accompanied intermittent Christian attacks on the Jews—

which possessed it. It was a call that aroused many thousands, if far from all of them, with purely spiritual motivations. The ambitious, the adventurous, the poor and desperate rallied to the cause. The assertive merchants of the Italian cities applauded it.

In a series of Crusades, one of which, in 1202–4, adjusted its purpose to target Constantinople, the capital of Christian Byzantium, the warriors of Christendom confronted Islam. At the height of their success, they expanded the goal of rescuing the Holy Sepulcher to encompass the conquest of Syria and part of Egypt. It was Saladin, of such chivalric renown, who stayed and then reversed the crucial momentum of the Crusaders' advance. Their ultimate defeat, however, was due to Baybars, a slave in the Mamluk dynasty that ruled Egypt from the middle of the thirteenth until well into the sixteenth century.

The Arabic word *mamlūk* means "possessed," or "slave," and the Mamluk dynasty was a succession of Sultans who had been military slaves, translated to freedom by their very accession to rule. Baybars, originally a Turkish military slave, had cut and thrust his way to the Sultanate, and it was his generalship that stopped the advance of the Mongols toward Egypt, at a battle near Nazareth in 1260. Then, turning his attention to the Crusaders, he inflicted one defeat after another on them. Neither chivalry nor compassion characterized his conduct. When he took Antioch in 1263, he had the entire garrison of sixteen thousand slaughtered and the hundred thousand other inhabitants — men, women, and children — seized to be sold as slaves. Baybars's successors, employing the military machine he had developed, dealt with the remnants of Christian conquest, which lost its final foothold in 1291.

The Mamluks eventually ruled Syria, Nubia, and the western slice of Arabia that included Mecca and Medina, as well as Egypt. Each Sultan succeeded to the throne by emerging as the most powerful or devious of the contenders or as the choice of whichever military faction happened to be dominant at the time. And if the consequences were often so dire, it may be argued that the principle of succession to rule by natural inheritance among the free had hardly proved markedly superior.

Under this extraordinary government, Cairo, which during its growth had simply absorbed the old capital of Fusṭāṭ, was the wonder of the West and the Middle East. A Persian, Khalil al-Zahiri, who visited it in the fourteenth century, declared that it was large enough to contain the ten largest towns in his own country. Leonardo Frescobaldi, a Florentine traveler, wrote in 1384 that there were more people living in a single Cairo street than in all of Florence, and that the number of vessels docking at the city's Nile port of Bulaq was equal to three times that in the harbors of Venice, Genoa, and Ancona combined.[18]

The Mamluk dynasty was, moreover, associated with an artistic and especially an architectural florescence—due in part to the settlement in Egypt by artists and artisans who had fled from Mongol rule elsewhere in Islam, in part to the influence of the precedent set by Baybars with his program of public works. Yet the costs of the construction involved only augmented the pressures, from an extravagant court and widespread corruption, on financial resources. One fifteenth-century Sultan, allured by the profits to be made from trading in commodities, cornered the market in pepper by buying up all existing supplies and then banning the import of all spices from India, before releasing his stocks at an inflated price to his subjects.

Taxes became ever more oppressive. Famine and revolt were frequent. And the regime, still able to repress, was unable to protect much of the population. The stricken peasantry was increasingly subjected to attacks from marauding Bedouin. Diseases thrived in such conditions. Plague killed three hundred thousand people in Cairo within three months. Philip K. Hitti writes: "It is estimated that in the course of the Mamluk period the population of Syria and Egypt was reduced by two-thirds."[19]

In the late thirteenth century, a new kingdom, that of the Ottoman Turks, emerged in Anatolia. By the end of the fifteenth century, the expanding Ottoman Empire had conquered all that remained of the Byzantine one and had reached deep into the Balkans. In 1516, directing their attention to the Mamluk possessions, the Ottomans took Damascus; and, in the very next year, Cairo. By 1520, the Ottoman Empire reached from the Red Sea in the south to Crimea in the north, from Kurdistan in the east to Bosnia in the west. In 1526, it would conquer Hungary and advance to the gates of Vienna.

Yet Islam was no more united than it had been since the eighth century, with the first of its rival Caliphates. The Safavid dynasty in Persia had created an empire that adhered to the Shi'a sect. It was a development that the orthodox Sunni Ottomans considered all the more dangerous for the signs that the Shi'a appeal was encouraging rebelliousness among some of the tribes in Anatolia. War between the two empires broke out in 1514, to resume repeatedly. In 1534 the Ottomans took Baghdad, and in 1546 they wrested Basra from the Safavids, who sought compensation for their losses in the west by expanding eastward.

Such was the hostility between the two empires that, far from combining to advance the cause of Islam against Christendom, each made an alliance with a Christian power: the Ottomans with France against the Hapsburg kingdom in Austria and its claim to Hungary, the Safavids with Austria against the Ottoman Turks. In the seventeenth century, after the two so-called Long Wars of 1578–90 and 1603–19 fought between them, both Muslim empires had so far bled themselves of men and money as to be in real if not yet correspondingly apparent decline.

In India, meanwhile, Islam had begun its conquests early in the eighth century and brought there black slaves, mainly from Ethiopia, some of whom rose to high positions in the armies and governments of independent Muslim rulers. A third great Muslim power, the Mughal Empire, instituted in 1526 after an invasion from Afghanistan, was both consolidated and expanded in the reign of Akbar (1556–1605). At the beginning of the eighteenth century, it attained its greatest extent, when it reached from Kabul and Kashmir in the north to all but a relatively small area in the south. Yet by then, Akbar's successful policy of reconciling the indigenous Hindu majority had given way to religious intolerance, and a decadent regime ruled over rising discontent.

In the course of the eighteenth century, as vast tracts of the empire were lost to conquest or, while yielding nominal allegiance, were effectively independent, it must have looked as though some indigenous power or coalition of forces might put an end to Mughal power altogether. The successful challenge, however, came from afar, through the trading interests of West European states, attracted to the spoils of imperial expansion in the East ever since the Portuguese had pioneered the sea route around the Cape to India. Dutch, Danish, French, and English enterprise followed the Portuguese in establishing trading posts that soon swelled into settlements along, or inland close to, the coast of India. By 1700, England's East India Company had several of these settlements, including one at Bombay and one at Calcutta. By the early years of the nineteenth century, British power had defeated or won over to submission—with offers of alliance that the recipients found it difficult to refuse—virtually all major Indian rulers, including the Mughal emperor. Effectively, the British Raj had arrived.[20]

The Ottoman Sultans, ruling the greatest of the three Muslim empires, had not been slow in assuming the prerogatives and eventually the title of Caliph. This could not, however, disguise the increasing inability of the later Sultans to preserve their vast possessions. By the nineteenth century, nationalist rebellion and Western imperialist expansionism combined to promote an accelerating dismemberment. By 1922, when Mustafa Kemal abolished the Ottoman Caliphate and declared Turkey an independent republic, the empire was already dead.

The Qajar dynasty, which succeeded the Safavid, governed Persia from 1794 to 1925, but its rule became increasingly nominal. In 1907, agreeing to a compromise between their ambitions, Britain and Russia divided the country into respective spheres of influence. What survived was an attachment to the Shi'a strain of Islam that would, in the late twentieth century, form the basis of a revolution that expelled the last of the Pehlevi Shahs and established a fundamentalist theocracy.

Yet it is important to recognize that the history of Islam involves very much more than its imperial forms. Philip Curtin has written that, for some 750 years, from the middle of the eighth century, "Islam was the central civilization of the Old World . . . serving as the carrier that transmitted innovations from one society to another."[21] The numerals adopted in Europe were an Indian invention subsequently learned from the Arabs, as the Chinese invention of the compass reached Europe through Arab intermediaries. Islam itself spread through trade at least as much as through conquest. "It is worth remembering," Curtin continues, "that the two countries with the largest Muslim populations in the last quarter of the twentieth century are Indonesia and China, where Arab armies never trod."[22]

FOUR

THE PRACTICE OF SLAVERY

Islamic tradition has it that the treatment of slaves featured in the final preoccupations of the Prophet. One or another ḥadīth reinforced the Koranic command that masters deal benevolently with them, not least the admonition "God has more power over you than you have over them." Specifically, the master was advised not to show contempt for his slave; to share his food with him and provide clothing similar to his own; to set him no more than moderate work; not to punish him excessively if he did wrong, but to forgive him "seventy times a day"; and, if they could not get on well together, to sell him to another master.[1]

The Koran, while upholding the distinction between owner and slave as part of the divine design, also expressly encouraged the freeing of slaves as an act of piety, whose merit might expiate particular crimes. And Muslim slaves were especially recommended for emancipation, in a celebrated saying attributed to the Prophet: "The man who frees a Muslim slave, God will free from hell, limb for limb."[2] It did not take long for pious Muslims to get the message. ʿAbd al-Raḥman bin ʿĀwf, one of the Prophet's ten closest so-called Companions, reportedly freed no fewer than thirty thousand of his slaves on his death, in 652.[3]

In particular, the Koran charged owners whose slaves asked for their freedom to provide them with an opportunity to purchase it:

Those your right hands own
who seek emancipation, contract with
them accordingly, if you know some good
in them, and give them of the wealth of God
that He has given you.[4]

Such a contract, or *mukātaba*, fixed the price of freedom, and the slaves involved in these contracts were entitled to earn money while still serving their owners until the stipulated payments had been made. This was not, however, the end of the relationship. A freed male slave, while immediately granted the same legal status as the freeborn, became — along with his male descendants in perpetuity — a client of his former owner, whose family, name, and even lineage he adopted as his own. This arrangement involved obligations on both sides: perpetuating deference while securing many former slaves and their descendants from want.

Masters were also required to treat their female slaves benevolently, though with qualifications as well as peculiar advantages. The Koran stipulated that female slaves might lawfully be enjoyed by their masters, but such lawful enjoyment passed to their husbands when the female slaves were married, and masters had a moral duty to marry off their virtuous slaves, male or female. Indeed, a twofold reward in heaven was due to the master who educated his female slave, then freed and married her. Furthermore, in contrast to laws and practices in the system of slavery centuries later in the Americas, it was forbidden in Islam to separate a slave mother and her young child up to the age of seven or so, by allowing them to become the property of different masters. A relevant ḥadīth declared: "Whoever separates a mother from her child, God will separate him from his dear ones on the Day of Resurrection."[5]

Muslim jurists tended to construe the injunctions or guidance expressed in the Koran and the sunnah in a generally humanitarian way, informed by the maxim *al-asl huwa 'l-hurriya*, or "the basic principle is liberty."[6] Thus, the assumption in all dubious cases, such as foundlings of unknown origin, was in favor of freedom. And Muslim law allowed only two passages to the status of slavery: birth to a slave mother and capture in warfare. Even these were qualified. The child born to a female slave and her master was automatically free, since otherwise the child would be its own father's slave. The enslavement of captives in warfare excluded Muslim ones, on the basis that Muslims would not war against each other, and the enslavement of unbelievers was both a compensation for Muslim deaths in lawful war and a way of promoting conversion to the faith.

Yet, given the encouragement to emancipation—indeed, its practice—and the effective limits to the Islamic conquest of infidel peoples, the supply of slaves would have fallen ever further behind the demand if the law had not come increasingly to be flouted. Muslims enslaved other Muslims, sometimes on doctrinal pretexts. Some Muslim movements considered those who were not adherents to be infidels, righteously to be attacked, captured, and enslaved. Rebellion provided another pretext; for instance, thousands of women belonging to a Berber tribe that had revolted were publicly sold at Cairo in 1077. More often, across the frontier from Muslim states, peoples of various faiths, including Islam, were subjected to war or raids, and captives were enslaved, regardless of whether they were Muslims. Even in Muslim states, the free were not safe from being kidnapped for subsequent sale as slaves.

Sometimes it might have seemed that no one was beyond the catchment area of such abuses. In 1391–92, for instance, King 'Uthmān ibn Idrīs, the ruler of Bornu, around Lake Chad in black Africa, sent a letter of protest to the Mamluk regime in Egypt: "The Arab tribes of Jodham and others have taken our free subjects, women and children and old men of our own family, and other Muslims . . . These Arabs have pillaged our land, the land of Bornu, and continue doing so. They have taken as slaves free men and our fathers, the Muslims, and they are selling them to the slave-dealers of Egypt, Syria, and elsewhere, and keep some of them for themselves."[7]

The early-nineteenth-century Swiss-born John Lewis Burckhardt, while journeying through Nubia, met up with a slave dealer, Hadji Aly el Bornawy, whose "apparent sanctity" of conduct and related "great reputation" did not preclude inconsistent practices:

> To hear him talk of morals and religion, one might have
> supposed that he knew vice only by the name; yet Hadji

Aly, who had spent half his life in devotion, sold last year, in the slave market at Medinah, his own cousin, whom he had recently married at Mekka . . . The circumstance was well known in the caravan, but the Hadji nevertheless still continued to enjoy all his wonted reputation.[8]

At one or another commercial center in Islam, the slave dealer would generally consign his stocks to a broker, or *dallāl*, who might dispose of the more desirable and correspondingly expensive items by private sale or otherwise include them with the rest for public sale in the slave market. A special official, the *muḥtasib*, policed various aspects of urban life, including the public markets. One of his related functions was to ensure that the broker recorded the name and description of every slave sold, in case any of them were stolen property.

Muslim propriety permitted no such scrutiny as came to be common in the slave markets of the Americas. Male slaves might be examined only above the navel and below the knees, female slaves only by viewing their faces and hands, though blacks were often so scantily clothed that much more was visible. By custom, the buyer enjoyed a trial period of three days before the sale was ratified, to allow for the discovery of undisclosed defects. A twelfth-century manual, written by al-Saqatī of Malaga in Islamic Spain for the use of the muḥtasib, suggests that brokers were given to practicing cosmetic deception.[9] Not all drawbacks were easily identifiable by the lay eye, and there were doctors who specialized in examining slaves for defects and signs of disease. Ibn Butlan, a tenth-century physician in Baghdad, was among those who wrote treatises on such expertise.

Female slaves were required in considerable numbers, for a variety of purposes. Some were musicians, singers, and dancers—neither the status nor the style of a great house could do without a *sitara*, or chamber orchestra—reciters and even composers of poetry. There were celebrated schools in Baghdad, Cordoba, and Medina that supplied tuition and training in both musical and literary skills. Such slaves were highly prized and costly. Many more were bought for domestic work as cleaners and cooks, washerwomen and nursemaids. And many were in demand as concubines.

The harems of rulers could be enormous. The harem of 'Abd al-Raḥman III (912–61) in Cordoba contained some six thousand concubines; and the one in the Fatimid palace in Cairo had twice as many. High officials and great merchants owned numbers of concubines in keeping with their position and resources. Nor was ownership conditional on riches. Even much lower down the social scale, tradesmen and artisans with the necessary means might boast a concubine or two, who were probably required to perform other domestic duties as well as provide sexual service.

There was no social degradation in being a concubine. For a master to marry his concubine was neither disreputable nor rare. Indeed, concubines were often bought to be tried out as potential wives. Furthermore, those who bore their masters' children were not to be sold or given away, a respect in which they were arguably more secure than wives, who might be divorced against their will.

Male slaves, too, were required for domestic purposes. Across the social range of people who could afford the necessary space, homes were functionally divided into areas reserved for women and those which men reserved to themselves. In the latter, male slaves would see to the needs of the master and his guests. They were employed also as grooms; as guards, both for the home and abroad, when master or mistress ventured through the crowded and hazardous streets of the cities; as messengers and porters. The households of great merchants would also have held other male slaves, from musicians and scholars to secretaries, agents, and clerks. And there was one further use for them.

To secure the virtue of the supposedly fallible female and preserve the honor of her husband or master, prevalent practice in Islam went beyond the veiling of women and their seclusion in special quarters. Where resources allowed, the harem was secured not only by locks but by slave guards, and these were invariably eunuchs.

The preoccupation with honor was far from peculiar to Islamic culture. It was crucial to the code of chivalry in medieval Christendom, for instance. It was—and still is—found in societies where, in the absence of relatively developed class distinctions, the honor of person, family, and clan was the determinant of respect. It was certainly central to pre-Islamic Arabian society, where it was accompanied by an attitude of men toward women that suggested an obsessively suspicious possessiveness. And, for all the compassionate precepts of the Koran, this attitude survived in the more sophisticated urban culture of Islam. Marshall G. S. Hodgson writes:

> Formalized sexual jealousy, even more than the simple spirit of vengeance, fills the popular stories that appear, for instance, in the *Thousand and One Nights*. One can sometimes get the impression that the most important source of an individual man's personal reassurance was his absolute control over his womenfolk. A woman's "honour," her shame, formed an important point in determining the honour of her man; indeed, perhaps the gravest insult to a man, which most insistently abridged his right to precedence and called for vengeance, was any impugning of the honour of his womenfolk.[10]

In ancient Arabia, castration seems to have had no place; and when it subsequently did acquire one, the practice was roundly condemned by early Muslims. Mutilation was forbidden by Muslim law, and a specific ban on castration was invested with the authority of the Prophet by a ḥadīth: "Whoever cuts off the nose of a slave, his nose will be cut off; and whoever castrates a slave, him also shall we castrate."[11] But the wealth acquired by conquest and the influence of cultures encompassed in the advance of Islam—eunuchs were employed for various purposes in both the Persian and Byzantine empires—proved more potent than precept.

The letter, if not the spirit, of the law was long observed by leaving to those beyond the territorial limits of Islam the act of castration and then importing the product. In the Middle Ages, Prague and Verdun became castration centers for the supply of European eunuchs; Kharazon, near the Caspian Sea, a center for the supply of central Asian ones. Further circumventions, on Islamic territory, were pursued on the basis that the operations were conducted by non-Muslims. In tenth-century Islamic Spain, Jewish merchants reportedly performed the operation.[12] In the nineteenth century, Christian monks ran a castration center at their monastery of Deir al-Jandala near Abu Tig, a small town in Upper Egypt.

Such circumventions, however, were not always necessary, as ready-made black eunuchs were available in Muslim areas where slaves could be bought. Having traveled in Muslim West Africa during 1353, Ibn Baṭṭūṭā wrote of Barnu (Bornu), a Muslim kingdom: "From this country come excellent slavegirls, eunuchs, and fabrics dyed with saffron."[13] From the seventeenth century, eunuchs were produced in Baghirmi, a state southeast of Lake Chad that was at least nominally Muslim. One nineteenth-century traveler reported that in Morocco some masters castrated their own slaves, to use them as concubines.[14] Moreover, across the centuries, Muslim slave traders sometimes performed the operation themselves, at the place of purchase or along the route to market centers.

The high price of slave eunuchs—up to seven times that of uncastrated male slaves in the nineteenth century—reflected both their relative scarcity, as a result of the high death rate which the operation involved, and an all-but-insatiable demand for them. While the reason for employing them as guardians of the harem is obvious, the reason for their widespread use also as administrators, tutors, secretaries, and commercial agents is less so. One can only speculate that eunuchs were regarded as likely to be more devoted and dependable in serving their masters than other males, with normal distractions, would be. Certainly, the numbers some rulers required could be huge. The Caliph in Baghdad at the beginning of the tenth century had seven thousand black eunuchs and four thousand white ones in his palace.[15]

The use of slave eunuchs as concubines by some merchants in nineteenth-century Morocco points to a feature of Islamic society that affected the treatment of young male slaves, whether they were eunuchs or not. The attitude toward women, formalized in the secured seclusion of the harem, can scarcely have failed to promote a measure of heterosexual frustration among young males not yet of an age or with adequate means to acquire concubines or to marry, and this might well have promoted the alternative of homosexual relations.

There was a further factor. The primacy, even glorification, of virile values influenced attitudes and conduct, most markedly in societies of militarized rule. In association with the courts of the generals or amirs, Hodgson explains, "sex between males entered pervasively into the ethic and aesthetic of the upper classes . . . As in some classical Athenian circles, it was assumed that a handsome adolescent ('beardless') youth or even a younger boy was naturally attractive to any full-grown man, and that the man would have sexual relations with him if the occasion arose (for instance, if the youth were his slave), alongside sex relations with his women."[16] Many love lyrics, particularly in Persia, were conventionally and explicitly addressed by male poets to males.

Yet, Hodgson adds, the "Muslim stereotype of such sexual relations answered the idea of the sex act as an act of domination. The adult male, as the lover, enjoyed a youth (probably anally) who was, in principle, passive; and while the relation was only improper, at most licentious, for the lover, it was very dishonourable for the youth who was enjoyed, who thus allowed himself to be cast in a woman's role."[17] In this context, whatever the sexual inclinations of the male slave might have been, he had no choice in the matter. And for those male slaves who were used against their will, in a culture so preoccupied with masculine honor, a special sense of shame might well have been involved.

Outside of domestic service, male slaves might be found in a variety of activities, from labor at the ports, in construction and transport, to employment in workshops and factories. Many were certainly black, as were those engaged in especially exacting labor beyond the mainly urban economy—working, for instance, in the gold mines of Wadi Allaqi in Egyptian Nubia, until the deposits there were exhausted in the fourteenth century, and the western Saharan salt pans.

It is clear, however, that there was no extensive and long-sustained commitment of black slave labor to the scale of commercial plantation agriculture that absorbed so many millions of black slaves in the Americas. This was not for want of trying. But the consequences of the commitment proved so devastating as to have a widespread and lasting effect.

As early as the late seventh century, black slaves known as the Zanj, associated with people from the East African coast, were put to agricultural work in a region that encompassed part of western Persia but mainly southern Iraq. They dug ditches, drained marshland, cleared salt flats of their crust; they cultivated sugar and cotton in plantations; and they were accommodated in camps that contained five hundred to five thousand each. Their living conditions were as harsh as the labor demands imposed on them. In 694, rebellion broke out among them, but this was crushed with such relative ease that there was no impact on the use of numerous black slaves in agricultural labor.

Then, in 868–69 (the year 255 of the Islamic Era), there arrived in the city of Basra a certain 'Alī ibn Muḥammad, who had previously proclaimed himself, without much success, the new Prophet in eastern Arabia. He rapidly acquired a following among the Zanj engaged in clearing the salt flats, by promising them power and property. With energy and resolution, he soon had an army of fifteen thousand rebels, formed into units under efficient commanders. In 869–70 (256), the rebels took two important towns, and the uprising spread among the Zanj in western Persia, where the support given it by the urban poor and disaffected peasants contributed to the capture of Ahwaz, the principal city of the region.

The defeat of a large force sent by the Caliph to crush the rebellion so alarmed the rich of Basra that many of them took flight. More Zanj victories followed in 870–71 (257). The Caliphate armies contained Zanj soldiers, who increasingly deserted, reinforcing the rebellion with their training and weapons. In the autumn of 871, Zanj forces captured and pillaged Basra itself. Much of the city was consumed by fire; three hundred thousand inhabitants lost their lives.[18]

The rebels were not so dazzled by the importance of their latest prize that they abandoned their base or their mobile strategy. In the Shaṭṭ-al-'Arab marshlands, they secured their strongholds by constructing earthen walls on islands or along canals among the concealing reeds. One such stronghold, where 'Alī ibn Muḥammad had his headquarters, became the fortified town of Mukhtāra and the capital of what was effectively an independent Zanj state. From this command center, Zanj forces raided army camps, towns, trade caravans, and commercial shipping.

In 878–79 (265), the Zanj captured Wasit, in a drive toward Baghdad itself, then the greatest city in all Islam. It proved to be the high point in their challenge. Muwaffaq, the new commander of the Caliphate armies, had strategic flair. He acquired an auxiliary fleet of boats that could navigate the channels and canals of the marshlands. And he abandoned the established policy of killing or torturing any captured Zanj rebels, with the hope of encouraging deserters from a cause whose popular support was now reportedly shrinking.

As the rebellion advanced to control more territory and take more plunder, the power and property once promised to the Zanj came increasingly to be concentrated in the possession of their leaders. Peasants, many of whom had rallied to the slave rebellion in despair at the tax exactions of the Caliphate, found themselves subjected to similar exactions from rebels turned rulers. Once sympathetic or simply neutral traders and artisans were alienated by the damage done to the economy within and beyond the compass of conquest. When 'Alī ibn Muḥammad proclaimed himself Caliph, ordered prayers to be said for him in the mosques, and coinage to be issued in his name, it might well have seemed that the regime of the rebellion was much like the one it had set out to displace.

Muwaffaq's forces reconquered more and more territory. And as the Zanj withdrew to defensive positions in the marshlands, Muwaffaq followed them there, his river boats mounting one successful assault after another. It was still a slow and costly process. Mukhtāra itself withstood three years of siege, despite a pledge of pardon if only 'Alī ibn Muḥammad would surrender and swear allegiance to the Caliph. By 883, however, hunger and desertions had so weakened the defenders that this last fortress fell. The head of 'Alī ibn Muḥammad was thrown down at Muwaffaq's feet.

A triumphant Caliphate slaughtered many of the defeated Zanj and restored the rest to slavery. Those inhabitants of Basra who had allied themselves with the rebellion and refused to renounce their allegiance were killed.[19] Yet, even crushed, the rebellion had a lasting impact. The use of large numbers of black slaves in plantation agriculture and irrigation schemes sharply declined; it was considered too dangerous.

Decline, to be sure, was not abandonment. During the tenth century, the date plantations of al-Ahsa', in northeast Arabia, used substantial numbers of black slaves, as did the Saharan oases where dates were produced along with grain and vegetables. As Nehemia Levtzion writes: "In the fifteenth century, slaves were in great demand for labor in expanding plantation agriculture in southern Morocco."[20] And in the nineteenth century, when the demand for cotton was high and the supply of slaves from Sudan plentiful, they were used to increase production of the crop in Egypt, while large numbers of slaves obtained from the interior were used for grain production on the East African coast and in the clove plantations on the islands of Zanzibar and Pemba. Nonetheless, without the great ninth-century Zanj rebellion, such usage might well have been more massive and sustained, arguably with economic and social consequences closer to the American experience.

Finally, there was a major use of black and other slaves for military service, in a systematic manner unique to Islam, reaching from Spain to Bengal and beyond. One scholar, Daniel Pipes, argues that the reasons for this were related to the very nature of Islamic politics.[21] Alone among universalist religions, Islam, in conformity with the career of its founder, made no distinction between the religious and the political. The umma, or community of believers, swept aside all other affiliation for a unity symbolized by the Caliph.

Yet soon there were rival Caliphs, political unity was never restored, and the Caliphate itself became a title that mocked its pretensions. Furthermore, many Muslims were increasingly estranged from rulers who neither in their policies nor in the conduct of their lives represented the principles and precepts of the faith they professed. Some took to boycotting government and all its works—refusing, for instance, to handle its coinage—while others engaged in militant movements of protest and reform.

The very success of the Zanj rebellion in attracting so much support from those who were free but poor exposed the economic fissures in Muslim society. Rulers, aware of the risks in relying on soldiers recruited from a population infected with discontent, were already using slaves to guard their palaces and augment their armies. The Zanj rebellion, reports of which resounded through Islam, advanced this process. Given the extent of desertion by Zanj military slaves to the rebellion, prudence might have prompted reliance on eastern Europe and central Asia as sources for the supply of such slaves. There were, however, not enough of these available to meet the need, and too great a reliance on a particular source raised the risk of an ethnically united disaffection. Black slaves continued to be used in substantial numbers.

Military slaves were distinctive in various ways. Other slaves might be required to fight, but this was in practice relatively rare. Military slaves might be required, in the course of campaigns, to do menial work, but only as subservient to their use as soldiers. Any free person with the means to buy a slave might own one. The ownership of military slaves was restricted to the ruler. Other slaves might be bought at any age. Military slaves were generally acquired as older children or adolescents, preferably at the age of twelve, since they needed years of training and the inculcation of loyalty in order to be of skilled and reliable use. To confirm this loyalty, they were compelled to become Muslims, while other slaves could adhere to their own religions, especially those with which Islam had concluded a covenant.[22]

Bernard Lewis argues that "pagan and early Islamic Arabia seems to have shared the general attitude of the ancient world, which attached no stigma to blackness,"[23] and that there were three factors that adversely affected this attitude. First was the very fact of conquest, in which "the normal distinctions inevitably appeared between the conquerors and the conquered."[24] The second was the advance of such conquest into areas of black Africa whose population seemed less "developed" than the Arabs or the conquered peoples "in Southwest Asia and Southern Europe."[25] Finally, "the large-scale importation of African slaves influenced Arab (and therefore Muslim) attitudes to the peoples of darker skin whom most Arabs and Muslims encountered only in this way."[26]

These explanations for the emergence of color prejudice seem broadly persuasive. Certainly, the Prophet himself counted among his early followers and persons close to him, known as the "Companions," those who were partly or wholly of Ethiopian descent—notably, Bilāl ibn Rabāh, his personal attendant and, when Muḥammad instituted the call to prayer, his first muezzin; 'Umar, who would later become Caliph; and 'Amr ibn al-'Ās, who would command the Arab invasion of Egypt in 639. Yet the Prophet also stated in his last sermon: "No Arab has any priority over a non-Arab and no white over a black except in righteousness."[27] This admonition would suggest that an Arab attitude of superiority toward others, and in particular toward blacks, was already being expressed in his lifetime. Moreover, the experience of such prejudice began to be reflected in the verses of black poets at an early stage in the history of Islam.

> *If my colour were pink, women would love me*
> *But the Lord has marred me with blackness,*

wrote Suḥaym, a slave of African origin who died in 660. He proclaimed his essential dignity in another poem:

> Though I am a slave my soul is nobly free
> Though I am black of colour my character
> is white.[28]

Nuṣayb ibn Rabāh, who died in 726, had his own cutting rejoinder to an attack on him for his color from an Arab poet:

> Blackness does not diminish me, as long as I
>   Have this tongue and this stout heart.
> Some are raised by means of their lineage; the
>   Verses of my poems are my lineage!
> How much better a keen-minded, clear-spoken
>   Black than a mute white![29]

One scholar argues that it was the great Zanj rebellion which led to a hardening of attitudes against blacks; that "the black Africans came to be held in contempt, in spite of the teachings of Islam, and there emerged in Muslim literature many previously unknown themes expressing a negative attitude towards blacks."[30] As certain poems suggest, a negative attitude had emerged much earlier, but the rebellion might well have intensified this. And the context of the rebellion does point to another factor in the development of color prejudice. Black slaves had come to be favored for forms of labor requiring physical strength, and such labor was generally at the bottom of the social scale. Essentially, too, Islamic culture prized intellectual qualities above physical ones, albeit with feminine beauty an exception. And the association of peculiar physical prowess with intellectual inferiority both rationalized and promoted the disparagement of blacks.

There were still other influences. As Islam expanded its sway, it encountered and encompassed peoples and cultures with beliefs and attitudes of their own. The Persian-based religion of Zoroastrianism, for instance, taught of a fundamental cosmic conflict between Good, as represented by Light, and Evil, as represented by Darkness. Whether or not the doctrine came to inform an explicit prejudice against blacks, it is easy to see how it may have reinforced an existing one.

There was a more specific line of influence, from science and learning, that—despite the supposed absence of any stigma attached to blackness in the ancient world—may be initially traceable to Galen, the renowned physician in the Roman Empire of the second century. His writings, in particular his textbook on anatomy, had a marked impact on the practice of medicine and related matters in medieval Islam. He listed ten characteristics of black males: thick lips, broad nostrils, frizzy hair, black eyes, furrowed hands and feet, thin eyebrows, pointed teeth, long penis, great merriment. And this great merriment, he wrote, "dominates the black man because of his defective brain, whence, also the weakness of his intelligence."[31]

The eminent writer al-Mas'ūdī, who died in 956, quoted the foregoing passage directly from Galen's writings. And whether or not related was the work of Ibn Sina (980–1037), a Persian physician in Baghdad who wrote on both medicine and philosophy and became so celebrated that his writings, translated into Latin, circulated in Europe, where he was known as Avicenna. Ibn Sina maintained that climate crucially affected human temperament, and that the extremes of heat or cold produced natures suitable to slavery, "for there must be masters and slaves."[32]

Almost certainly influenced by Ibn Sina's theories were the writings of Sā'id al-Andalusī (died 1070), a qāḍī, or judge, at Toledo, an important city in Islamic Spain. He could scarcely have expressed his rationalization of slavery in terms further from the spirit and the letter of what the founder of the faith had taught. He characterized the Slavs, the Bulgars, and their neighbors, living at an "excessive distance" from the sun, as frigid in temperament, with raw humors: "Thus they lack keenness of understanding and clarity of intelligence, and are overcome by ignorance and dullness, lack of discernment, and stupidity."

At the other extreme, he wrote, were those living under the "long presence of the sun at the zenith," because of which "their temperaments become hot and their humors fiery, their color black and their hair woolly." In consequence, too, "they lack self-control and steadiness of mind and are overcome by fickleness, foolishness, and ignorance. Such are the blacks, who live at the extremity of the land of Ethiopia, the

Nubians, the Zanj and the like." He went still further, to distinguish between "even the most ignorant peoples" who "have some kind of monarchical government and some kind of religious law" and those "who diverge from this human order and depart from this rational association . . . such as the rabble of Bujja, the savages of Ghana, the scum of Zanj, and their like."[33]

Even Ibn Khaldūn (1332–1406), the preeminent medieval historian and social thinker in Islam, slid easily from prevailing theories on climatic impact to those of ethnic inferiority. Elaborating on the association between exposure to the heat of the sun and the generic merriment of blacks, he likened the effect to that of alcohol on the drinker and of warm air in the bath, which induced the bather to sing. He went on to claim that "the Negro nations are, as a rule, submissive to slavery," because they "have attributes that are quite similar to those of dumb animals."[34] Apparently such momentous events as the great rebellion of the Zanj were exceptions that only proved the rule.

For much of Islamic history, however, there was no such virtually exclusive identification of slavery with blackness as came to exist in the Christian West with colonial expansion and the Atlantic Trade. This would not have been compatible with the widespread use of white slaves. However, prejudice did promote discriminations. By the Middle Ages, the Arabic word 'abd was in general use to denote a black slave, while the word mamlūk referred to a white one.

The processes of enslaving blacks did come, in the nineteenth century, to involve violence and brutality on a gigantic scale. But many of the leading slavers then were Afro-Arab blacks themselves, and there is no evidence that it was blackness which motivated such ruthlessness. The market demand for black slaves seemed virtually insatiable, a result of the need to provide labor for the plantation economies in Muslim East Africa, the mounting apprehension across Islam that Western pressures against the trade might soon end it, and a sharpening decline in the availability of white slaves. The related rewards of black enslavement excited greed, and traders, turned conquerors in the catchment areas of supplies, were involved in incessant raiding and warfare.

Even then, however, black slaves were still mainly treated by their masters with relative benevolence; and many of them enjoyed the favor traditionally due to their real or supposed attributes. Nubian women, for instance, were highly prized as concubines, and the great twelfth-century geographer al-Idrīsī (1110–65) was eloquently expressive of their attractions:

> Their women are of surpassing beauty. They are circum-cised and fragrant-smelling . . . their lips are thin, their mouths small and their hair flowing. Of all black women, they are the best for the pleasures of the bed . . . It is on ac-count of these qualities of theirs that the rulers of Egypt were so desirous of them and outbid others to purchase them, afterwards fathering children from them.[35]

In the early nineteenth century, Burckhardt found that at Mekka (Mecca) there was a general choice of Abyssinian (Ethiopian) women as concubines and, among many Meccans, as wives:

> There are few families at Mekka, in moderate circum-stances, that do not keep slaves . . . the concubines are al-ways Abyssinian slaves. No wealthy Mekkawy [Meccan] prefers domestic peace to the gratification of his passions; they all keep mistresses in common with their lawful wives: but if a slave gives birth to a child, the master generally marries her, or, if he fails to do so, is censured by the com-munity . . . Many Mekkawys have no other than Abyssinian wives, finding the Arabians more expensive, and less dis-posed to yield to the will of the husband . . . The same practice is adopted by many foreigners, who reside in the Hedjaz for a short time. Upon their arrival, they buy a fe-male companion, with the design of selling her at their de-parture; but sometimes their stay is protracted; the slave bears a child; they marry her, and become stationary in the town. There are very few unmarried, or without a slave. This, indeed, is general in the East, and no where more so than at Mekka. The mixture of Abyssinian blood has, no doubt, given to the Mekkawys that yellow tinge of the skin which distinguishes them from the natives of the Desert.[36]

Such preferences for Abyssinians among African women were clearly influenced by standards of beauty set by the dominant peoples—Arabs, Persians, Turks—of Islam, rather than the standards that most black Africans would have recognized as natural. And other physical features seem to have been more important than color itself, since some Abyssinians were a good deal darker than others. Burckhardt observed: "The Mekkawys make no distinction whatever between sons born of Abyssinian slaves and those of free Arabian women . . . Sherif Ghaleb Yahya, the present Sherif, is of a very dark complexion, like that of his father; his mother was a dark brown Abyssinian slave."[37] This was the case, too, for Nubian women, whose appeal so captivated al-Idrīsī.

Special talents or circumstances might make such considerations irrelevant. Ishraq as-Suwaida, a black girl, was celebrated throughout tenth-century Islamic Spain for her knowledge of grammar and prosody. In Egypt the longest reigning of the Fatimid Caliphs, al-Mustanṣir (1036–94), was the son of a Sudanese black concubine. In fact, since he was only seven when he became Caliph, it was she, with the help of the Jewish merchant responsible for her sale to the royal harem, who effectively ruled for the first fifteen years of his reign.

Subjective aesthetic judgments did, however, influence presumptions of other characteristics, especially among male African slaves. Burckhardt expressed early-nineteenth-century prejudices, along with his own, in writing about this:

> The male Noubas in Egypt, as well as in Arabia, are preferred to all others for labour: they bear a good character, and sell at Shendy [in Nubia] and in Egypt twenty per cent. dearer than the Negroes. The male Abyssinians, on the contrary, are known to be little fit for bodily work, but they are esteemed for their fidelity, and make excellent house servants, and often clerks, their intellects being certainly much superior to those of Blacks. The Noubas are said to be of a healthier constitution, and to suffer less from disease than the Abyssinians. The greatest part of them are exported to Egypt; but some are sent to Souakin [the Red Sea port for shipment to Jiddah on the Arabian coast].[38]

Nonetheless, for black male slaves of varying complexions and features, two institutionalized practices in Islam afforded peculiar opportunities for vertical mobility.

Unlike white eunuchs, deprived only of their testicles, black ones were subjected to the most radical form of castration, known, according to John Laffin, as "level with the abdomen . . . based on the assumption that the blacks had an ungovernable sexual appetite."[39] Whether out of consideration for the sacrifice they had suffered or in the belief that, freed from the distractions of carnal appetites, they were more devoted to their masters or to spiritual concerns, black eunuchs were treated with particular consideration. Indeed, many of them were appointed to offices of high responsibility, respect, and reward.

One black eunuch of probable Nubian origin, Abu'l-Misk Kafur, eventually rose to rule Egypt during the tenth century. The Ikhshidid ruler, Muḥammad b. Tughi, who had bought Kafur, invested him with increasingly important political and military responsibilities, including the position of tutor to his two sons. With the death of Muḥammad b. Tughi in 946, Kafur became regent to each of his sons in turn until, with the death of the second in 966, he declared himself ruler and remained such for the two years until his own death. In fifteenth-century Egypt, under Mamluk rule, one black eunuch was appointed governor of Aden, and another was sent on a special mission to his Ethiopian homeland.

At Mecca, Burckhardt found that most of the eunuchs were blacks, with a few "copper-coloured Indians;" that they were all married to black slaves; maintained several male and female slaves as servants in their homes; and had a large income through the revenues of the mosque, private donations from pilgrims, regular stipends from Constantinople, and profit from their engagement in trade. Burckhardt continues: "Their chief, or Aga, whom they elect among themselves, is a great personage, and is entitled to sit in the presence of the Pasha and the Sherif."[40] Still greater, he found, in the respect shown to them and in their self-regard, were the "forty or fifty" eunuchs at Medina.

There,

> they are more richly dressed, though in the same costume;
> usually wear fine Cashmere shawls and gowns of the best

Indian silk stuffs, and assume airs of great importance. When they pass through the Bazar, every body hastens to kiss their hands; and they exercise considerable influence in the internal affairs of the town . . . They live together in one of the best quarters of Medina, to the eastward of the mosque, and their houses are said to be furnished in a more costly manner than any others in the town. The adults are all married to black or Abyssinian slaves . . .

The chief of the eunuchs is called Sheikh el Haram; he is also the chief of the mosque, and the principal person in the town; being consequently of much higher rank than the Aga, or chief of the eunuchs at Mekka . . . A eunuch of the mosque would be highly affronted if he were so termed by any person. Their usual title is Aga. Their chief takes the title of Highness or Sadetkom, like a Pasha, or the Sherif of Mekka.[41]

Substantial numbers of blacks were used as military slaves, which provided opportunities for advancement to power and riches. Some of these slaves rose to positions from which they made and unmade rulers, while in Islamic India there were some who became rulers themselves. Collective ethnic selection, however, could carry collective ethnic risk.

The first recorded use of black military slaves was in early-ninth-century Ifriqiya (Tunisia), where the Aghlabid ruler formed them into a special corps, as a potential countervailing force to the Arab soldiery, and his dynastic successors continued the practice. When the Fatimids displaced that ruling dynasty, they slaughtered all the black military slaves, evidently in distrust of their loyalty, since they then enlisted a black corps of their own. In 972, the Fatimids moved their capital to Egypt and left their North African lieutenants, the Zirids, to hold Ifriqiya. These not only maintained but much augmented the black military slave force there; the Zirid ruler Mu'izz bought thirty thousand black slaves. Then disputes over the succession led to armed conflict between black troops of differing allegiance, so the use of such troops in Ifriqiya was abandoned from the middle of the eleventh century.

Aḥmad b. Ṭūlūn, the Ṭūlūnid ruler from 868 to 884, introduced black military slaves to Egypt in 870 and left at his death, among his other properties, twenty-four thousand white slaves and forty-five thousand black ones.[42] He ordered special quarters to be built for the black slaves in the barrack town set aside for his imported soldiery, though this segregation was almost certainly directed at securing a separate force of allegiance rather than a formalized color prejudice.

The Fatimid rulers of Egypt (969–1171) raised large black battalions as a counterweight to their Berber and Turkish troops. While visiting Cairo in 1046–49, the Persian Nasir-I Khusraw estimated that there were some thirty thousand black soldiers in an army exceeding a hundred thousand.[43] What ensued was a brittle coexistence among the three ethnic groups of military slaves, intermittently fractured by conflict between one and another. Sometimes Berber and Turk combined against black, and it was this which reached a climax in 1169, when fifty thousand black soldiers fought fiercely for two days in the capital before being forced to flee into southern Egypt.

The Ayyūbid successors to the Fatimids avoided using black military slaves altogether. The armies of the following Mamluk regime consisted essentially of slaves from the Turkish and Circassian peoples of the Black Sea region. And the Ottomans relied for military slaves mainly on the Slavic and Albanian populations of the Balkans. It was only in the early nineteenth century, under the rule of Muḥammad 'Alī, that large numbers of black military slaves would be used again in Egypt.

In Morocco the Almoravid ruler Yūsuf b. Tāshfīn (1061–1106) was the first to use black military slaves, for a special two-thousand-man bodyguard. Black military slaves then came to be used in the regular Almoravid army, which lost on a single day of battle against insurgent Almohad forces in 1129 about three thousand soldiers, most of them blacks. The triumphant Almohads also made use of black military slaves, though, for unrecorded reasons, they later abandoned the practice. It was only in 1591, after his conquest of Timbuktu, that the Sa'dian ruler al-Manṣūr again brought military slaves into the Moroccan army, selected from among the captives. And their descendants are likely to have been a part of that great black military slave force which, for a time under the 'Alawid dynasty, became first the guardians and then the commanders of rule.

Mūlāy Ismā'il, the second 'Alawid Sultan (1672–1727), was himself the son of a black concubine. Early in his reign, he instituted a system by which black slave children over the age of ten were conscripted. The girls were educated and trained in domestic virtues by the women of his household. The boys worked with carpenters and other craftsmen, learned related skills and also how to handle horses, were trained in various martial abilities, and then enlisted in the army. Presented with the now accomplished young women in marriage and with funds to build their own homes, the young men were expected not only to provide military service but, with their wives, to create a new generation for similar treatment.

The resultant black slave army was certainly large; estimates of its numbers vary widely—from as many as 250,000 to fewer than 50,000.[44] A figure of 150,000, based on the ledgers of the Sultan's chief secretary, might have included black slaves assigned to public works as well as those devoted to military service. Whatever the case, this army gave loyal service to Mūlāy Ismā'il, a ruler as ruthless and cruel as he was energetic and efficient, who succeeded in uniting at last a long-torn and troubled kingdom. After his death the black slave army made and unmade, within a span of thirty years, no fewer than seven Sultans from among his five hundred sons, until a strong ruler, enthroned in 1757, recruited an Arab army to disperse the black one. At the end of the eighteenth century, however, black slaves were once again being integrated into the army. And late in the nineteenth century, an army of five thousand black slaves served the ruler of Iligh, a small principality in southern Morocco.[45]

The uses to which black slaves were put in Islam are relatively well documented. There is much more uncertainty about the overall numbers exported in the trade. One scholar, Ralph Austen, has provided rough calculations, albeit based mainly on sparse indicative records for particular periods. These figures show fluctuations that may correspond to times of economic expansion or contraction; the availability of black slaves and, alternatively, of white ones; and the growth or decline in demand for particular purposes, as for military service or plantation labor.

Austen's calculations encompass the three sectors of the export trade in black slaves: across the Sahara, from the coast of the Red Sea, and from East Africa. For the trans-Saharan trade, conducted along six major routes, he estimates a total of 4,820,000 for the 950 years between 650 and 1600. He suggests that this sector began with an annual average of 1,000 for the period 650–800 (a total of 150,000); then tripled to an annual average of 3,000 in the ninth century (300,000); almost tripled again, to an annual average of 8,700 in the tenth and eleventh centuries (1,740,000); declined to an annual average of 5,500 in the twelfth to fourteenth centuries (1,650,000); declined even further to an annual average of 4,300 in the fifteenth century; then rose again to an annual average of 5,500 in the sixteenth century (550,000). For the Red Sea coast trade, he estimates a total of 1,600,000; for the East African one, 800,000, in the period 800–1600.[46]

Another scholar, Paul Lovejoy, has commented: "The figures cited here, 4,820,000 for the Saharan trade between 650 and 1600 and 2,400,000 for the Red Sea and Indian Ocean trade between 800 and 1600, could be twice as many slaves as the number actually exported or considerably less than the total volume. The time span is so great and the supply area so extensive that the estimated figure (7,220,000) is a rough approximation indeed; a range of 3.5 to 10 million is more accurate."[47]

It is estimated that in the seventeenth century 700,000 slaves were exported along the trans-Saharan routes, 100,000 from the Red Sea coast, and another 100,000 from East African ports, for an annual average of 9,000, or 900,000 in all. Estimated numbers for the eighteenth century are still larger: 700,000 across the Sahara, 200,000 from the Red Sea, and 400,000 from East Africa, for an annual average of 11,300, or a total of 1,300,000.[48] By the end of the eighteenth century, therefore, a rough total of 9,420,000 slaves might have been dispatched from black Africa to the markets of Islam.

The nineteenth century exceeded any of the previous twelve centuries in the volume of this trade, and the related documentary evidence is more extensive and exact than it is for any previous century. Some 1,200,000 have been estimated for the trans-Saharan routes, 450,000 for the Red Sea route, and 442,000 for East African coastal exports: an annual average of over 20,000, or more than 2,000,000 in all.[49] This figure, added to the previous estimated numbers, makes a total, for twelve and a half centuries, of 11,512,000, a figure not far short of the 11,863,000 estimated to have been loaded onto ships during the four centuries of the Atlantic slave trade.[50]

Nor was this the end. Raymond Mauvy has estimated that 300,000 black slaves were traded in Islam in the first half of the twentieth century. And his own estimates for the total of the trade since its start substantially exceed Austen's. He has suggested a figure of 100,000 for the seventh century; 200,000 for the eighth; 400,000 for the ninth; 500,000 for each of the next four centuries; 1,000,000 for the fourteenth century; and 2,000,000 for each of the following five centuries—or, with his estimate of 300,000 for part of the twentieth century, a total of 14,000,000.[51]

Estimates as enormous as those of Austen or Lovejoy, let alone Mauvy, are disputed. Basil Davidson, whose distinguished work on the history of Africa and, in particular, the Atlantic slave trade requires respect for his judgments, is one such critic. He argues: "Slaves were expensive. For the most part, only the rich man was able to purchase them. Being expensive, they were cherished as individuals, often they were regarded as irreplaceable."[52]

The question of expense remains crucial. E. S. Goitein, who drew on the mass of documents discovered in a Cairo *geniza*, or storeroom, for his work on Jewish social history and Islamic civilization in the Mediterranean area from the tenth to the thirteenth century, gave the standard price of a slave in Cairo during the Fatimid period as twenty gold dinars. Davidson cites this, as well as the report of the Andalusian historian al-Bakri, who, writing in 1067 about the excellence of black female cooks in the western Sudanic trading city of Awdaghost, added that such a cook could cost a hundred dinars or more.[53] Furthermore, in Islamic Spain, records of the period 1065–67 reveal that a black slave cost 160 *mictals*— the local term for dinars—while a house in the city of Cordoba sold for a similar sum, another house for 280 mictals, a horse for 24, and a mule for 60.[54]

Against this expense should be set the pressure of need. Goitein himself, dealing with one aspect of such need, describes it as follows: "This study shows that the female slaves formed a vital section of the working population, insofar as they provided domestic help, a type of work shunned by free women. We, with electricity and gas and countless gadgets at our disposal, can easily forgo the services of a maid. But in the

Geniza period, as in the time of our own grandparents, a larger house-hold could hardly do without domestic help. This explains why female slavery looms so large in the Geniza papers."[55]

Furthermore, the rich in Islam could be very rich indeed. The tenth-century Arab traveler Ibn Ḥawqal, visiting the self-same Awdaghost where a good female cook cost a hundred dinars or more, reported see-ing a check for forty-two thousand dinars—enough to buy over four hun-dred cooks—issued to a merchant in southern Morocco.[56] And the ownership of slaves, for all their relatively high price, could grow with the economic context. Times and places set their own standards.

In the eleventh century in al-Andalus, or Islamic Spain, when a black slave cost the equivalent of 160 dinars, there was an economic boom, fed not only by West African gold flows but by also the export of products from specialized agriculture and manufacturing. The result was inflation at home and so much purchasing power abroad that it dominated some foreign markets. As Thomas Glick writes: "The sale of the Egyptian flax crop in the eleventh century was coordinated with the arrival of Andalusi merchants . . . Viewed from al-Andalus, the Islamic world was a vast em-porium where finished products and highly valued raw materials could be purchased for gold."[57] In so far as slaves came to be a luxury, it was one that so much prosperity was well able to afford.

That price might have been a poor guide to numbers is strongly sug-gested by a period and place for which extensive information on the mar-keting of slaves is available—late-nineteenth-century Morocco. Market sales were by auction, and prices varied according to age, gender, origin, and condition. Females comprised the large majority of imports, with the pubescent generally fetching the highest prices. In 1876, at the market in Essaouira, prices ranged between £10 ($48) and £30 ($144): £10–15 ($48–72) for males five to ten years of age; £15–20 ($72–96) for males ten to fifteen years old and females five to ten years old; and £20–30 ($96–144) for females aged ten to fifteen. Once trained for agricultural, domestic, or other work, they could then be resold for appreciably higher prices, in accordance with their skills and appearance. Attractive virgins could fetch £40–80 ($192–386) and even more.[58]

These were serious sums in the nineteenth century. Yet tax returns for the slave market in Marrakesh reveal that the average annual number of slaves sold there was 3,788 in the period 1876–78 and 4,781 in the

period 1884–94, with annual peaks of 6,305 in 1890–91 and 6,302 in
1893–94. (These figures apply to the Islamic calendar year, which encompasses parts of two years in the Christian Era calendar.)

Some of these slaves were related to the internal trade, sold by their
Moroccan owners or speculatively bought elsewhere in Morocco by
dealers looking to higher prices in the leading market. Certainly, too, the
Marrakesh market was so predominant at this period that it might well
have accounted for three-quarters of all recorded sales in the urban markets of Morocco. But it is likely that such sales represented at most a
quarter of the total. Slave dealers were notorious for flouting Muslim law
and doubtless found various ways of evading taxes by clandestine sales.
Even within the law, many sales were conducted on commission and
never reached the markets for inclusion in the records. Not least, many
imported slaves were traded in rural or tribal areas where the tax authorities had little or only intermittent control. On this basis, Daniel
Schroeter states that "a conservative estimate of annual slave imports
from the 1870s to 1894 would range between 4,000 and 7,000, with an
apparent upward trend until at least 1894."[59]

Many slaves auctioned in the urban markets might well have fetched
prices beyond the reach of all but the rich — mainly merchants, landowners, and high officials. Yet there were clearly enough of these to sustain a
sizable trade. The Sultan himself contributed mightily to its prosperity as
well as to its protection. An estimated 5 percent of all slaves sold in the
markets were bound for the royal household.[60] There were also many
Moroccans of no great wealth, however, who could afford a slave or two
at a suitable price, in the major urban markets and especially in the un-
regulated rural or tribal areas.

No less relevant to the argument on the overall volume of the Islamic
trade in black slaves are the particular reports of the large numbers transported or on sale at various times. In the 1570s, a Frenchman visiting
Egypt found "many thousands" of blacks on sale in Cairo on market
days.[61] In 1665–66, Father Antonius Gonzales, a Spanish-Belgian traveler, reported seeing eight hundred to one thousand slaves in the Cairo
market on a single day.[62] In 1796, a British traveler reported a caravan of
five thousand slaves departing from Dar Fur.[63] In 1849, the British vice
consul reported the arrival of 2,384 slaves at Murzuq in the Fezzan.[64]

These numbers may seem small alongside Mauvy's estimate of

14,000,000 for the total volume of the Islamic black slave trade. Yet even that total, spread across thirteen and a half centuries, represents an annual average of 10,370, or little more than twice the number in the single caravan that reportedly departed from Dar Fur in 1796. The lower total of some 11,500,000, based on the Austen estimates for twelve and a half centuries, represents an annual average of 9,200. Furthermore, if the figure of 2,000,000 for the nineteenth century, hardly disputed even by the critics of high numbers, were excluded as distortingly exceptional, the annual average for eleven and a half centuries would have been 8,270.

Nor was demand necessarily related to need. Status, custom, and the simple pleasure of possession were also factors. In today's Western culture, so driven by competitive consumption, there can be no difficulty in understanding an Islamic culture in which the ownership of slaves was a form of conspicuous consumption. An eleventh-century traveler, visiting Awdaghost, reported that a rich man there might own as many as a thousand slaves.[65] At the other extreme, a nineteenth-century British visitor, told by a local shaykh that there were thirty slaves in his poor mountainous district between Tripoli and Ghadames in the Sahara, wondered "how the people could keep slaves when they could scarcely keep themselves."[66]

Another explanation for the large numbers of black slaves was the very variety of occupations for which they were required. By 1838, for instance, an estimated ten thousand to twelve thousand slaves were arriving in Egypt alone each year, some of them doubtless bound for domestic service there or for export to undertake similar service, but others for use as concubines, construction and factory workers, porters, dockers, clerks, soldiers, and cultivators.

Despite the impact of the ninth-century Zanj rebellion in discouraging the large-scale engagement of black slave labor in agriculture, there were still times and places of just such an engagement. In the most notable instance, during the nineteenth century, the numbers acquired to work on clove plantations on the East African offshore islands of Zanzibar and Pemba, and other plantations mainly devoted to growing grain, in the vicinity of Mombasa and Malindi along the East African coast, totaled some 769,000.[67]

Such numbers are excluded from the cited volume of the nineteenth-century East African black slave trade, whose total of 442,000 includes 347,000 for Arabia, Persia, and India, and 95,000 for the Mascarene Islands.[68] While the use of slaves at the coast and on the offshore islands was strictly an aspect of the internal black African trade, it was also directly connected to the external Islamic network. The trade itself was conducted by Arab or Afro-Arab slavers; most of the plantations were owned by Omani Arabs; and the sovereign authority was the Zanzibari Sultanate. This presents an argument for raising the total volume of the Islamic trade for the nineteenth century and overall.

Where, however, is the evidence in Islam today, as there is in the Americas, of a historical trade in black slaves that amounted to so many millions? One answer is that there are, in fact, considerable numbers of blacks whose origin was overwhelmingly in the Islamic Trade. They are visible enough across North Africa, from Morocco to Egypt; in Yemen and the Gulf States; and from evidence of a darkening gene in other parts of Islam where such slaves were dispatched.

However, the main answer is that there was simply a much higher rate of social assimilation in Islam than in the Americas. As H. J. Fisher has written: "Indeed, it is arguable that a considerable majority of the slaves crossing the Sahara were destined to become concubines in North Africa, the Middle East, and occasionally even further afield. And it may be this, in turn, which helps to explain why a flow of slaves possibly greater in total than that across the Atlantic has not led to any comparably dramatic racial confrontation in North African society, although distinctions there of course are."[69]

The crucially different gender ratios—two females to every male in the Islamic Trade and two males to every female in the Atlantic one—would support this argument. Certainly, female slaves in a domestic environment were far more the means of assimilation than were male slaves in the plantation environment. Further, the higher rate of manumission in Islam and the absence of institutionalized racism made social assimilation so much the easier. And even if the volumes of the two trades were roughly the same, the Atlantic Trade involved only four centuries, while the Islamic one stretched well beyond that. Manumission and social assimilation were not only more acceptable and widespread in

Islam for doctrinal reasons but arguably also for the gradual character of the process.

There were two final factors. Lewis has cited "the high proportion of eunuchs among black slaves entering the Islamic lands" and "the high death rate and low birth rate among black slaves in North Africa and the Middle East."[70] There is much evidence for the second—as, already indicated, for the first—claim. Court probate records attest to an "astonishingly low" birth rate among black slave women in Cairo during the eighteenth century and most of the nineteenth century. Louis Frank, a French physician who resided in Tunisia during the early 1800s, remarked on the high mortality rate in early childhood among blacks there. In 1834, local French physicians reported an exceptionally high death rate from plague in Alexandria for "Negroes and Berbers." In 1838, a French government census revealed a low reproduction rate among blacks in Algiers.[71]

There may be various reasons for this. Recent slaves, weakened by their initial captivity and debilitating journey, would have been easy victims to climate changes and infections. Children were especially at risk, and the Islamic market demand for children was much greater than the American one. Many black slave women were not used for procreation or provided with the opportunities for it. Not least, many blacks, both slave and free, lived in conditions conducive to malnutrition and disease, with effects on their own life expectancy, the fertility of women, and the infant mortality rate. For all the heights that Islamic civilization had scaled, it lagged increasingly behind the West in protecting public health.

The arithmetic of the Islamic black slave trade must also not ignore the lives of those men, women, and children taken or lost during procurement, storage, and transport. One late-nineteenth-century writer held that the sale of a single captive for slavery might represent a loss of ten in the population—from defenders killed in attacks on villages, the deaths of women and children from related famine, and the loss of children, the old, and the sick unable to keep up with their captors or killed along the way in hostile encounters or dying of sheer misery.[72]

Terror, suffering, and death did not end with the raiding and wars that provided the captives. And of the subsequent trials and dangers that took their own toll of death, there is ample evidence in the writings of those Western travelers and explorers who witnessed them. If such costs were known or at least suspected by the purchasers of black slaves in their market destinations, it clearly did not affect the demand that sustained the markets themselves.

Gustav Nachtigal, a German physician, traveled from 1869 to 1874 through various parts of the black African interior, and his reports, published in three volumes from 1879 to 1889, include vivid accounts of the storage and transport conditions in the slave trade.[73] At the marshaling yards of 'Abū Sekkin, the ruler of Bagirmi, newly captured slaves were kept in chains or, when there were no chains left, were tied together by strips of rawhide, even though some of them were so weak that they were scarcely able to move.[74] On a subsequent journey to the marketing center at Kuka, on the shore of Lake Chad, Nachtigal accompanied a caravan with hundreds of slaves and observed such hardships that for every slave who survived, he estimated that three or four had died or, desperate to escape, had disappeared.[75]

Crossing the Sahara was itself a hazardous undertaking and thus more likely to prove fatal for slaves in a weakened condition. On his way both into and back from the Tibesti region, Nachtigal encountered numerous bleached human bones and the skeletons of camels, the remains of slave caravans that had reached local springs only to find them choked.[76]

Cold could be as lethal as heat. The explorer Heinrich Barth recorded that his friend Bashir, wazir of Bornu, while on pilgrimage with numerous slaves he intended selling, lost forty of them in the course of a single night, killed by the cold in the mountains between Fezzan and Benghazi.[77]

Sometimes the caravan ran short of food, either because the journey took longer than expected or because the supplies had been stinted at the start to reduce expenses. In such cases, the traders were likely to distribute whatever food was still available with a mind more to their own survival than to that of their slaves. A British explorer encountered over one hundred skeletons from a slave caravan that had left Bornu with insufficient food stocks, and recorded that the survivors, when they reached Fezzan, were then fed to fatten them for the market in Tripoli.[78]

Not least, disease was a constant threat and as likely to spread as quickly in a caravan as on a ship. The British explorer Richard Lander came across a group of thirty slaves on the way to Zaria, in West Africa, all of them apparently stricken with smallpox, and the men were bound neck to neck with twisted strips of bullock hide.[79] The distress of such groups was often increased by their being shunned along the way, without help or haven.

Some caravans suffered more than a single adversity. One caravan, with three thousand slaves, proceeding toward the coast from Manyuema in East Africa, lost two-thirds of its numbers from starvation, disease, and murder. Joseph Thomson, a British explorer, found the remainder surviving on grass and roots along the western bank of Lake Tanganyika.[80]

Other caravans, with large numbers of slaves, disappeared altogether, without attributable cause. One with two thousand slaves was reported to have vanished in the Libyan desert.[81] In 1850, a caravan of twenty-five hundred to three thousand slaves was reported by the Sardinian consul in Tripoli to have been lost along the route between Wadai and Benghazi.[82]

For slaves who survived the journey to East Coast, Red Sea, or North African ports, for onward transport, there were further tribulations. The dhows on which they were conveyed were generally small and closely packed to cut costs. In such conditions, the sea voyage was scarcely more congenial or less dangerous than caravan travel had been. One estimate of a 9 percent mortality rate among East African slave exports to Arabia, Persia, and India in the nineteenth century seems safe from any charge of exaggeration.[83]

The nineteenth century, from which such detailed reports derive, was distinctive both for the sheer volume of the Islamic black slave trade and for the recorded brutality with which so much of the trade was conducted. Yet the cause and character of fatalities in the reports were far from peculiar to that century. They were inherent in the very difficulties and dangers of the transit routes.

This was all a far cry from the call to compassion, justice, tolerance, the respect for human dignity, that belonged to the divine design communicated by the Prophet. Though never remotely institutionalized as they eventually became in the West, racist attitudes did emerge in Islam as a rationalization or result of the trade in black slaves. And that such attitudes should have developed to condone even the enslavement and marketing of Muslim blacks fired one nineteenth-century Moroccan historian, Aḥmad ibn Khalid al-Nasiri (1834–97), to an impassioned denunciation:

> It will be clear to you from what we have related of the history of the Sudan how far the people of these lands had taken to Islam from ancient times. It will also be clear that they are among the best peoples in regard to Islam, the most religiously upright, the most avid for learning and the most devoted to men of learning . . .
>
> Thus will be apparent to you the heinousness of the affliction which has beset the lands of the Maghreb since ancient times in regard to the indiscriminate enslaving of the people of the Sudan and the importation of droves of them every year to be sold in the market places in town and country where men trade in them as one would trade in beasts—nay worse than that. People have become so inured to that, generation after generation, that many common folk believe that the reason for being enslaved according to the Holy Law is merely that a man should be black in colour and come from those regions. This, by God's life, is one of the foulest and gravest evils perpetrated upon God's religion, for the people of the Sudan are Muslims having the same rights and responsibilities as ourselves.
>
> Even . . . if you suppose that Muslims are not a majority and that Islam and unbelief claim equal numbers there, who among us can tell whether those imported are Muslims or unbelievers. For the basic assumption in regard to the human species is freedom and lack of any cause for being enslaved.[84]

FIVE

THE FARTHER REACHES

China, India, and Spain represented three different aspects of the black slave experience at the farther reaches of Islamic conquest and beyond. In China black slavery was peripheral and connected to the currents of trade. In India, all but encompassed by Islamic rule at one time, individual black slaves came to play a major part in government, and the descendants of black slaves retain a vestigial identity today. In Spain, blacks—whether slave or free—were a significant part of a Muslim state with a high distinctive culture, before civil strife, political fragmentation, and Christian conquest led to the expulsion of Islam from the Iberian peninsula.

CHINA

The early-tenth-century Muslim geographer Ibn al-Faqīh described the inhabited world as all that "is known between al-Andalus [Islamic Spain] and China."[1] Occasional references provide only enticing hints of a black presence in China. Joseph Needham's great study, *Science and Civilisation in China*, notes: "The Chinese and other Asian nations had been using negro slaves for many centuries, but the fact that their slavery

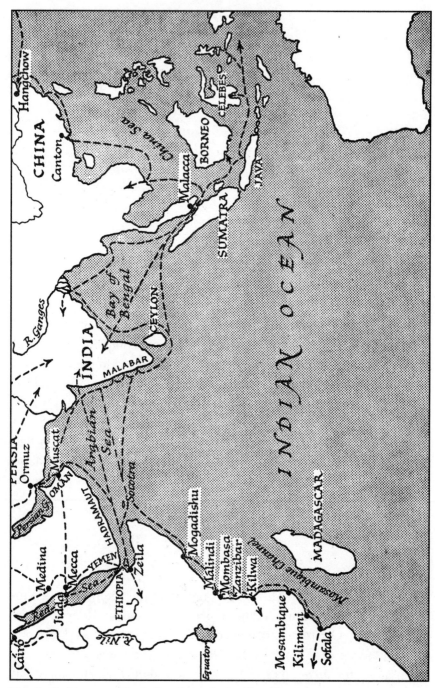

Map 1: Trade routes of the Indian Ocean in the fifteenth century

was basically domestic kept the practice within bounds [short of the massive imports for plantation labor that dominated the Atlantic Trade.]"[2]

In the Chronicle of the T'ang Dynasty, events for the year 724 included the presentation of a black girl to the Emperor, and the same form of tribute is recorded in ninth-century events. The Chronicle of the Sung Dynasty records that in 976 an Arab merchant brought to the imperial court "a black K'un Lun slave with deep-set eyes and black body."[3] Then, in the twelfth century, black slaves came to be imported in larger numbers.

In 1119, Chu Yu, a Chinese scholar of the Sung era, wrote: "In Kuang-chou [Canton] most of the wealthy people keep devil-slaves [kuei-nu], who are very strong and can lift [weights of] several hundred catties. Their language and tastes are unintelligible [to the Chinese]. Their nature is simple and they do not abscond. They are also called 'wild men' [yeh-jen]. Their colour is as black as [Chinese] ink, their lips are red, their teeth white and their hair curly and yellow [sic]. There are both males and females among them . . . They live on the islands beyond the sea."[4]

Canton was the main port of entry and distribution center for the trade, and though black slaves would doubtless have been dispatched to other cities, many would have stayed in Canton. There was even a fashion, starting in Canton and spreading elsewhere, to employ black slaves as doorkeepers. And these, it was remarked, looked sad from homesickness. Not all blacks or their descendants, however, remained in menial occupations. The Asian Art Museum in San Francisco possesses a fourteenth-century Chinese painting of a black whose high status is apparent from his costume and bearing.[5]

Another Chinese writer, Chan Ju-kua, referred to African slaves in a work dated 1226. They were, he wrote, "enticed by offers of food and then caught and carried off from Pemba for slaves to the Ta-shi [Arab] Countries, where they fetch a high price."[6] The source suggests that part of this trade was conducted by Muslim Arab merchants specifically for the Chinese market.

Arab seafarers were active across the Indian Ocean, and the Arab geographer al-Mas'ūdī, writing in the middle of the eleventh century, mentioned the trade in which slaves, ivory, and iron were exported from

Mogadishu and Pemba in exchange for pottery from China and Persia. The eunuch admiral Chêng Ho, himself a Muslim from the province of Yunnan whose father had made the pilgrimage to Mecca, led seven successive naval expeditions, the first in 1405–7.[7] The fourth expedition, in 1413–15, had Muslim interpreters attached to its staff and visited Hormuz and the Persian Gulf. The final three, in 1417–19, 1421–22, and 1431–33, explored the east coast of Africa, including Mogadishu and Malinda (Malindi).

In a subsequent Chinese text from *Li-Tai Thung Chien Chi Lan* (*Essentials of History*), Li Hsi-Hsiung, the editor and compiler in 1767, records: "Chêng Ho was commissioned on no less than seven embassies, and thrice he made prisoners of foreign chiefs . . . At the same time, the different peoples, attracted by the profit of Chinese merchandise, enlarged their mutual intercourse for purposes of trade, and there was uninterrupted going to and fro."[8] It is not extravagant to infer that black captives were taken back to China and arrangements made with Muslim merchants to include black slaves in further trade.

From the twelfth century to the beginning of the sixteenth century, when the Portuguese began displacing them, Muslim merchants from the Persian Gulf, Arabia, and Islamic India controlled the Indian Ocean trade essentially as middlemen. Small trading towns along the East African coast became important merchant cities, and from the ruins of one of these towns, the Songo Mnara palace city on a coral island off Tanganyika, search has yielded "broken glazed pottery from the Persian area, stoneware from Burma and Siam, pieces of Cornelian, and amber, crystal and topaz and a mass of Chinese porcelain from late Sung to early Ming."[9] Along with African ivory, known to have been needed in China, slaves may well have been taken there, in part or whole exchange for so much porcelain.

In the first half of the seventeenth century, the Portuguese lost control of the Indian Ocean trade routes, and commercial towns, governed by Swahili-speaking Muslims and trading in ivory and slaves, flourished along the east coast of Africa. Sites dating roughly from 1637 to 1810 have yielded "great quantities of Chinese blue and white porcelain."[10] Again, this may argue that there was some export trade in black slaves as well as ivory for China, though it is also possible that purchasing such large quantities of porcelain was simply part of a complex pattern. Muslim merchants might have bought and sold with small regard to particular territorial imbalances in goods, since such imbalances could be settled easily enough by payment in precious metals or the related acceptable coinage.

There is one further aspect of the connection between black slaves and China. In Chinese folklore, Africans are credited with peculiar strength and resourcefulness. In particular, they are celebrated as capable of diving to exceptional depths. Indeed, they were used to caulk the seams of ships at sea. Chu Yu, whose father, Chu Fu, had been Superintendent of Merchant Shipping in eleventh-century Canton, wrote *Phing-Chou Kho Than* (*Table Talk at Phingchow*) in 1119. In it he remarked of seafaring at the time: "If the ship suddenly springs a leak, [the mariners] cannot mend it from the inside, but they order their foreign blackamoor slaves [*kuei-nu*] to take chisels and oakum [*hsü*] and mend it from outside, for these men are expert swimmers and do not close their eyes when under water."[11]

INDIA

Islam expanded into India behind the sword, seizing Sind in 712 and the Punjab in 986, before spreading eastward and southward, albeit alongside fluctuations in power and the rivalries of various Muslim rulers. Black slaves were imported in its wake, for all the usual purposes but mainly for military service. Ethiopians were particularly favored; the term *Habashi* or *Habshi*—from the Arabic word for Ethiopian—came to be applied to other Africans as well, and referred not only to the freed but to their descendants.

Freed blacks, however, upon their conversion to Islam, took to calling themselves "Sayyad," or descendants of Muḥammad, and became known as *Siddis*. As a group, they were both cohesive and aggressive, were formidable in battle, and were especially renowned as excellent sailors. As early as 1100, they established kingdoms of their own in Janjira and Jaffrabad in western India. Siddis were also increasingly employed as security forces for the Muslim fleets. Siddi commanders even rose to become admirals of the Mughal Empire, at annual salaries of 300,000 rupees.

That great fourteenth-century traveler Ibn Baṭṭūṭa, during his long visit to India and accompanying sea voyages, embarked on a ship that had sixty oars and was "covered with a roof during battle in order to protect the rowers from arrows and stones." It "had a complement of fifty rowers and fifty Abyssinian men-at-arms." He commented: "These latter are the guarantors of safety on the Indian Ocean; let there be but one of them on a ship and it will be avoided by the Indian pirates and idolators." Such men were almost certainly Siddis.

By the thirteenth century, substantial numbers of black slaves—still mainly Ethiopian—were being imported from East Africa, and even larger numbers arrived in the fifteenth century. In the late 1300s, one Habshi eunuch, Malik Sarwar, became vizier to the Sultan of Delhi, Muḥammad b. Firuz, and in 1394 was appointed governor of the turbulent eastern province, with his capital at Jawnpur. He not only pacified the province but extended its frontier and was, on his death in 1399, succeeded by his adopted son, another black slave, Qaranful, who took the title of Mubarak Shah and displayed such effective independence during his three years of rule as to command the striking of his own coinage. His brother, Ibrahim Shah, who succeeded him in 1402, ruled for thirty-eight years, to sustain complete independence from Delhi by the strength of his armed forces. He was no mere militarist, however. Ibrahim Shah became as renowned for the art and scholarship he encouraged at his court as for the many impressive new buildings that distinguished his reign.

From the second half of the fifteenth century, black slave soldiers were increasingly used in Bengal. Sultan Rukn al-Din Barbak Shah, who ruled there from 1459 to 1474, is reputed to have had eight thousand of them, some holding high rank. His successor was assassinated by a Habshi eunuch who used his command of the army to seize the throne. During the seven tumultuous years that followed, various Habshis ruled for short periods until an Arab vizier took power and expelled the Habshis from Bengal. Clearly more valued than feared, they found new homes in Gujarat and the Deccan.

Habshis also wielded influence under the Bahmani dynasty in the Deccan. Sultan Firuz, who ruled from 1397 to 1422, had Habshi women in his harem and Habshi men among his personal attendants. One of the latter was responsible for the Sultan's assassination, but evidently this did not cause any decline in Habshi fortunes. The Habshis were Sunni Muslims and accordingly aligned with the so-called Deccan party against the growing influence of Shi'a Muslims and Turks in the Sultanate. Under Ahmad Shah, who ruled from 1422 to 1435, the Deccan party was ascendant, and Habshis were appointed governors for two of the Sultanate's four provinces. During the 1480s, another period of Sunni ascendancy, a Habshi was appointed minister of finance.

Gujarat was a maritime power, with corresponding access to black slaves. Sultan Bahadar, who ruled from 1526 to 1537, reportedly had five thousand of them in his service. Among those attaining riches and power was Shaykh Sa'id, a soldier of learning and taste as well as military prowess, who had a famous library and was responsible for building a beautiful mosque in Ahmadabad. Indeed, a Habshi nobility took form that came into conflict with the established nobility of Gujarat. Exploiting the division, the Mughal Empire in the north conquered the Sultanate in 1573.[13]

It was in the Deccan in the latter part of the sixteenth century that the most illustrious Habshi of all rose to power.[14] Born Shambu, around 1550 in Ethiopia, Ambar was sold into slavery and then resold to successive owners in the Hejaz, Baghdad, and Mocha. His earlier masters evidently failed to provide him with either a secure home or the encouragement to embrace Islam. For it was only his master in Mocha who promoted his conversion; renamed him Ambar; and, recognizing his abilities, taught him something of finance and administration. Then, after his master died, Ambar was sold to a slave dealer who took him to India, where around 1575 he was bought by Chingiz Khan, Habshi prime minister to the Sultan of Ahmadnagar.

Indian history had long been—and, until the nineteenth century, would continue to be—dominated by the geographical division of the country into three parts: the northern plains, with the basins of the Indus and Ganges rivers; the Deccan plateau to the south; and, south of this, the lands beyond the Krishna and Tungabhadra rivers. In the sixteenth century, the Mughal Muslims controlled the north; the far south was composed of the Tamil states; and five Sultanates—Ahmadnagar, Berat, Bijapur, Bidar, and Golconda—emerged after the collapse of the Bahmani dynasty to command the Deccan. All five Sultanates were within Islam, but this did not deter them from contending with one another, any more than it persuaded them to acquiesce in the expansionism of the Mughal Empire.

The death of Chingiz Khan led to civil dissension in the Sultanate of Ahmadnagar. Ambar was sold yet again, first to the Sultan of Golconda and then to the Sultan of Bijapur, who invested him with the military command and the title of Malik, "Kinglike." This display of trust gave way to reservations, however. The Sultan came to resist the mounting financial costs incurred by Ambar's policy of recruiting Arabs for the army. Around the year 1590, Ambar deserted, together with a number of his Arab soldiers. Then, seeking others for his independent force, he found them from among the Deccanis, or the indigenous people of the region, as well as from among the Habshis, who shared his origin.

He soon commanded more than fifteen hundred men, fighting as mercenaries for one or another ruler. It was clearly a force that, left unattached, presented both a temptation and a threat. In 1595, the Sultan of Ahmadnagar established an army of Habshis, and his prime minister, himself a Habshi, invited Ambar to unite his own force with it. Ambar readily agreed. He had no doubt of his ability to dominate the augmented army and accordingly advance his leadership of Deccan resistance to the increasing threat from the Mughal Empire. His successes in beating back attacks from that empire made him so powerful that in 1602 he simply imprisoned the Sultan and declared himself Regent-Minister.

His army grew into a force of sixty thousand horsemen, supported by artillery that he obtained from the English. He also won over to his side the naval prowess of the Siddis in Janjira, who cut Mughal supply lines and conducted other disruptive or distracting missions. Having frustrated the design of the great Mughal Emperor Akbar to conquer the Deccan, Ambar then dealt just as effectively with the efforts of Akbar's successor, Jahangir. And, intermittently, he fought and defeated rivals for leadership of the region. Nor was it only his success on the battlefield that secured his supremacy. The rulers of Bijapur and Golconda, mindful of his previous associations with their Sultanates and of his proven abilities, became important allies in the common cause of resisting Mughal might.

For all that, by the time of his death in 1626, there was spreading discontent with his rule, even among the officers in his army. The drain in men and money from more than twenty years of warfare was proving too much. His son, Fettah Khan, succeeded him as Regent-Minister, but remained so only until 1629. Malik Ambar's own preeminent achievement became more evident with his absence. The Mughal Empire had repeatedly failed to conquer the Deccan during his lifetime. It succeeded after his death.

His outstanding generalship was based on the mobility for which he trained and equipped his troops, along with his recourse to guerrilla warfare whenever circumstances advised it. Even his most arrogant adversary, the Mughal Emperor Jahangir, who had lost no opportunity to disparage him, not least for his color, was moved to pay him a belated tribute. "In the art of soldiering," he would write in his memoirs, "Ambar was unique in his age."[15] Yet Ambar was scarcely less remarkable for the social, economic, and cultural policies he pursued.

Doubtless influenced by his own origin and color, with the prejudice that he experienced especially during his early years as a slave, he used the power he had achieved to provide the various ethnic and religious groups in the Sultanate with a sense of having some stake in its progress. Not surprisingly, he favored the enlistment of Habshis in the army— reportedly he even bought one thousand Habshi slaves for his private guard—and appointed them, as well as Arabs, to high military posts. But he also gave grants of land to Hindus, chose Brahmins as his top financial officials and tax collectors, and promoted the employment of Marathas in the civil service. Habshis, Arabs, and Persians dominated the sector of small-scale businesses. Arabs and Persians developed a foreign trade primarily with the Persian Gulf, though also increasingly with the English and the Portuguese. Under his rule the Sultanate manufactured much silk and paper which, with swords, axes, and guns, were exported to other parts of India, to Persia, and to Arabia.

Given his own training and experience in administration, Ambar was concerned to promote efficiency and ready to pursue sometimes bold innovations. He introduced and developed a postal service whose messengers ranged throughout the region. He encouraged trade and agriculture with new canals and innovative irrigation schemes, levying taxes in kind on the use of such facilities. His taxation policies were, for the age, remarkably progressive and responsive to changing conditions. Poorer parts of the realm paid lower tax rates, as did richer ones stricken by crop failures. He did not interfere with the traditional system of community land ownership in the villages; but elsewhere, especially in prosperous districts, he encouraged private ownership to promote competitive production.

He established a new capital at Kirkee and enticed poets and scholars, mainly Arab and Persian, to his court there. Devout Muslim that he was, he also encouraged Hindu scholars and even provided a center in the capital where they could meet. And with a passion for planned civic development and embellishment, he furnished his capital with wide roads, canals, drains, public gardens, and buildings. His use of only black stone for such buildings, including his own tomb, when other sorts of stone were more readily available, suggests more than mere coincidence.

Ambar was certainly not the last Habshi to leave a mark on Indian history, though he remained the most notable. In the seventeenth century, a number of Habshis held high posts in the Muslim courts of the Deccan and in the Mughal Empire. In the eighteenth and well into the nineteenth century, the Siddi rulers of Janjira commanded a strategic island fortress off the west coast of India. It was only in 1834 that British forces finally confronted them, destroying the Siddi fleet and declaring the island a colony. In the mid-nineteenth century, Siddi 'Anbar was steward—in practice, first secretary or personal assistant—to the Vizier of Hyderabad. He received such recompense or exploited his position to such effect that he came to own a sizable slice of real estate in the center of Hyderabad City, an achievement commemorated in the Siddi 'Anbar Bazar [sic] there.

Habshi communities still reportedly exist in several Indian states, though widespread intermarriage and a pressure to adopt the norms of the wider Muslim community have accelerated assimilation.[16]

SPAIN

Far to the west, conquering Islam crossed the straits between Africa and Europe in 711, defeated the Vandal rulers of Spain in a series of battles, and by 720 commanded all of the Iberian peninsula except Galicia in the northwest, which remained under Christian control. The conquerors, having seized much of southern France, might well have spread right across Europe, had it not been for their defeat by a Frankish army at the Battle of Poitiers in 732. Instead, they consolidated their occupation of the Iberian domain, which they named al-Andalus.

A prince of the Umayyad dynasty, escaping the slaughter that accompanied the 'Abbasid conquest of the Caliphate in Damascus, reached al-Andalus and established a rival emirate there. Reigning from 756 to 788, 'Abd al-Rahman I made Cordoba his capital. In his palace, named Ar-Rusafa, after one of the former Umayyad palaces in his Syrian homeland, he wrote a poem that concluded with a prayer:

> A *palm tree* I beheld in Ar-Rusafa,
> Far in the West, far from the palm-tree land:
> I said: You, like myself, are far away, in a strange land!
> How long have I been far away from my people!
> You grew up in a land where you are a stranger,
> And like myself, are living in the farthest corner of the earth:
> May the morning clouds refresh you at this distance,
> And may abundant rains comfort you forever.[17]

The Islamic palm would flourish wonderfully in its new home, but not forever. And its loss would long be—indeed, still is—lamented in Arabic literature.

The invading army was composed less of Arabs than of North African Berbers converted to Islam, and it was from among such Berbers rather than the Arabs that the early colonists of conquest were drawn. The Berbers had experienced the scorn of their own Arab conquerors toward them. They were correspondingly receptive to Kharidjism, a revolutionary sect of political theology within Islam that propagated the principle of an elected imam, or leader of the Muslim community, without distinction of race, color, or country, "even were he an Abyssinian slave with a slit nose."[18]

Duly incorporated into the trade routes of Islam, al-Andalus thrived from an abundance of raw materials, from a vigorous agriculture, and from the development of manufacturing with the deployment of specialist skills. Related to this was the relatively tolerant Muslim regime, which attracted corresponding support not only from many Christians but especially from Jews, whose previous treatment had been harsh under the influence of a Catholic Church less concerned with charity than with faith. Rapid urbanization promoted social mobility and communal harmony. Ethnic and religious intermarriage became quite common, as Muslims acquired *djariyas*, or slave wives, who were permitted to retain their Christian or Jewish convictions. As M. Talki explains: "Black *djariyas* were appreciated no less than others, and mulattoes, free from any complex whatsoever, moved freely at any level in the social hierarchy."[19]

The extent of urbanization was remarkable. Ibn Ḥawqal, the tenth-century Arab geographer, who had traveled widely, described Cordoba, the largest city in al-Andalus, as having "no equal in the Maghrib, or in the Jazira or Syria, or Egypt, to approximate the size of its population, extent of its territory, area of its markets, cleanliness of its inhabitants, construction of its mosques, and number of its baths and hostelries."[20]

One modern historian, E. Lévi-Provençal, has estimated the population of Cordoba in the tenth century at one million.[21] Thomas Glick gives the much lower figure of a hundred thousand, but he bases his estimate on the number of male worshippers who could be accommodated in the city's main mosque.[22] Yet the urban populations of al-Andalus contained sizable components of Christians and Jews. Furthermore, there were extensive suburbs of Cordoba, along the local commercial roads or around palaces and military establishments.[23] Not least, Glick excludes from his estimate slaves who were not devout Muslims. Still another historian, Philip Hitti, has cited the city's "one hundred and thirteen thousand homes" and "twenty one suburbs,"[24] which would support the higher figure. Yet, even if the lower estimate is accepted, the population of tenth-century Cordoba would still have been much larger than that reached by Paris and more than double that reached by London, four centuries later.

Slaves are estimated to have composed around a fifth of the population in the major cities of al-Andalus, and they were also used as rural laborers, mainly on the large estates. White slaves, from Christian Spain, central or eastern Europe, and black ones, newly brought from beyond

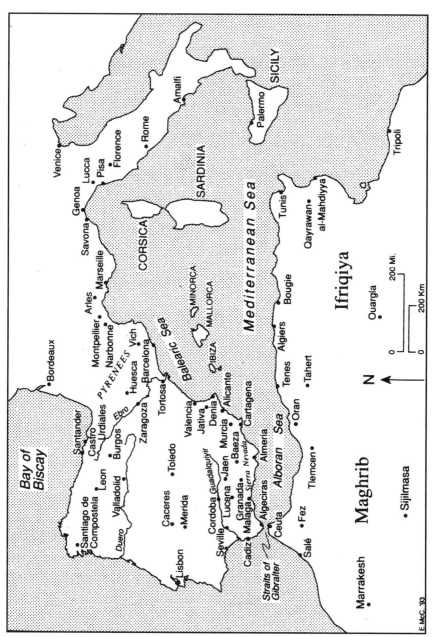

Map 2: Spain and the Maghrib

the Sahara or drawn from among those already in North Africa, served together both in the palaces of rulers and the establishments of the rich. There they might be menial domestics, concubines, eunuchs, musicians and dancers, stewards or agents, soldiers and guards.

Many, perhaps most, of the white slaves brought to al-Andalus apparently did not remain there. Ibn Ḥawqal, writing in the 970s, remarked that "among the most famous exports [from al-Andalus to other Muslim lands] are comely slaves, both male and female from Frankish and Galician regions" and that "all Slavic eunuchs on earth come from al-Andalus, because they are castrated in that region and the operation is performed by Jewish merchants."[25] This last statement needs to be qualified by a report from Ibrāhīm b. al-Qāsim al-Qarawī (died 1026) that in al-Andalus Muslims as well as Jews castrated slaves for export abroad.[26] It is possible that some black slaves were among them, but few others are likely to have been brought there for export to other parts of Islam, which needed no such detour from shorter, direct routes in the black slave trade. Most would have been imported mainly for use in al-Andalus itself.

'Abd al-Raḥman II, who reigned from 822 to 852, did much to centralize the administration of al-Andalus, concentrating power in the person of the ruler and securing the financial sustenance of his rule by the development of state monopolies. A new bureaucratic class, drawn from merchants and the ruler's clients, provided the mechanism of control and confronted divergent or divisive tendencies. The resources channeled to the court by such changes supported a splendor modeled on the Persian manners of the court in Baghdad.

In the stylistic revolution that followed, the crucial figure was a black singer, musician, and poet named Abū'l-Hasian 'Ali ibn Nāfi' but generally known as Ziryāb (789–857). Born in Iraq, he rose to high favor at the court of the Caliphate in Baghdad, but then apparently fell victim to jealousy and made his way to al-Andalus, where he arrived just before 'Abd al-Raḥman II began his reign. He was soon exercising such influence over the new ruler as to become the very arbiter of taste. He imposed Iraqi styles of singing, added a fifth string to the lute, and founded a school of music. He introduced the use of toothpaste and underarm deodorants, promoted particular hairstyles and the clean-shaven look for men, and set a new fashion for changing dress to correspond with all four seasons of the year instead of only summer and winter. He also introduced asparagus, spread the knowledge of Iraqi cuisine, and gave his name to numerous recipes.[27]

Not least, he is credited with having made the drinking of wine a more acceptable and widespread practice among the Muslims of al-Andalus. Vineyards had initially been cultivated for grapes and raisins, with wine a minor product, mainly for the domestic market of the Christian and Jewish communities. The impact of the influence attributed to Ziryāb not only boosted the production of wine but led to enrichment of choice, as new varieties of grape were introduced. Andalusi jurists, in line with the generally relaxed attitude of their rulers toward Islamic doctrine, declared that the drinking of wine was permissible,[28] despite all Orthodox teaching to the contrary.

Olives, figs, and grapes had been staples of Hispano-Roman agriculture, and it was a prime achievement of al-Andalus to have renewed and intensified their production after so long a period of neglect and decay. Andalusi olive oil was so plentiful that its markets extended from Christian Spain to the eastern Mediterranean. Quality was not sacrificed to quantity; Malagan figs, for instance, became so famous for their taste that they were sought not only in Baghdad but as far away as China.

Crops wholly new to the Iberian peninsula, such as sugar cane and cotton, were also introduced, augmenting agricultural prosperity. Enhanced domestic purchasing power fueled the further development of manufacturing, with new products that in turn were profitably exported. Andalusi textiles (mainly silk), leather goods and paper, copperware, and even ships were held in high regard and widely sought. Andalusi merchants explored markets well beyond the eastern Mediterranean, often earning large sums on a single trip, though not without evident risk. 'Abū Bakr Muḥammad b. Muʻāwiya al-Marwānī (died 968), a merchant and scholar related to the ruling Umayyad family, visited the markets of Iraq and India, where he made a profit of thirty thousand dinars in trade before losing all he had in a shipwreck on his way home.[29]

Contributing significantly to this economic growth was the continuing flow of gold, brought directly across the Sahara in return for trade goods or received in payment for exports elsewhere. Initially, Andalusi rulers produced a silver coinage that came to be so widely acceptable that small numbers of such dirhems have been found in Britain, Scandinavia, and eastern Europe. By the first half of the tenth century, locally minted gold dinars were highly prized in western Europe and helped to boost trade. In such congenial conditions, and under a regime remarkably tolerant for the times, many non-Muslims converted to Islam.

By the tenth century, 'Abd al-Raḥman III, who reigned from 912 to 961, ruled over a state so powerful, rich, and secure that it had no equal in Europe. Such was its status in Islam that he confidently assumed the title of Caliph in 929 and began to build a suitable palace-city outside Cordoba. Under his immediate successors, the unity and strength of the state remained unchallenged and might well have seemed eternal. Then, in the early eleventh century, the edifice collapsed, in what came to be known as the *fitna al-barbariyya*, or Berber-based civil strife.

Berbers from the Maghrib had settled in various parts of al-Andalus and become a major ingredient in the ethnic concord that Arab rule there had promoted with such apparent success. Yet this concord was either less sound than it appeared or was being undermined by other policies that the Arab rulers pursued. In their commitment to centralizing power and ensuring their own hold on it, they came increasingly to rely on the service of slaves and, in particular for the army, Berbers. This process markedly accelerated in the reign of 'Abd al-Raḥman III, who imported large numbers of Berbers to protect his Caliphate against Arab rivals.

These Berbers were viewed differently from the descendants of their predecessors, now largely and indistinguishably assimilated. They were resented for their privileges, such as the land and homes and payment they were given to secure their loyalty; their distinctive appearance, conspicuous in their dress; their very isolation in the areas of settlement with which they were provided. Seen as intrusive and foreign, they were the more easily targeted as the scapegoat for popular grievances against the regime because of their role in sustaining it. And nobles with their own ambition to rule promoted such prejudice to their advantage.

Accordingly, when the line of succession to the Caliphate came to be disputed, the conflict quickly acquired an ethnic cast. At Cordoba in 1009, a mob was incited by local nobles to assault the Berber suburbs, burning the houses and murdering the women. The city itself was then besieged by vengeful Berber soldiers, and anyone within its walls who was suspected of being a Berber risked attack. A contemporary historian reported various instances of the ethnic violence that ensued. One woman in the city, returning from a visit to an oven, dropped her pot and by doing so drew attention to herself. Bystanders cried, "There is a black Berber," and she was killed.[30]

This episode invites speculation. Most Berbers were light-skinned and blue-eyed, though there were also some dark-skinned ones, the progeny, near or distant, of miscegenation. Blacks were not Berbers. Was the victim seen as Berber because of her dress, and as black because of her dark complexion? Was she black and called a Berber because it was the Berbers against whom the rampant rage and fear were primarily directed? Or were there so many blacks as well as Berbers in the army of the regime that they were lumped together as targets while still distinguished from each other? Perhaps it was enough for the woman to have had some perceived characteristic of one targeted ethnic group for the prejudice against both groups to be invoked.

In 1013, Cordoba and the palace complexes outside the city were sacked by Berber armies, the princely libraries were dispersed, and the pretensions to an Andalusi Caliphate were drained of all credibility by claimants that rival generals and their armies advanced. What emerged were three dozen small Islamic states, called "Party Kingdoms" (*Mulūk al-ṭawāʾif*), reflecting and promoting ethnic divisions. For instance, an Arab dynasty held Seville; two different Berber dynasties, Malaga and Granada; while successive *saqāliba* (Slav eunuchs) governed the coastal cities of Almeria, Valencia, and Tortosa.[31] The lofty titles of the rulers did nothing to disguise a weakness that their rivalries only underscored and that the Christian kingdoms were quick to exploit, exacting tribute in return for support or proceeding to outright conquest.

Yet political and military weakness did not spell commensurate economic and cultural decline. The rich Party Kings competed to adorn their courts with writers, who might also be employed as diplomats. Andalusi poetry in particular acquired an identity all its own. Two Kings of Seville themselves came to be celebrated as among the greatest poets in the history of Islamic Spain. But division had its price. In 1085, Toledo fell to the Christian King of Castile. This so alarmed the Party Kings that they temporarily joined in an appeal for armed intervention to the ruling dynasty of the Almoravids in the Maghrib.

This dynasty had arisen from a Saharan movement of austere nomads committed to a puritanical and legalistic version of Islam. The Almoravids had then extended their rule southward, to encompass parts of the black African Sudan, and northward to Ceuta, which commanded the straits between Africa and Europe. In 1086 and again in 1088, in response to the cry for help from the Party Kings, the Almoravid leader Ibn Tāshfīn crossed the straits with a considerable army and crushed the Christian forces that took the field against it. No sooner had he returned to North Africa, however, than the Party Kings returned to their former rivalries. Finally, in 1090, Ibn Tāshfīn crossed the straits again to denounce the Party Kings for their corrupt practices and their collaboration with the Christians. Within four years he had deposed them all and restored Muslim unity, in all that remained of al-Andalus, under Almoravid rule.

Almoravid control over the trans-Saharan trade routes ensured a continuing and, indeed, an augmented flow of gold to al-Andalus. The widely valued dinars of the dynasty—one of the most used and copied currencies of the medieval western Mediterranean region—were minted in Seville, Cordoba, Malaga, and Almeria, as well as in the Moroccan cities of Fez and Marrakesh. And, almost certainly, along with the gold came an augmented supply of black slaves.

What had jubilantly been greeted as rescue, however, was soon resented as repression. By those who had grown accustomed to religious tolerance and an advanced culture, prosperity was not considered adequate recompense for the imposition of *Shari'a*, or strict religious law, on both private conduct and public affairs. Non-Muslim communities had reason to feel insecure. Although Andalusi Jewish merchants were allowed to continue trading, the Jewish quarter in Cordoba was plundered and burned in 1135.[32] Aware of the spreading popular discontent in al-Andalus, the Christian kingdoms resumed their campaign of conquest. And in 1144, encouraged perhaps by reports of opposition to Almoravid rule in the Maghrib itself, Muslims, along with others targeted by intolerance in al-Andalus, rose in revolt.

Ironically, Ibn Tāshfīn's son ʿAlī, who ruled the Almoravid Empire from 1120 to 1143, had become so influenced by Andalusi culture that he ordered the abandonment of the veil for men, a distinguishing feature of the movement and its followers. Furthermore, he had enlisted Andalusi poets and other artists to embellish his court, which assumed much of the ease and luxury that had been the mark of the Caliphate court in Cordoba; he had appointed Andalusi scholars to high administrative posts in the empire; and he had employed Andalusi architects to help plan urban expansion in Morocco.

It was in al-Andalus that Sufism, the Islamic strain of mysticism that placed personal piety and the love of God above mere rigid observance of the law, began to have a spreading, subversive impact; and in the Maghrib, Sufi ideas influenced a Berber to found the Almohad movement, which would overwhelm Almoravid rule.

Muḥammad b. Tūmart (c. 1080–1128), from one of the Masmuda tribes in the Anti-Atlas Mountains, visited Baghdad early in the twelfth century and encountered there the teachings of Sufism. On his return to the Maghrib, he secured widespread support among the Masmuda for his claim to be the *mahdī*, or inspired leader, sent to confront the Almoravid rulers, whose prevalent morality and obsession with the letter of the law were distorting the true faith. He died soon after his Berber army was defeated at the gates of Marrakesh, the Almoravid capital. Yet, within less than two decades, his disciple and successor ʿAbd al-Muʾmin had defeated the Almoravid army, had captured the Almoravid ruler, and had conquered Marrakesh. Then, under ʿAbd al-Muʾmin's successors, the Almohads crossed the straits to pursue their doctrinal jihad, turned back the advance of Christianity, and asserted their own authority over al-Andalus.

As so often in Islamic history, successful dissent became a new and repressive orthodoxy. Like the Almoravids before them, the Almohads waged holy war against other Muslims, whom they denounced as heretics; and, having acquired their initial impulse in the resistance of mountain Berbers to centralized authority, they proceeded to extend their own centralized authority across the Maghrib. ʿAbd al-Muʾmin even proclaimed himself Commander of the Faithful and instituted a Maghribi Caliphate.

Inheriting Almoravid control of the trans-Saharan trade routes, the Almohad Caliphs maintained the flow of gold from the Sudan, for the minting of dinars which soon acquired no less an international acceptance than those of their predecessors had done. Along with the gold came black slaves, both for domestic and military service in al-Andalus and elsewhere in the empire. According to the historian Nehemia Levtzion: "Indeed, if one goes by the repeated accounts of slave raids in the Sudan and of the arrival of Sudanese slaves in the Maghrib, it is possible that the export of slaves from the Sudan increased in the twelfth and thirteenth centuries."[33]

Meanwhile, the apparent cohesion of the Almohad Empire masked serious internal strains. Various Berber shaykhs were alienated by a bureaucracy, most of it drawn from al-Andalus, that sustained and promoted the centralized power of the Caliphate. Increasingly, the Almohad Caliphs relied on Arabs from the eastern Maghrib, who had resettled in Morocco, to reinforce their regime. It was a development that augmented both the ethnic complexity and conflicts within the region. Another threat was emerging from the very growth in prosperity.

Trade, much of it conducted by Jewish intermediaries, expanded between the Almohad Empire and an economically resurgent Christian Europe, with Italian cities and their banking houses financing commercial and industrial enterprise. Christian Spain was a major beneficiary of this expansion, through its proximity to a thriving al-Andalus and, through al-Andalus, to the North African market and beyond. Yet this was less an inhibition than an incentive to renewed conquest. In 1212, the Christian kingdoms in Spain combined to field an army that defeated the Almohad forces and captured their treasury. Valencia, Cordoba, and Seville fell in turn. By 1276, only the kingdom of Granada, with a line of ports to Cadiz, remained of what had once so extensively and richly been al-Andalus.

It was not only territory that was lost. By the beginning of the twelfth century, with a high rate of voluntary conversions and of widespread intermarriage, al-Andalus contained some 5.6 million *muwalladūn*, or indigenous Muslims, out of an estimated total population of 7 million.[34] But a decline in popular allegiance had already begun. Almoravid and then Almohad intolerance led some Jews and Christians to take flight.

And there were some Muslims, alienated or made apprehensive by repression, who resisted less fervently the advance of Christian conquest and stayed in the lost cities rather than retreat to the contracting territory of al-Andalus.

For all that, Almohad rule itself came to an end, and the Andalusi kingdom of Granada had much to offer. The ruling Nasirid dynasty survived for more than two and a half centuries, sometimes bribing Christian kings with sufficient payment of tribute, sometimes exploiting their divisions with the deployment of its own military resources, and meanwhile presiding over a brilliant intellectual culture from its citadel of interlinked palaces and gardens in the Alhambra.

The great Muslim traveler Ibn Baṭṭūṭa visited al-Andalus in the middle of the fourteenth century, where he found, at Málaqa (Malaga),

> one of the largest and most beautiful towns of Andalusia. It unites the conveniences of both sea and land, and is abundantly supplied with foodstuffs and fruits. I saw grapes being sold in its bazaars at the rate of eight pounds for a small dirham, and its ruby-coloured Murcian pomegranates have no equal in the world. As for figs and almonds, they are exported from Málaqa and its outlying districts to the lands both of the East and the West. At Málaqa there is manufactured excellent gilded pottery, which is exported thence to the most distant lands. Its mosque covers a large area and has a reputation for sanctity; the court of the mosque is of unequalled beauty, and contains exceptionally tall orange trees . . .
>
> Thence I went on to the city of Gharnáta [Granada], the metropolis of Andalusia and the bride of its cities. Its environs have not their equal in any country in the world. They extend for the space of forty miles, and are traversed by the celebrated river of Shanníl [Xenil] and many other streams. Around it on every side are orchards, gardens, flowery meads, noble buildings, and vineyards . . . There is also at Gharnáta a company of Persian darwishes, who have made their homes there because of its resemblance to their

native lands. One is from Samarqand, another from Tabríz, a third from Qúniya [Konia], one from Khurásán, two from India, and so on.[35]

Christian Spain, united under a single monarchy, secured the surrender of Granada in 1492, on the pledge of religious tolerance toward Muslims. But this was a monarchy whose interpretation of the Gospel required the tortures and burnings of the Inquisition to ensure its acceptance. It expelled professing Jews in 1492, and then, despite its pledge, professing Muslims ten years later. Conversion to Christianity provided no lasting protection. Jews and Muslims who had converted, but whose original faiths, practiced in secret, were discovered or suspected by the preying Inquisition, were expelled or otherwise eradicated along with much else. There was no statute of limitations even for the inanimate. For, as Robert Irwin states, "in the centuries that followed, Muslims and books written in Arabic were thrown onto the bonfires of the Inquisition."[36] The loss to the cultural and economic life of Spain from the expulsion of the Jews has long been recognized. The expulsion of the Muslims was scarcely less damaging.

The Christian reconquest of Spain brought with it the capture of black slaves whom al-Andalus had imported, some of them certainly employed in the cultivation of sugar. The year in which this was accomplished was also the same year Christopher Columbus set out on the voyage that led to European conquest of the Americas. In 1511, the Spanish Crown licensed the dispatch of fifty black slaves to the conquered island of Hispaniola, initially for work in the mines, and then for sugar production. From this tiny beginning would develop the immense Atlantic Trade.

INTO BLACK AFRICA

By the beginning of the eighth century, Islam's conquests had spread westward across Africa north of the Sahara. And by the late eighth century, caravans from the north were regularly crossing the desert to trade with black Africa. Any military invasion there in the cause of Islam, however, was avoided until, in 1062, the Moroccan-based Almoravids set out to subjugate the kingdom of Ghana in the western Sudan. They met with such resistance that it was only in 1076 that they succeeded in taking and plundering the capital of the kingdom, and by the beginning of the twelfth century, the conquerors had lost the last remnants of direct control. Meanwhile, the king and people had become Muslims, and they remained so after Ghana successfully asserted its independence.

In 1154, al-Idrīsī (1100–62), one of the great medieval chroniclers, described Ghana as "the greatest country in the land of the Sudan, the most populous, and having the most extensive trade."[1] Yet all was not well with the kingdom. Agriculture around the capital had not recovered from the damage done by the Almoravid nomads and their flocks during the occupation. The goldfields of Bambuk, between the Senegal and Faleme rivers, were becoming exhausted after centuries of exploitation. To the southeast, at Bure on the Upper Niger, rich new deposits were being mined. And it was in the Upper Niger Valley that Sundiata, leader of

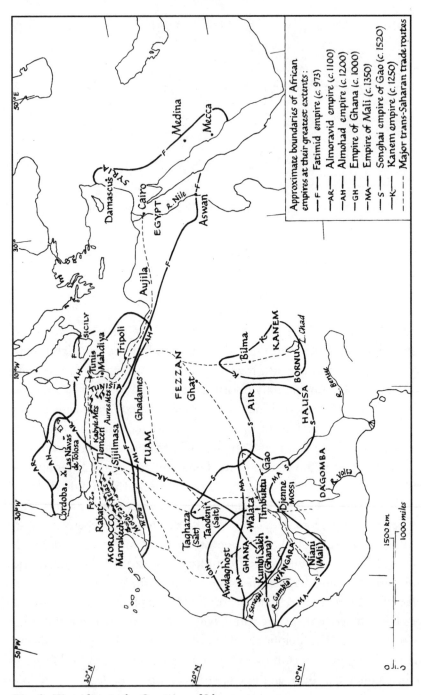

Map 3: West Africa in the Great Age of Islam

one of the Mande clans there, set out on a career of conquest. The result was the empire of Mali, over which he reigned for a quarter of a century from 1230.

The Almoravid conquest had spread Islam farther and more lastingly than its exercise of control had ever reached. Sundiata seems to have been at least nominally a convert, and his successors as *Mansa* (Emperor) were Muslims, though some of them were less devout than others.

In the middle of the fourteenth century, Mansa Musa, the most celebrated of Mali's rulers, caused a great stir in Cairo, where, stopping on his way to Mecca, he expended so much gold that the value of the metal fell substantially. However, these riches, which spread his fame beyond Islam to the Christian world, were not his only distinction. Visiting the empire of Mali in 1352–53 during Musa's reign, Ibn Baṭṭūṭa reported the facility and safety with which traders and foreigners were able to move about, the flourishing agriculture and commerce, and the stern administration of justice.

By the beginning of the fifteenth century, the empire was in decline. From their capital at Gao, on the Niger bend, some seven hundred miles east of Niani, the capital of Mali, the kings of the Songhai broke from their allegiance. The armies of Sonni ʻAlī (c. 1464–92) advanced, turning more and more of Mali's dependencies into Songhai ones. This expansion initially confronted Islamic influence, but then Sonni ʻAlī's successor, Muḥammad (1493–1528), proceeded to restore and augment this. The Songhai Empire became the greatest yet in the region. It reached northward almost to Morocco, and from the mouth of the Gambia River on the Atlantic coast eastward almost to Bornu (Borno), the state encompassing Lake Chad.

Such a vast advance of Islam in black Africa was due to factors other than conquest from the north. Rulers of successive empires in the region were ready to adopt Islam because it lent them a certain legitimacy in their dealings with rulers and merchants of the Maghrib, on which so much of their trade and prosperity depended. Relatedly, most of the merchants in the region became Muslims and, given their prestige as well as their mobility, they were especially influential in the spread of Islam. Indeed, some merchants were also Muslim clerics and accorded a corresponding respect for the supernatural sanctions that they were believed able to invoke. Richard Jobson, a seventeenth-century Englishman traveling in the Gambia, reported of these mercantile clerics: "They have free recourse through all places, so that howsoever the King and Countries are at warres and up in armes, the one against the other, yet still the Marybucke [marabout] is a privileged person, and many follow his trade or course of travelling, without any let or interruption of either side."[2]

Furthermore, and perhaps above all, Islam provided or promised a solution to the central problem of expansionist rule. A ruler traditionally and primarily relied on the allegiance of those related to him, by such kinship as came from a common ancestor. The wider the bounds of empire were set, however, the farther such allegiance was stretched. Local leaders might all too easily invoke local kinship loyalties to raise resistance. Appointing members of the ruling family to serve as governors, along with a suitable supply of soldiers, raised the risk that such governors might form a rebellious alliance with disaffected subjects for an attempt to capture the imperial throne. Emperors took instead to appointing provincial governors from among those of their slaves who possessed the necessary qualities as well as personal allegiance to a principle beyond that of kinship.

Such qualities and allegiance were found among those, slave or free, who were educated at the growing number of Muslim schools and colleges in the region, which attracted scholars from elsewhere in Islam. Yet, if the rulers were generally successful in making use of Islam to organize and maintain an effective administration of government and trade, they proved to be less successful at the lower, popular level. For there, Islam did not, at least until the nineteenth century, permeate societies. Traditional kinship allegiances reasserted themselves and revealed the vulnerability of empires.[3]

Gold and slaves traveled directly northward, from the successive Sudanic empires of West Africa to Morocco. But this was far from being the only route or destination. In the ninth century, there was a diagonal route from Ghana to Gao and then across the Sahara to Egypt. This seems to have gradually declined in importance, while another route, from Mali to Upper Egypt, rose to prominence in the fourteenth century, and in the sixteenth century, yet another one, from Timbuktu to Cairo.

The sixteenth-century travel writer al-Ḥasan ben Muḥammad el Wazzan es Zayyati, known also as Leo Africanus, recorded of certain Saharan oases along the route that their inhabitants were wealthy from the trade between Egypt and Gaogao (Gao) and were black. Some of these people may well have been Songhai merchants, their slave agents, or other slaves who had settled there to exploit and secure such staging posts in the slave trade.[4]

Another early and important route reached from the central Sudanic belt to Tripoli, on the Mediterranean coast, through the complex of oases in the Fezzan, where Zawila was the principal staging post. Without the gold that was a crucial component in the trade from West Africa, slaves were the staple export. As early as the late ninth century, al-Ya'qūbī, a contemporary Arab geographer and historian, reported that Zawila was important to the slave trade and a stronghold of the Ibāḍī Berbers, who were also trading farther south. Al-Istakhrī, a tenth-century writer, in contrasting slaves from various parts of Africa, asserted that those who arrived from the central Sudan and passed through Zawila on the route north were blacker and better than the others. As H. J. Fisher writes: "The slave revolt in Iraq, late in the ninth century, particularly associated with Zanj slaves, may have given all those from eastern Africa a bad name, and correspondingly heightened the demand for those from the central Sudan."[5]

It is probable that the central Sudanic kingdom of Kanem, which emerged in the ninth or tenth century, did so in response to the slave trade. What is certain is that the formation of the state involved military conquest. In the eleventh century, a Muslim missionary, Muḥammad Mani, converted the Mai Humai of Kanem, and received, in gratitude for the Koranic instruction he had given the monarch, alms of a hundred slaves, a hundred camels, a hundred gold and a hundred silver coins.

Subsequent rulers were renowned for their devotion to Islam, and Muslim divines enjoyed a privileged position in the kingdom. At the height of its power in the early thirteenth century, Kanem conquered the Fezzan, probably to control or secure the trade route across the Sahara, and even opened a hostel in Cairo for Kanemis in that city. Then, in the middle of the fourteenth century, the kingdom came under serious pressure, from quarrels over the succession within and from Arabs in the east who were seizing Kanemi Muslims to sell as slaves. In the last decade, the *Mai* (King) fled with his court and followers into Bornu, southwest of Kanem, and established there a new state, which expanded and would survive unconquered until late in the nineteenth century.

Many of the black slaves exported from the central Sudan were destined for military service in North Africa. The trade also supplied eunuchs for employment in harems or in government service, and female slaves for sale as concubines. Ibn Baṭṭūṭa, who crossed the Sahara in the middle of the fourteenth century and traveled with a caravan of six hundred female slaves, wrote favorably of both the eunuchs and the slave girls from Bornu. The trade supplied many other slaves for more menial purposes. Still others were not provided to the trade but used as the currency of tribute or of gifts. In 1257, for instance, a contingent was sent from the King of Kanem and the Lord of Bornu to the ruler in the eastern Maghrib.

Slaves were procured not only to serve the trans-Saharan demand but also for central Sudanic rulers who sought them as a source of prestige and a demonstration of wealth, for employment in retinues, or as laborers with or without special skills. Moreover, population decline from drought and famine, epidemic and war, was an intermittent pressure. Slaves were needed to replenish such losses. A nineteenth-century Hausa, who had been a slave in Bornu, would remark: "The country of Bornu—I am telling the truth—is a country of slaves."[6]

From 969, when the Fatimids conquered the country, and through the successive dynasties of Ayyūbids and Mamluks—a period of five and a half centuries—Egypt developed from a mere province of empire to an independent state and then the paramount power in the Near East. To the south, in Nubia, where two Christian kingdoms were heirs to an ancient African civilization, Muslim merchants settled in separate quarters of the towns to conduct a trade with Egypt based on the export of cattle, ivory, ostrich feathers, and, above all, slaves. These slaves, known as *al-Nuba* or *al-Sudan* (blacks), were sought for various purposes: the females as concubines or nurses; the males as domestic servants or, mainly, as soldiers.[7]

They were imported in such numbers that the relatively sparse population of Nubia could hardly have provided them, and the likelihood is

that many, if not most, of them came from the large area to the south
that reached westward from the border of Ethiopia to Darfur and beyond. The end of the Fatimid dynasty led to a sharp decline in the demand for black military slaves, not least because they had proved so loyal
to the Fatimid cause that they rebelled in its interest. However, the
demand for "Nubian" slaves, to provide domestic and other services,
continued for markets not only in Egypt but in many other Islamic countries. By the late fourteenth century, Arab raiders were supplying Egyptian markets with slaves from the vicinity of Lake Chad; these even
included, to his protests, some relatives of the Muslim king of Bornu.

Egyptian merchants were also active in Ethiopia, trading both with
the independent Christian kingdom and with Muslim states to the south
of it. They supplied linen, cotton, and silk textiles as well as weapons,
and returned with ivory, spices, and especially slaves. These slaves were
highly prized throughout Islam for their reputed reliability; among them
were eunuchs, exported mainly from Hadya in southwest Ethiopia,
where they were brought after having been castrated elsewhere in the region.

The advance of Islam southward along the East African coast came
mainly by a sea route long established in conformity with the annual
shifts in the direction of the monsoons. As Hippalos, a first-century
Greek, had observed, for four months of the year around winter, the
northeast winds carried ships from Arabia and northwest India to the east
coast of Africa, and for six months of the year around summertime,
southwest winds carried ships in the opposite direction. Written at some
time in the second century by an anonymous Egyptian Greek, *The
Periplus of the Erythraean Sea* reported that slaves were exported from
the Horn of Africa and that southern Arabs were settled along the East
African coast.[8] These Arab settlers were joined by Muslims late in the
seventh century; and by the ninth century, Islam had rooted itself in
the coastal regions. Muslim settlements, established and developed by
merchants from Arabia and countries around the Persian Gulf, were
strengthened by intermarriage between the newcomers and the indigenous people of the Horn, who were called Berbers or sometimes, to distinguish them from the Berbers of North Africa, "black Berbers" by Arab
geographers.

A foreign, mainly Arab, component infuses the genealogical traditions of the Somali people today. These traditions, confirmed by Arabic
inscriptions, date the first Arab settlement at Mogadishu to the second
half of the eighth century. The first major migration, however, occurred
in the early years of the tenth century, and was followed by other waves
of Arab and Persian settlers. By the thirteenth century, when the Sultanate of Mogadishu was established, this prominent commercial port
was attracting regular visits by merchants from India as well as Arabia
and Persia to transact business with local traders.

Northward along the African coast and across the Gulf from Aden
was the Somali town of Zeila, whose inhabitants were Muslim. So dominant did this port become in the commerce of the region that all the
Muslim communities along the trade routes into central and southeastern Ethiopia were, by the fourteenth century, collectively known in Syria
and Egypt as "the country of Zeila."[9] Already in the twelfth century, the
Moroccan scholar al-Idrīsī described Zeila as "a town of small size but
highly populated," whose "export consists of slaves and silver."[10]

Zeila might well have been the departure point for those who migrated to establish Muslim communities and even polities in the
Ethiopian region. By the early fourteenth century, after perhaps two
hundred years of development, many of these polities still existed. Most
were merely minor sheikhdoms, but several were sizable kingdoms, and
Ifat, the predominant one, commanded most of the long-distance trade
between the Ethiopian interior and Zeila on the coast. Yet, big or small,
these Muslim polities were more disposed to compete than to collaborate with one another, despite the threat from a reinvigorated and militant Christian kingdom. In fact, Muslim Hyda, already a regional center
of the slave trade in the thirteenth century, made a preemptive peace
with the Christian kingdom by becoming its tributary. And by the end
of the fourteenth century, war between that kingdom and Ifat resulted in
the latter's extinction as an independent Muslim power.

Arab geographers divided the east coast of Africa into four regions:
the Land of Barbar, which reached around the Horn and ended north of
Mogadishu; the Land of Zanj, which extended southward to beyond
Pemba but short of Zanzibar; the Land of Sofala, which ended probably
at the mouth of the Limpopo River; and, beyond that, the little-known
Land of Waq-Waq. Al-Mas'ūdī journeyed from Oman to Qanbalu, as

Pemba was then called, in 916–17. He wrote that the island contained Muslims, with a Muslim ruling family who spoke the Zanj language, and that Muslims had conquered the place around the end of Umayyad rule in Baghdad, or roughly 750.

Approximately a third of the way northward up the coast of Zanj, at Manda, there is archaeological evidence of a ninth-century town, remarkable for the apparent extent of its riches. Some of its buildings were of coral stone, which was also used for walls, made of large blocks weighing up to a ton each, probably against encroachments by the sea. Not only Chinese stoneware and porcelain have been discovered but imported pottery much like that found at Siraf on the eastern side of the Persian Gulf. That an extensive trade existed at the time between Manda and the Gulf, and particularly with Siraf, seems virtually certain. Since elephants were common on the mainland then, as they are today, it may reasonably be supposed that ivory acquired there was a major export from Manda.[11]

To the south of Pemba, on the island of Zanzibar, discoveries have included Islamic pottery of the ninth and tenth centuries and gold coins, one of which, a dinar struck by a vizier of Hārūn al-Rashīd, is dated the equivalent of 798–99. In the middle of the twelfth century al-Idrīsī wrote that the inhabitants of an island (Zanzibar seems, from the context, to be the one he had in mind) were mainly Muslims, and that iron was produced in the middle area of the Sofala coast. The iron, he added, was of such reputed excellence that people from Java—clearly, visiting traders—transported it to India, where it was used to make swords of exceptional quality. It is unlikely, however, that iron would have been the only export from the region.

This first phase in communication with Islam seems largely to have been limited to trade and traders, but was no less influential for that. By the early eleventh century, if not still earlier, a distinctive coastal language, Kiswahili, was emerging from a Bantu language core, and around 1100, a related and distinctive Swahili coastal culture began developing in various settlements. During this second phase, roughly 1100 to 1300, there was a marked increase in trade and commercial wealth, a correspondingly augmented use of coral stone for buildings, and the spread of Islam by contact with Middle Eastern and Indian merchants.

Early in the twelfth century, for instance, the first stage of the Great

Mosque at Kilwa was constructed, and in the twelfth and thirteenth centuries, Lamu, Malindi, Mogadishu, Mombasa, and Zanzibar town became major coastal settlements. Associated with this was the migration of Arab clans from Yemen, in particular to Mogadishu, which acquired a series of Arab ruling dynasties, developed a flourishing coastal commerce, and earned renown as a center of Muslim learning; and to Kilwa, which acquired, near the end of the thirteenth century, a ruling dynasty of Yemeni *sharifs* (asserted descendants of the Prophet) and dominance of the gold trade from Sofala.

In the third phase, roughly 1300 to 1600, which would come to be called the golden age of coastal history, the region reached a peak of prosperity, with half of all known coastal settlements being founded. To the north, Mombasa and Malindi became prosperous commercial centers, challenging Kilwa's dominance. Direct trading contacts, until then mainly with the Persian Gulf, became part of the wider Indian Ocean network, extending from Egypt to the Far East. Philip Curtin writes: "A little before 1500, the annual northward flow of gold into the general commercial system of the Indian Ocean . . . reached at least a metric ton on the average. This linked Zimbabwe to the world economic system based on gold and silver, just as the western Sudan had already joined through the trans-Sahara trade."[12] In addition, ivory, skins, ambergris, cowries, and agricultural products were dispatched from East African ports, which received spices, jewels, silks, brocades, celadons, and porcelains from China and Malacca.

Islam became the dominant coastal religion. Larger and more elaborate mosques were constructed with varieties of coral. Yet the culture, far from being an imposed foreign one, remained distinctively Swahili. Indigenous African social traditions of matrilineal inheritance seem to have successfully withstood the influence of Islamic patrilineage in the northern cities before the seventeenth century. There is considerable evidence that women, not least as queens, were prominent in public life. They participated in important ceremonies, attended mosques along with men, and were encouraged to become literate and to study Islamic sciences (*elimu*). They enjoyed equal rights of inheritance and property ownership with men, and in some coastal settlements, succession to rule proceeded through female members of the royal lineage.

The coastal settlements were not, however, left to pursue their prosperity in peace. Increasingly, they came under pressure from two sides. One threat was from "northern" Arabs as well as the Portuguese, who would arrive suddenly by sea to pillage and to seize people for enslavement. Another came from the interior, where some indigenous peoples attacked Swahili agricultural communities along the coast. One early Portuguese commentator remarked that Swahili towns were "oft-times at war but seldom at peace with those of the mainland"; another observed of the coastal towns that "none of them owns a yard of land in the hinterland because the Kafirs do not allow them to have it, and they are in fact afraid of them. For this reason their towns are surrounded by walls."[13] Walls had not been a feature of Swahili towns in the previous phase, but by 1505, both Kilwa and Mombasa to the south and most of the known major towns along the northern coast had defensive barriers.

One reason could have been that some, if not all, of the coastal settlements were involved in slave trading and even slave raiding. That there were slaves in their populations is certain. Muslim societies would have regarded the absence rather than the presence of slaves as extraordinary. The early Portuguese remarked not only on the luxury of the clothes, silk as well as cotton, and the impressive amount of gold and silver jewelry worn by the upper classes in the coastal towns, but also on the loincloths worn by slaves.[14]

Ibn Baṭṭūṭa, having visited the region in the middle of the fourteenth century, described Kilwa as "a large town on the coast. The majority of its inhabitants are Zanj, jet-black in colour, and with tattoo-marks on their faces . . . Its inhabitants are constantly engaged in military expeditions, for their country is contiguous to the heathen Zanj. The sultan at the time of my visit was Abd'l-Muzzafar Hasan, who was noted for his gifts and generosity. He used to devote the fifth part of the booty made on his expeditions to pious and charitable purposes."[15] If slaving was not a prime purpose of such military expeditions, as it might well have been, slaves doubtless represented at least part of the booty.

The existence of protective walls did not signify isolation. The coastal settlements continued to absorb immigrants from southern Arabia, along with Africans fleeing from danger, persecution, warfare, or simply drawn by the reported prosperity and associated delights of coastal society, for assimilation into the distinctive Swahili culture. This proved to be both resourceful and resolute.

In the sixteenth century, Islam south of the Horn came under increasing pressure from the Portuguese, whose naval power now dominated the western Indian Ocean and whose control of the Zambezi route cut the coastal trade for gold and ivory through Sofala. The religious as well as commercial aggressiveness of the Portuguese—whose Inquisition proved as intrusive and repressive as its counterpart in Spain—only strengthened the resistance of the coastal societies, which would defy and finally defeat them. The very failure of a jihad to conquer Christian Ethiopia was a factor in the growth of the region, for it brought new migrants from Arab clans, who mainly settled on the Pate and Lamu offshore islands. These developed into major trading centers, through the commercial contacts that such clans enjoyed as far east as Indonesia, and the wealth accordingly generated drew older coastal clans—the *waungwana*, or free, "civilized" townspeople of the coast with their Swahili language, learning, and traditions.

In Pate and Lamu, in the seventeenth and eighteenth centuries, the rich Arabs and waungwana built "magnificent, multi-storied mansions," as symbols of their social dominance.[16] Below them, in descending order, came the middle layer of poorer waungwana, such as artisans, the *wageni* (Muslim newcomers or "foreigners"), the *washenzi* (non-Muslim "barbarians"), and, at the bottom, the slaves. These served not only as concubines and servants in the households of their owners but as laborers on the mainland agricultural estates that provided much of the material for trade. Randall Pouwels states that at Lamu in the eighteenth century, for instance, the trading wealth amassed by certain clans—from extensive mainland plantations and links with settled Somali and other peoples on the mainland—"was augmented by the acquisition and employment of huge numbers of slaves."[17]

In coastal society, wealth was the decisive factor. It brought such attributes of status as the size of house and style of household, family alliances, religious duties. Indeed, Pouwels adds, "even genealogy changed fluidly with the achievement of wealth."[18] There was only one barrier. This was a plutocracy wedded to religion. Social advancement was allowable only to Muslims.

It was in this period, too, that the Omani Arabs began substantially to affect coastal society and politics. British assistance enabled them successfully to confront Portuguese power in much of the region. By the middle of the eighteenth century, the Busaidi dynasty had won control not only of Oman itself but of Zanzibar as well. Then, in the early 1800s, the Busaidi ruler, Sayyid Said b. Sultan, who would reign for more than half a century from 1806, set out from the strategic bases of Zanzibar and Kilwa to conquer the coast. It would prove to be a protracted engagement, with resistance from other clan and factional interests. Mombasa, for instance, was not captured until 1837. But by the time of his death, in 1856, he had wrested control of all the principal coastal towns. It would still take until 1895 before Busaidi authority over the whole coastal strip was recognized, and by then, real power was wielded by Britain. Meanwhile, the trading towns had retained substantial control over their own affairs. The Sultans had been more suzerains than sovereigns over the conquests.

Resistance to the Sultans surfaced intermittently until the 1880s. And even in Zanzibar, to which Sayyid Said had moved his capital and court, the Sultan's writ might be defied by nobles from rival clans. As Richard Burton observed: "Sometime a noble, when ordered into arrest at Zanzibar, has collected his friends, armed his slaves, and fortified his house. One Salim b. Abdallah, who had a gang of 2,000 musketeer negroes, used to wage a petty war with the Sayyid's servile hosts."[19]

Sayyid Said used his power to amass riches, and his riches to maintain his power. His revenues were immense. Commercial treaties with Britain, France, and the United States supplied him with a 5 percent duty on goods brought by their nationals into coastal ports, while an excise duty of 5 percent on exports supplied another lucrative flow. He was not, however, satisfied to be just a tax collector. He had agents who traded on his behalf. One American reported that the Sultan dispatched every year a hundred men to collect ivory.[20] Along with members of his family, Sayyid Said was heavily involved in the slave trade, which was profitable enough in itself but especially important as the source of labor for his prime enterprise: the cultivation and export of cloves, centered on Zanzibar, where he personally owned numerous plantations.

Questions remain over the extent and duration of the Islamic slave trade from East Africa south of the Horn. Historical records leave no room for doubt that it was the black slaves known as the Zanj, mainly put to work on irrigation projects in southern Iraq, who had mounted the great rebellion in the ninth century there. It is likely that they would have come from the East African coastal area known by that name, though it is also possible that others from a wider region were associated with them as the dominant group. What seems certain is that a considerable slave trade from East Africa existed at least as far back as the ninth century, and many references to Zanj slaves in medieval writings strongly suggest that the trade in Zanj slaves continued, if not in such concentrated numbers.

The historian and archaeologist Gervase Mathew, in discussing the period from the twelfth century to the fifteenth century, when Muslims dominated the Indian Ocean trade, has written that the trading towns along the East African coast provided two particular exports eastward: "African ivory was much needed in China and much prized in India, while in Islamic India and in Mesopotamia [Iraq] there was an insatiable demand for slaves."[21] The historian Neville Chittick, while accepting that a slave trade from East Africa was already in existence by the ninth century, asserts that there is very little evidence for exports except in the north, from what is now the Somali coast: "It seems most likely that the Horn continued to be the main source of slaves; human beings are comparatively expensive to transport and subject to loss by disease, so that the shorter voyage from the Horn would have been advantageous."[22]

It is not improbable that both historians are right, and that Zanj slaves were transported overland to the Horn and shipped from there. In any case, there was certainly a flow of black slaves from the east coast of Africa to various parts of Islam over the centuries, and if it was not as large overall as that in the Red Sea trade, let alone the predominant overland trade across the Sahara, it involved very considerable numbers.

SEVEN

THE OTTOMAN EMPIRE

Of all the empires that rose and fell within Islam, the Ottoman was the largest and most enduring. At its greatest extent, it reached, in the north, from east of the Black Sea to the border of Austria; in the south, from the Persian Gulf, through Iraq, Syria, and the Hijaz, to include Yemen; and across Egypt, along the coastal region of North Africa, to the border of Morocco. The last of its Sultans was thrust from his throne almost six centuries after the death of its progenitor in 1324.

The empire derived its name from Osman I, a clan leader among the nomadic Turkish tribes that had swept from the plains of central Asia to conquer and settle in Anatolia. Within slightly more than a century, almost all of Anatolia had succumbed to Ottoman rule. Then, in 1453, Mehmed II captured Constantinople, known as the Queen of Cities, and the report of the capture was received by the Doge and Senate of Venice as "the darkest day in the history of the world."[1] The fall of Constantinople marked the end of the Byzantine Empire, heir to the Classical and then Christian heritage of the ancient Roman Empire for a thousand years after that empire's collapse in the West.

The Christian powers, for all their expressions of distress, soon demonstrated that they were more dedicated to doing business with the Ottomans than with supplying any material support for the summons from the Pope to a new crusade. Mehmed II himself, meanwhile, made no secret of the ultimate purpose that his latest conquest was intended to serve. To a young Venetian, he declared that "he would go from the East to the West as the Westerners had gone to the East. The Empire of the world, he says, must be one, one faith and one kingdom. To make this unity, there is no place more worthy than Constantinople."[2]

Western Christians who had carried the sword along with the cross eastward in the Crusades and would, sometimes on the pretext of saving souls, subsequently carve out colonies across much of the world, were scarcely in a moral position to condemn their Muslim counterparts for religious imperialism. Indeed, in its dealings with the adherents of other religions, the Ottoman Empire proved overall a good deal more tolerant than much of Christendom showed itself to be. Jews who were expelled from Spain, and who found few havens in Europe open to them, chose to settle in the empire, where they received a ready welcome. Neither they nor even Christians, the historical adversaries since the Crusades, who were encompassed by Ottoman conquests or who simply settled in the empire, encountered serious discrimination against the practice of their faith or their commercial enterprise.

Along with this productive tolerance, the empire's vast domestic market in three continents and its trade relations with countries beyond its borders should have enabled it to pioneer or at least exploit the development of capitalism and the industrial revolution it promoted. Instead, it became the victim of both. Already by the seventeenth century, the Ottoman economy was being confronted by the West's colonial production of sugar, cotton, and tobacco in the Americas. Cheaper sugar from American plantations put an end to Ottoman refineries in Cyprus and Egypt. Increasing demand for cotton fabrics, within the empire as well as the West, inflicted further damage on an Ottoman silk trade already in difficulties. Even Cairo's seventeenth-century command of the transit trade in coffee, much of it from Yemen for markets in the empire and elsewhere, was gone by the middle of the eighteenth century, because of the competition from cheaper American supplies.

The West's colonial production was not the only problem. By the early sixteenth century, the Anatolian city of Bursa had developed a flourishing silk industry. This was soon confronted by mounting compe-

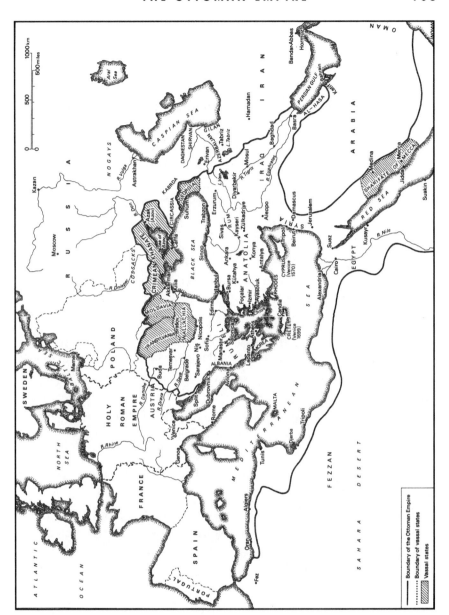

Map 4: The Ottoman Empire, c. 1550

tition from the products of mechanized silk reeling in northern Italy. With correspondingly reduced labor costs, Italian manufacturers were able to pay more for raw silk—driving up its price internationally—while still exporting fabrics cheaper than those produced in the empire. Foreign manufacturers also took to exporting still lower-priced, lighter fabrics from a mixture of silk and cotton. These fabrics became popular in the empire but were resisted by the craftsmen in Bursa and rejected by the Ottoman palace, the single most important customer for high-quality fabrics. Paradoxically, the difficulties of the industry were augmented by the reliance of many Ottoman manufacturers on slave labor, which was profitable only when profit margins were high. As profits came to be ever more tightly squeezed in the late seventeeth and eighteenth centuries, the silk industry in Bursa declined unremittingly.[3]

One element of the Ottoman Empire's long economic decline is evident here. There are varying opinions on the importance of the slave trade and the institution of slavery itself to the development of capitalism and the industrial revolution in the West. What is certain, however, is that the Atlantic slave trade was a markedly profitable commercial operation, that part of these profits was reinvested in an industrial growth already being promoted by the provision of barter goods for the trade, and that large profits came from the use of slaves, defined and treated as units of labor, in the commercial plantations of colonial agriculture.

Slaves in the Ottoman Empire were differently regarded and treated. In conformity with Islamic teaching and law, slaves were people who had stipulated rights. In practice, many—for example, soldiers and civil servants who were slaves of the Sultan—rose to become generals and governors. Indeed, there were free-born Muslims, doctrinally protected from enslavement, who bribed or otherwise insinuated their way into becoming slaves of the Sultan, for the related prospect of attaining high office. A slave concubine whose son became the Sultan acquired accordingly an institutionalized high status and large financial resources of her own. Certainly, there were countless other slaves whose fate was menial and sometimes brutal. Yet a populous and productive peasantry preempted the need for slave labor in agriculture, and though there were slaves on the great estates of Ottoman landlords, it was not in such numbers or for such purposes that they provided the profits for significant capital accumulation.

Essentially, the distinction between Western and Ottoman—indeed Islamic—slavery was that between the commercial and the domestic. This is not to ignore the existence of domestic slaves in the Western colonies, any more than one can ignore the use of slave labor in a variety of commercial activities in the Ottoman Empire. But the basis of slavery in the West was, simply, the economic exploitation of slave labor. In the Ottoman Empire, the slaves provided personal services. While slavery in the West was directed to the productive economy, in the Ottoman Empire it was a form of consumption.

As such, the marketing of slaves was closely regulated. Along with certain designated precious goods, such as silk and arms, slaves had to be sold only through officially appointed brokers in the bazaar, so as to ensure that buyers were not cheated and that a fair price was paid. Furthermore, from the late sixteenth century onward, the state became increasingly hostile to the accumulation of commercial capital—especially where speculative gains were suspected—since this was held to exploit rather than benefit the community. Successful slave dealers might, like other merchants who attracted suspicion, be conscripted to provide particular services notorious for the risks of large financial loss that they entailed. Supplying camels for the Ḥijāz caravan was one such costly punishment.

This points to a related reason for the failure of the Ottoman Empire to keep pace with, let alone outstrip, economic developments in the West. The empire was a religious construct, and Islam, while far from indifferent to the benefits of trade, did not itself rate trading high in the order of human pursuits. The advancement of the faith, through scholarship or soldiering, was considered a much more meritorious calling. Nationalism, which the community of Islam confronted, promoted more material priorities in the West. There, not least in its colonial extension, it provided both incentive and opportunity for the advancement of capitalism. And the prime beneficiaries, the merchants and industrialists, exercised increasing influence over government, whose policies were adapted to correspond ever more closely to their interests.

The contrast presented by the Ottoman Empire could scarcely have been more striking. The concept of the state as a means of promoting the faith and expressing its moral principles was profoundly formative. The doctrinal charge to serve the welfare of the whole community, for instance, infused such economic practices as the regulation of markets, the fixing of prices, and the restraint of profit, to ensure the provision of necessities to the populace. Crucially, in this last regard, the state largely denied itself such protectionist devices as were employed in Western countries to promote their own industries. Ottoman markets were left open to cheaper foreign cloth because the poor might not be able to afford the domestic products available.

In the Ottoman Empire, a major repository of capital were the charitable foundations established by successive Sultans. Their function as a source of venture capitalism was severely restricted, however, by their primary obligation to spend their revenues on good works, such as building mosques, supporting schools, and distributing alms. The dynamic of social distinction and religious directives ensured the spread of this obligation widely among the rich, who were given to establishing charitable foundations of their own.

Yet this early Muslim version of the welfare state was also an absolute autocracy, whose elaborate isolation might have been designed to promote the waywardness and corruptions of rule. Both symbol and substance of this was the new palace, built by Mehmed II, in the capital. It had three courts, of which only the outermost was accessible to the public, and then only on holidays or when the Sultan's *divan*, or council, was in session. Few of the thousands of palace guards and servants were permitted to penetrate farther, except on rare occasions. Beyond this, through the Gate of Salutation, was the second court, with its Hall of the Divan, sumptuously furnished to represent the power and riches of the Sultan. There, his acceptable officers of state and religion met to advise him, sometimes in his visible presence and sometimes merely in his hearing as he sat behind a curtained grille. Then, beyond this, was the third, innermost court, a palace within the palace, ḥarām (forbidden) to all but the Sultan himself and those whom he allowed to be associated with him in the seclusion of his greatness.

His singularity was demonstrated as well as secured by the character of his servants and guards. These were young male white slaves, mainly acquired as tribute from the conquered Christian peoples of the empire, who were circumcised and converted to Islam, given the status of royal pages, and trained for a variety of offices and functions, military and civil, in the service of the Sultan. In time, as the era of conquest gave way to one of containment and then contraction, the supply of suitable white slaves sharply diminished, and the ranks of royal pages were replenished by inheritance from father to son. White eunuchs, most of them bought from castration centers in Christian Europe and Circassia, were responsible for much of the domestic administration in the new palace, and had particular charge of the royal pages and their training.

It was in the old palace, inherited from the Byzantine Empire, that the harem of the Sultan's women was initially situated. There, black eunuchs, who had undergone the most radical form of castration and were accordingly considered most suited to their sensitive responsibilities, were the only male slaves employed. Their duties went far beyond the domestic ones of attendance and watchfulness. They came to be charged, for instance, with administering the various properties and investments of the Sultan's mother, known as the Valide Sultan, of his favorite concubine, and of his daughters and sisters. The chief black eunuch, or *kizlar ağasi*, in particular, eventually wielded power and influence of an extent that can only be understood in terms of the peculiar role played by royal women in the system.

The use of slave concubines as reproductive partners, in addition to the doctrinally allowable limit of four wives, was a practice commonly pursued by Muslims who could afford them. Muslim rulers were no exception, and their wealth often enabled them to afford numbers of women more representative of status than need. The Ottoman dynasty took the practice to an extreme. After those children mothered by the wives of the first two Sultans, virtually all children of Sultans were born of concubines. Indeed, marriage was avoided as a rule, with rare exceptions presented by an especially beloved concubine or the need formally to bind some Anatolian tribe or clan. Marriage to a woman of another Anatolian house ran the risk of endowing it with ideas beyond its station, and marriage with women from other ruling dynasties, Muslim or not, was regarded as conferring more distinction on them than the Ottoman dynasty itself could gain by the alliance.

Given the patriarchal nature of political power in Islam, slave maternity was no barrier to inheriting the Ottoman Sultanate. The very extent of royal reproduction through concubines, however, led to frequent disputes over the succession, some of which involved costly conflict. To preclude such disputes, from the middle of the fifteenth century, the accession of a new Sultan was confirmed by the execution of his brothers and their sons. Then, in the second half of the sixteenth century, further measures were taken. The practice of appointing princes to provincial governorships was abandoned, since it provided presumptive claimants with a power base on which to build, and the Sultan's sons, whatever their age, were confined to the palace and forbidden to father a child unless and until they succeeded to the throne.

The practice of royal fratricide, though, grew to be so unpopular that it was abandoned. When Ahmed I died in 1617, he was succeeded, for the first time in fourteen generations of Ottoman rule, by his brother. And, as Leslie Peirce has written: "In the twenty-two generations of the Ottoman dynasty that followed Ahmed I, the throne always passed to the eldest living male Ottoman, and only three times did a son succeed his father: for the most part, sultans were followed by their brothers, less frequently by nephews, and once by a cousin."[4] Given a princely life expectancy rate that was subject to every sudden start of suspicion, jealousy, or resentment in the Sultan's mind, the principle of succession by seniority must have been at least as much a source of apprehension as of pleasurable anticipation to the next in line.

For all its intermittent internal turbulence, the dynasty was considered so sacred that its right to rule was never seriously questioned, until close to its republican conclusion in the twentieth century. Yet this sacredness did not preclude connections that must have seemed bizarre, if not abhorrent, to royalty in the West. From the middle of the fifteenth century, princesses—daughters or sisters of the Sultan—were commonly married to high officials in the slave military and civil administration, who were already or might then be made grand viziers. These *damad* viziers, sons-in-law, though sometimes brothers-in-law, of the Sultan, as Leslie Peirce explains, "were thus in many respects the male parallels of the sultan's concubines, the women who rose to the top of the female slave hierarchy."[5] They were commensurately enriched and had their own grand establishments in the capital. One was said to own thirteen hundred slaves, another, seventeen hundred. Some were invested with governor-generalships or given army or navy commands. But their very eminence was also invested with risk, from which the royalty of their wives could not protect them. One grand vizier was executed in 1536, another in 1614, both for having provoked the Sultan by their supposed pride.

In practice, often more important and powerful than any princess was the favorite concubine of the Sultan. She had her own high title and income and the assurance of a corresponding retirement allowance. But supreme among the women in the empire was the Valide Sultan, whose status and role went far beyond simply being the Sultan's mother. She was the imperial matriarch, symbol of the dynasty's legitimacy and responsible for ensuring its continuity by promoting the birth of princes for the succession and preventing as far as possible their execution by too wary or wayward a Sultan. The Valide Sultan generally acted as Regent when the Sultan was a child or when he went abroad, and some played a constantly active role in statecraft. They corresponded with foreign rulers, especially when these were women; they advised the Sultan; and, when he was away, they kept him informed of developments at home.

Since she was granted large stipends and properties that provided additional revenues, the Valide Sultan had ample resources to perform charitable works, such as building mosques and schools, that augmented her independent popularity. Indeed, alone among the women in the imperial harem, she was entitled to leave it, and even the palace itself, for public appearances. Her prime domain, however, was the harem, and her sway there became increasingly influential as the Sultanate, after its era of imperial conquest, became a sedentary one, with the Sultan no longer leading his army in battle and seldom emerging from the palace.

The black eunuchs, not only the guardians and attendants of the Valide Sultan and the royal concubines but the managers of their financial affairs, were crucially placed to exercise influence, and during the reign of Suleiman I (1520–66), their role was much augmented. In 1541, after a fire in the old palace that housed the imperial harem, Suleiman brought his favorite concubine to live in the new palace, followed by the whole harem, albeit so gradually that the transfer was completed only by the middle of the seventeenth century. The early impact, however, with the installation of the Valide Sultan in particular, was immense. The new palace became the center of the Sultan's private life as well as of his

public one, and this close coexistence all but inevitably promoted the
force of the former over the latter.

Black eunuchs came to occupy strategic positions of authority and access, until they were the very valves controlling the flow of blood to and
from the heart of government. Already in 1595, the first year in the reign
of Mehmed III, the ascendancy of the chief black eunuch was such that
he was given the office, until then held by the chief white eunuch, of
administering the supreme holy places—the mosques of Mecca and
Medina—with their vast annual revenues. His office was subsequently responsible for administering the charitable foundations established by
the Sultans themselves. Some of these foundations were beneficiaries of
continuing tax revenues: all non-Muslims in Istanbul paid their head
taxes to the foundation of Mehmed the Conqueror (1451–81), while one
of the major trade fairs in the Balkans served to finance that of Ahmed I
(1604–17). All in all, a substantial sector of Ottoman public finances was
placed under the chief black eunuch's control.

His essential sphere remained the imperial harem, while the grand
vizier, whose sphere was the state, was the equivalent of chief minister
and ranked second only to the Sultan. Yet, where the Sultan was the
state—more so even than France's King Louis XIV envisaged, since the
Sultan was indivisibly the religious as well as secular embodiment of
the empire—the influence that access to him provided could mean
more than any formal status conveyed. Living in such proximity, and
with virtually unrestricted access to the Sultan, the chief black eunuch
effectively came close to being his private chief minister. In fact, his public role as councillor and administrator was formalized by membership
in the imperial divan.

The extent to which the status and prestige of the chief black eunuch could be deployed was demonstrated in 1617, when Ahmed I died,
and it was not his eldest son, Osman—nor any of his other five sons—
who mounted the throne, but his brother Mustafa. The contemporary
historian Ibrahim Peçevi ascribed this first break with the principle of
succession from father to son to the influence of the chief black eunuch,
Mustafa Agha, who persuaded leading statesmen that Osman was too
young—although, at fourteen, he was the same age at which his father
had become Sultan. Mustafa Agha's motive was allegedly his determina-

tion to retain the power he had wielded under Ahmed I, when all affairs of state had been committed to his management.[6]

When a chief black eunuch was not able to influence the Sultan directly, his alliance with the Valide Sultan could be formidable enough, especially if the Sultan was young, weak-willed, or unpopular. Moreover, other black eunuchs were so situated as significantly to affect the course of events. This, along with the power of the Valide Sultan, came to be demonstrated most dramatically in the seventeeth century.

Murad IV, who reigned from 1623 to 1640, was one of the last Sultans to lead his army into battle, and Kösem, his mother, was the greatest of the Valide Sultans, in the range and quality of her statecraft. Both were ruthless. Murad, indeed, disposed of all his brothers but one, İbrāhīm, who survived only because Kösem had persuaded Murad that İbrāhīm was incapable of governing and accordingly posed no threat.

Having secured his eventual succession, Kösem set about encouraging İbrāhīm to father an heir. He responded so readily that his sexual excesses earned him the historical title of İbrāhīm the Debauched. This rampant libido had implications that threatened Kösem's own dominance. She dealt with the ascendancy of one favorite concubine by inviting her to a feast and having her strangled there. İbrāhīm, however, had no fewer than eight favorites, and by 1648, he was so far beyond his mother's control that he exiled her to one of the capital's imperial gardens. Kösem set out to remove him, and his increasing unpopularity provided her with the means. She enlisted the support of the janissaries (royal guards), along with a *fatwa* (judgment) from the religious authorities stating that a madman was disqualified from rule. İbrāhīm was deposed and shortly afterward murdered, leaving the way clear for Kösem's seven-year-old grandson to mount the throne as Mehmed IV.

This concluded Kösem's role and authority as Valide Sultan, an office to which Turhan, the mother of the new Sultan, now acceded. But given the relative youth of Turhan, who was still in her early twenties, and Kösem's own developed network of allies, which must have included the chief black eunuch, Kösem secured the necessary support to have herself declared Regent.

This was such a breach of custom that it became a source of scandal, and Turhan was encouraged in her resistance by Süleyman Agha, the head of the black eunuchs in her service. Suspecting a conspiracy, Kösem planned a preemptive strike. She would have her eldest grandson displaced on the throne by his younger brother, whose mother, she was satisfied, was likely to prove more submissive than Turhan.

One of Kösem's maidservants, however, betrayed this plan to Turhan, who might well have sanctioned—if not instigated—what ensued. Süleyman Agha and the other black eunuchs under his command murdered Kösem. The popular response in the capital to the killing of such a venerable personage was to shut the mosques and markets for three days of mourning. Yet, in the Ottoman system, status was sacred. However widespread the belief in her complicity might have been, Turhan was Valide Sultan and now became Regent, while Süleyman Agha was raised to the office of chief black eunuch. His, however, proved to be a short tenure of power. He was dismissed some nine months later, when Turhan began to regard his political objectives as in conflict with her own.

Turhan was the last of the Valide Sultans to act as Regent, but the role of Valide Sultan remained vital, and the influence of the black eunuchs in the palace, however attenuated from time to time, continued to affect the conduct of government. While they certainly were the most prominent black slaves in the empire, they were never more than a minute proportion of the total number of blacks there.

A customs register for the port of Antalya in 1559 reveals that among the considerable variety of exports from Egypt by sea, "Black slaves, both male and female, constituted the bulk of the traffic. Many ships carried slaves exclusively."[7] Some black slaves who were imported through Antalya probably went to Anatolian cities, among them Bursa, for employment in the labor-intensive manufacture of heavy brocades. Declines in particular modes of production were likely to be met by increases in the demand for black slaves elsewhere in the economy. Such demand increased markedly in Cairo, for instance, during the second half of the seventeenth century, when merchants and artisans enjoyed a particular period of prosperity.

Black slaves and freedmen were so numerous in the Aegean province of Aydin by the last quarter of the sixteenth century that an edict was dispatched from the capital proscribing their assemblies, perhaps because some of the rites or customs they practiced were regarded as religiously suspect.[8] The frequent mention of black slaves and freedmen in the judicial registers of Cyprus suggests that there were sizable numbers of them on the island. And the trade continued to flourish in the empire during the eighteenth century. Wealthier households of every faith usually had slaves, and demand was conditioned by different ethnic priorities: "Greeks are said to have preferred Bulgars as slaves, while Turks preferred Africans."[9]

In the absence of adequate records, there are grounds only for guesswork on the magnitude of the Ottoman demand for black slaves. Certainly, the reliance on slaves, both white and black, was extensive from the start. As early as 1453, Mehmed the Conqueror actually imposed strict controls on their export. And as the supply of white slaves declined, the Ottomans became more dependent on slaves from black Africa. In the great households of the rich, and even in those lower down on the social scale, blacks were sought for various domestic purposes. They were used for large building projects and in transportation, as well as in the small workshops of artisans. They also came increasingly to be used as military slaves in one or more regions.

The continuous demand for black slaves was effectively sustained by obedience to the Koran, with its encouragement of manumission, either through gratuitous acts of benevolence or through limited service contracts by which slaves bought their freedom with their earnings. There is evidence that this practice was extensive in the craft sector of the empire. Moreover, it was not uncommon for masters to free and marry women slaves, who appear in estate inventories under the patronymic "b. Abdullah."[10]

The cost of sustaining the Sultanate in a style suitable to its pretensions, and of waging war to maintain an empire whose enrichment by conquest receded ever further into the past, drained tax revenues. In the budget of 1669–70, for instance, when warfare was limited to the Ukraine, 62.5 percent of expenditure went on military purposes and no less than 29.5 percent on the Sultan and his palaces.[11] One devious and dangerous way of meeting the huge financial costs of the military machine was the issuance of pay tickets or promissory notes by the Ottoman treasury instead of money. In 1782, an inspection ordered by the grand vizier found that only 10 percent of the names on these pay tickets corresponded to real people who could be brought to battle.[12] It is not surprising that the royal janissaries were in intermittent revolt, as their pay fell more than two years in arrears, or that the army was more formidable on paper than in the field.

While social, political, and, above all, economic innovation swept the West, the Ottoman Empire remained steeped in sterile ceremonial. The color of robes and of slippers, the cut of sleeves, the shape of turbans, the length of beards defined in scrupulous detail the difference between one set of officials and another. It took until the reign of Mahmud II (1808–39) for a modernizing Sultan to replace the ornate distinctions of dress with a new uniform for officials: a black frock coat and red conical fez. Expecting particular trouble from the clergy, Mahmud permitted them to keep their traditional flowing robes and large turbans. Even so, demonstrations and rioting accompanied the abandonment of custom for a costume associated with the worldly West.

Modernizing the economy, however, was a very different matter from modernizing the dress. Later in the nineteenth century, the empire borrowed from the main industrial states of Western Europe large sums, whose interest costs and capital repayment inevitably led to borrowing even larger sums on ever more costly terms. This made pressure from Britain against the slave trade more difficult to resist. In 1846, the slave market in Istanbul was closed, though sales were then held in private houses. In 1855, moves to impose a ban on the trade throughout the Ottoman Empire led Shaykh Jamāl, head of the Muslim community in Mecca, to issue a fatwa declaring that the ban was a breach of Islamic holy law and that the Turks were apostates and heathens against whom it was obligatory to wage holy war. Revolt in the Hijāz followed fast, and though it was defeated by June 1856, the ban, when promulgated in 1857, expressly exempted the Hijāz from its provisions. This gave the slave traders a base from which to operate, and the flow of black slaves to Arabia and the Gulf continued, although the numbers diminished as Western states extended their conquests and control to catchment areas and supply routes in Africa.[13]

Wars and rebellions, directly or indirectly involving one or more of the so-called great powers—Britain, France, Germany, Austria, and Russia—deprived the empire of its richest provinces, weakening it further and quickening the pace of its dismemberment. Then, in a final misjudgment, the empire chose the losing side in World War I. It emerged from the war to linger awhile on its deathbed and was buried in 1923, when the republic of Turkey came into being. The formal abolition of the Caliphate and the inception of a secular state followed in 1924. Slavery itself, abolished by the government in 1889 but still legal under Islamic jurisdiction, lost its last protection.[14]

For all its oppressions and corruptions, the Ottoman Empire had, within a Muslim ascendancy, pursued in general a policy of religious tolerance by which other confessional communities coexisted in comparative peace. The process and aftermath of its contraction were accompanied, most notably in the Balkans, by the development of contending nationalisms and confessional adherences that developed an ethnic or "racial" ferocity that would be lasting and terrible in its effects.[15] For Islam itself, the secularization of Turkey was the gravestone on the Caliphate, which had long been the last living symbol of a global state uniting the community of the faithful.

EIGHT

THE "HERETIC" STATE: IRAN

Nowhere else in Islam was the early emergent Shi'a (separatist) sect more successful than in Iran, or Persia, which came to be seen by the Sunni (orthodox) strain as the heretic state. The doctrinal difference was far from trivial, since it involved no less than the nature of Islam's proper spiritual and temporal government. The association of this dissent with what amounted to a Persian nationalism was expressed in the Shi'ite claim that Husayn, son of the "martyred" 'Alī, had married a daughter of the Persian king Yezdigird—of the Sassanid dynasty swept away by the Arab conquest—and that it was only from among their descendants that the imamate, or divinely ordained succession to the spiritual and temporal leadership of Islam, could come.

As one historian has described this development: "In the field of religion, the Persians resisted conversion to Islam for a long time and, in the end, devised a new religion of their own, Shiaism, perhaps because they did not want to profess the same religion as the Arabs."[1] That the Persians devised "Shiaism" is surely a patriotic fantasy, but one that, in so far as it was believed, proved particularly potent.

Certainly, unlike so many other peoples and cultures engulfed by the seventh-century Arab conquests in the cause of Islam, the Persians came to resist Arab rule through the Caliphate and the resultant dominion of

Arabic as the holy language in which the Koran had been revealed. The efforts of the Umayyad Caliph 'Abdul Malik (685–705) to impose Arabic as the official language throughout the empire fomented Persian dis-affection, which surfaced in successive uprisings promoted by Shi'ite preachers. Then, in 747, the Umayyads were challenged by a rebellion, with Persian support, led by their own cousins, the 'Abbasids, descended from al-'Abbas, an uncle of the Prophet. The success of the rebellion opened a wide breach in Islam.

An Umayyad dynasty would come to rule al-Andalus and establish a rival Caliphate there. The 'Abbasid Caliphate lost control of North Africa, too. Meanwhile, the establishment of the 'Abbasid capital in Baghdad brought it closer to the ideas and traditions of the East, most markedly the Persian. The 'Abbasid Caliphs assumed more of the powers and dignities of Persian kings than those of Arabian sheikhs, and their court was distinguished by the promotion of the arts, science, and schol-arship. According to Hitti in *The Arabs*: "In two fields only did the Ara-bian hold his own: Islam remained the religion of the state and Arabic continued to be the official language of the state registers."[2]

The adoption of Persian wine, women, and song did not, however, satisfy Persian or Shi'ite aspirations. In Persia, from his base as ruler of Sistan, Ya'qūb (died 879) went to war against the 'Abbasid Caliphate. He failed to defeat it, but he had already promoted a revival of the Persian language, and the Samanid dynasty (900–1229), which ruled most of Persia, presided over a florescence in Persian arts and scholarship. But it was only in the sixteenth century that another Persian dynasty, the Safavids (1499–1736), who claimed direct descent from the seventh imam, would set out to unite Persia as a Shi'a state and separate it finally from Sunni domination. This came to involve a series of wars with the Ottoman Empire, by then the greatest power in Orthodox Islam. And it was the decisive victory of Persian forces in 1603, during the reign of Shah 'Abbas I, that not only restored to Persia its so-called lost provinces but secured the identity of a Shi'a Iran.

Such turbulence is unlikely ever to have interrupted the demand in Iran for black slaves. Shah 'Abbas himself, rather than training his sons in the practice of arms that he himself had so profitably employed, jeal-ously confined them to harems and the tutelage of eunuchs.[3] It would not have been remarkable if some of these eunuchs had come from Africa. The fact is, however, that relatively little is known about black slaves in Iran.

An American scholar, Joseph Harris, researching in the late 1960s for a book subsequently published under the title *The African Presence in Asia: Consequences of the East African Slave Trade*, experienced particular difficulties in acquiring information on the Iranian involvement in the black slave trade.[4] He found virtually no published material in English or French on the subject, and there was no Iranian who knew of any such study in Arabic or Persian. A history of Iran, published in 1961, provided brief references to African slaves and small settlements of African descendants such as Zanjiabad (village built by Africans), Gala-Zanjian (castle of Africans) near the "Mount of the Blacks" in Baluchistan, and Deh-Zanjian (village built by Africans) in Kerman Province.[5]

Then there is enticing evidence that black slaves from the coastlands of modern Kenya and Tanzania, the so-called Zanj, were imported in the early centuries of Islam for labor on the sugar plantations in Khūzistān.[6] And the success of the late-ninth-century Zanj rebellion in spreading from Iraq to Persia, where it captured the province of Ahwāz, was due to the large numbers of Zanj laborers, who were disaffected by work and living conditions on the sugar plantations there. One scholar, indeed, identifies the leader of the rebellion as Persian.[7]

Recently, an American scholar, Thomas Ricks, has provided invaluable further information from his research.[8] In 936, an Iranian slave trader reportedly had as many as twelve thousand black slaves.[9] And in the fifteenth century, there were hundreds of black slaves in Bam.[10] Shah Sultan Husayn (died 1722), with his entire court, visited the markets in Isfahan on the first days of the Iranian New Year. A contemporary chronicler estimated that, among the five thousand from the royal harem accompanying him, there were "100 white eunuchs and 100 black eunuchs."[11] Eighteenth-century accounts make it clear that black slaves were sometimes entrusted with various, even high, administrative responsibilities in the provinces. In 1717, for instance, Ya'qūb Sultan, identified as a black slave in one such contemporary account, was appointed Governor of Bandar Abbas, the principal port serving southern and central Iran.[12]

Jiruft was long a market center for a trade that included African slaves, and Harris found living near it a separate black community whose members, he supposed, were very likely the descendants of African merchants and slaves. They spoke a dialect that most Iranians did not understand and that may have accounted for their declared "strangeness." Another black community living near the port of Bandar Abbas would have been descended from the black slaves employed on dhows or on date plantations in the vicinity. No such community existed in Shiraz, but some people there recalled reports of black slave men and women who accompanied Iranian Muslims returning from the pilgrimage to the holy places in Arabia.[13]

The *Encyclopaedia of Islam* yields other, albeit meager, information. Treating of slavery in the Middle Ages, it refers to "the enormous slave-militias, black or white, frequently in rivalry, which speedily reinforce or replace the Arab, Berber and Iranian fighting-men."[14] Subsequently, "[in] modern Persia, it is essentially in the domestic form that slavery has been practised. There one meets with the general characteristics already noted: usually good treatment, integration in the family, ease of enfranchisement, with some modifications belonging to Imami Sh'ite law." Seventeenth-century Europeans traveling in Iran were struck by the high number of eunuchs and the power they had, both at the Safavid court and in the houses of the great, though the majority of them were white. The *Encyclopaedia* continues: "In the first half of the 19th century, under the Kadjars, white slaves became few and soon disappeared altogether, except for the pretty Caucasian girls who continued to enter the *harims* . . . The numbers of the black slaves had increased; they were either Ethiopians who had crossed Arabia, or Zandj of east Africa who came by way of Zanzibar, Mascat and Bushire . . . to draw custom to the market of Shiraz."[15]

The "usually good treatment" of slaves in Iran is confirmed by Lady Mary Eleanor Sheil, writing about the country in 1849–50 from the perspective of the British embassy, and it is clear from her observations that she was dealing with the treatment of black slaves:

> They are highly esteemed as being mild, faithful, brave and intelligent, and are generally confidential servants in Persian households. Ill-treatment must of course sometimes

take place when there is unlimited power on one hand, and entire submission on the other. The fact is proved by the occasional instances in which slaves have taken refuge in the [British] Mission to escape from punishment by their masters. Still it is believed that in general, cruelty, or even harshness, is rarely practised towards slaves in Persia. Their customary treatment is similar to that of the other servants of a family, or even something better, particularly when they happen to be Nubees [Nubians] or Habeshees [Ethiopians]. They are never employed as field labourers, their occupations being confined to the duties of the household.

She pointedly contrasted their condition with that of American slaves: "They are not treated with contempt as in America; there are no special laws to hold them in a state of degradation; they are frequently restored to freedom, and when this happens, they take their station in society without any reference to their colour or descent."

She even addressed the difficult question of numbers annually imported from the Red Sea and Zanzibar:

They certainly are not numerous, judging by the few to be seen in the streets of the large towns in the north of Persia. In those of the south they are doubtless in greater numbers, and particularly in the low, level tract bordering the coast . . . The difficulty of forming a correct calculation on the subject, arises from the practice of each petty chief in the Persian Gulf being an importer in his own vessels, and from the slaves being landed at a variety of small harbours extending over a great length of coast. The number is supposed not to exceed two or three thousand annually, of whom a great many die after leaving the hot region of the Persian coast.[16]

Lady Sheil's comments on the absence of color discrimination in Iran must be considered alongside the very different evidence adduced, albeit more than a century later, by Joseph Harris. Conducting interviews at

Tehran, Isfahan, Shiraz, and Bandar Abbas in 1967, Harris encountered
attitudes that seemed similar to those among northern Indians of Aryan
origin: a color consciousness that identified a fair or light complexion as
the ideal of human beauty and attached a corresponding stigma to blackness. In widely separated parts of the country, he came across proverbial
expressions that attested to such prejudice. Someone neglected by relatives or friends might issue the rebuke "Am I your child of a Negress?"
And irresponsibility or lack of sound judgment might be castigated in the
criticism "It is like putting a sword in the hands of a drunken Negro."[17]

Iranians of African descent, such as those in the black community living near Bandar Abbas, complained to Harris of the scorn directed at
them, and he attributed such scorn to the legacy of centuries:

> Asians, like Europeans, were primarily interested in exploit-
> ing African labour; therefore they nourished ideas in sup-
> port of social and political systems that protected and
> perpetuated those interests. In Asia, Africans provided the
> labour for the date plantations and the pearl-diving indus-
> try; they were the principal stevedores, crew hands and do-
> mestics, the troops of Asian rulers, and the eunuchs and
> concubines of Asian elites. All of these roles satisfied the
> psychological, social, and economic needs of the Asian
> slaveholder and contributed to the devaluation of the worth
> of Africans.[18]

This view seems incompatible with that of Lady Sheil. Yet it is possible that each provided a different side of the truth. Lady Sheil observed
that the treatment of slaves was "even something better" than that of
other servants "particularly" when they were Nubians or Ethiopians, and
there would have been nothing peculiar to Iran within Islam in a color
prejudice that differentiated between the less and the more "Negroid" in
complexion and other features among African slaves. Lady Sheil may
also have formed her impressions from an Iranian upper social class in
no need of asserting its superiority of color. And it is arguable that color
prejudice intensified—as it did in the United States—after the end of
slavery.

Certainly, color prejudice, whatever its extent, did not preclude, in Iran as elsewhere in Islam, the humane treatment of black slaves, their frequent freeing and, for some at least, the relative ease of social assimilation. Indeed, Iranians had a special reason for treating their slaves humanely.

During the eighteenth century and part of the nineteenth century, Iran itself was a source of slaves. Its people in Khurasan and Gurgan were subjected to continual slave raiding by the Turkmens, and large numbers were slaves of the Uzbeks. Large numbers, too, were taken as slaves by the Ottomans, as evidenced for instance by a treaty in 1736 that provided for the return of several thousand Persian slaves to Iran from Ottoman Iraq.[19] Iranians in their turn seized Christian Armenians and Georgians in border raids or warfare, though after the Treaty of Turkmanchai in 1828, the supply of Christian slaves declined sharply and Iran became ever more dependent on black slaves.

Sparse figures exist, for particular periods, in reports to the British Foreign Office. In 1842, the number of African slaves who landed at Persian ports was estimated at 1,080, and a questionnaire elicited the response that about 3,000 slaves (roughly 2,000 males and 1,000 females) arrived in Bushire each year, with only 170 or 180 sold locally and the large majority dispatched to Muhammarah (Khurramshahr) and Basra.[20] According to such dispatches, the trade in Ethiopian slaves was especially profitable. A girl bought at Berbera for 40 Maria Theresa dollars (£8 sterling) could fetch as much as 150 at Bushire. Yet even the profits on other African slaves reaching Bushire were "never less than 50 per Cent." Almost all such sources agreed that once these slaves arrived at their ultimate destination, "their condition was little worse than that of the free population around them."[21]

British pressure against the slave trade in the region intensified from 1821 onward and achieved its most notable success in an agreement from the Sultan of Muscat to collaborate in its suppression. Yet, as John Barrett Kelly recorded, "the volume of slaves imported into the Gulf between 1848 and 1850 was almost as great as it had been before the conclusion of the 1845 and 1847 treaties," when the fall in exports from Zanzibar was offset by the rise in those from Ethiopia.[22] Lewis specifically cites the Arabia-Iran connection: "Thanks to the exemption from the ban on the slave trade, the flow of slaves from Africa into Arabia and through the Gulf into Iran continued for a long time."[23]

Thomas Ricks draws on contemporary nineteenth-century accounts to indicate "the extensive nature of the slave community within Iranian society . . . as a result of long-term slave trading and new demands for slave labor within the Iranian economy."[24] In 1868, a census in Tehran found that, of the 147,256 civilians, 12 percent were black slaves or servants, and 756 were male black slaves (*ghulam*) and 3,014 female ones (*kaniz*), or 2 percent of a population which, with 8,480 military troops, totaled 155,736.[25] But only urban household members were counted in the census. Slaves used in agricultural work, in the irrigation systems within and outside the city, and in the gardens surrounding it were excluded. Ricks concluded that the census of Tehran might well have represented "a fraction of that city's slave population," and with other numbers, such as roughly seven thousand in the Gulf region, he suggests a probable figure of eighty thousand for the "overall number of slaves in mid-19th century Iran."[26]

The number of blacks is another matter. Some were almost certainly counted as servants rather than slaves. In 1877, a high-ranking officer of the religious center in Mashad, leaving home on a business trip to Tehran, left instructions for the management of his household and village land in his absence. He mentioned in particular the "black servants" in his household, of whose well-being he was clearly solicitous.[27] In the same year, the principal financial officer of Isfahan, commissioned to survey associations and properties in the city, reported on "The Association of Male and Female Slaves" in the following expansive terms: "In Isfahan, there are many slaves. Some are free, some remain as slaves. The majority are children of slaves [*khanehzad*]. At one time when the sale of slaves . . . flourished, many were brought to Isfahan and sold. All of them have reproduced [among themselves] while some of them are half-breeds. While it is some years now that the sale of slaves is forbidden, a few are [still] brought into this region from Ethiopia and Zanzibar."[28]

It took until 1882 for Iran to renounce the trade in a treaty with Britain, and even then, slaves continued to be smuggled into Iran with the collaboration of bribed officials. Certainly, slavery itself survived. In 1898, the Anti-Slavery Society reported an estimate, from its correspondent in Iran, of between twenty-five and fifty thousand black slaves still in the country;[29] and eunuchs, not necessarily all of them freed, were still a feature of Iranian upper-class establishments in the 1890s.[30]

Subsequently, a certain Dr. A. Miller, after serving as Russian consul in Sistan, reported in a book published at St. Petersburg in 1907: "In Sistan they sell slaves, white and black, delivered openly in Baluchistan and other regions. Almost every village headman in Sistan has a male or female slave. The price of a strong young male slave in Sistan is an average 50 to 80 tumans. The female slaves are cheaper. Relations with slaves are humane."[31] Only in October 1907 did the newly established National Assembly enact a "fundamental law" in favor of individual freedom.[32]

There remains the vexed and vexing question of numbers. The mean vestiges of black survival in modern Iran bear little relation to the extent of imports for which there is evidence. The ease of social assimilation to which Lady Sheil referred would provide one explanation; her reference to the "great many" who died after leaving the hot region of the coast, another. The *Encyclopaedia of Islam* deals with the issue in exclusively male terms: "The high mortality rate which overtook these coloured men in Persia prevented their forming an important element in the population."[33] Ricks has a broader answer to the disappearing numbers of slaves: "High mortality among slaves and failure to reproduce slave children—since Muslims married slave women who bore them children and freed the offspring—reduced the surviving slave population."[34] Since assimilation was easier for those who were free than for slaves, Ricks's explanation would account as well for the all but complete disappearance of a black diaspora in Persia.

NINE

THE LIBYAN CONNECTION

In the fifth century B.C., the Greek historian Herodotus wrote of people in the Fezzan (situated in southern Libya) who went south into the desert and used four-horse chariots to chase "Troglodyte Ethiopians."[1] The ancient Greeks distinguished two categories of color among Africans. Libya was the homeland of the light-skinned, and Ethiopia was that of the dark. Hence, the charioteering Garamantes were Libyans, while the "Troglodyte Ethiopians" were not actually Ethiopians but were probably the Teda, or Tubu, nomadic black people of Tibesti in the Sahara. Herodotus's reference was long discounted on the grounds that there was no evidence of horse-drawn chariots ever having reached so far south. Recently discovered Saharan cave paintings of such chariots, however, suggest that Herodotus might well have been accurately informed, in that respect at least.[2]

Nonetheless, the lack of other records, such as relevant artifacts in Africa's southern savannah, suggests that any trade across the Sahara in ancient times was small and rare. It was the spreading use of camels during the third and fourth centuries of the Christian Era, and then the Islamic conquest of North Africa in the seventh century, that promoted a flourishing trans-Saharan trade. And by the beginning of the eleventh century, four main routes had developed, one of which reached from

Tripoli on the North African coast, through the Fezzan, to Hausaland and the region of Lake Chad.

The fourteenth-century Islamic traveler Ibn Baṭṭūṭa visited the area of Tagadda, along this trade route from Tripoli. At one day's journey from the town, he met the "Sultan," who seems to have been a Tuareg tribal chief. "In place of a saddle he had a gorgeous saddle-cloth, and he was wearing a cloak, trousers, and turban, all in blue," he reported. "I left Tagaddá on Thursday 11th Sha'bán of the year [seven hundred and] fifty-four [September 11, 1353] with a large caravan which included six hundred women slaves."[3] The caravan spent a month in Ahaggar—"the country of Haggar, who are a tribe of Berbers: they wear face veils and are a rascally lot"[4]—before Ibn Baṭṭūṭa left it at Búdá in the west, to join another caravan for the journey to Sijilmása and onward to his Moroccan home. The caravan with its female slaves was evidently elsewhere bound, for Tunis, Tripoli, or farther east, via the Awjila oasis south of Benghazi, to Cairo.

Ibn Baṭṭūṭa's account points to two essential features of the medieval trans-Saharan trade that would persist in the following centuries. Black slaves were the dominant export to the north, and, as Magali Morsy notes, the traders relied on a "working partnership with the nomads who were the masters of the desert and were therefore necessary for safe traveling."[5] These nomads, mainly Berbers but Bedouin Arabs as well, not only protected the caravans, or at least abstained from attacking them, but even provided guides and camel drivers. Furthermore, their military prowess might be directed against black Muslim states in the south, to supply the caravans in their tireless quest for slaves.

Muslim governments in the north accordingly tended to concede the autonomy and respect the institutions of the various tribal confederacies in the Sahara, treating these as agents or allies rather than adversaries. The more powerful Sudanic black kingdoms in the south, controlling the markets to which the Saharan nomads needed access, reached their own accommodation, using some of the tribal confederacies as associates in warfare, or in raiding other Sudanic peoples and states.

The central Sahara was home to the Berber Tuareg, whose traditions and dialect were related to the culture of ancient Libyan society. The men rather than the women wore veils, and their costume, which was made of cloth dyed dark blue, gave them the popular name of the "Blue People." Their various tribal confederacies were so strong that some of them came respectfully to be distinguished as "Sultanates." It was the pragmatic accommodation between these Tuareg and Tripolitania that, from the seventeenth century on, and especially in the nineteenth century, contributed to the mounting importance of the trade route between Tripoli and two major Sudanic slave-supplying markets: Bornu (later Kanem), in the region of Lake Chad, and the Hausa states to the west.

Long-distance trade across the Sahara required both camels and the date-producing oases for stations along the way. The Libyan oases of Awjila, Ghadames, and Kufra provided such stations for moving slaves across the Sahara not only from south to north but also from the western Sudan or Morocco east to Egypt. Nomads in the vicinity had numerous camels that could be hired or bought to furnish new caravans or replenish those in passage.

The great commercial center of Ghadames was an independent municipality, with a settled community swollen by sojourning merchants, and with official representatives of the authorities in Tripoli backed by an occasional reinforcing military expedition. Though the Tuareg controlled the surrounding territory and visited the town at their pleasure, for the sales or purchases on which they relied, they "avoided spending the night within its walls."[6] Likewise, the Sultanate of Fezzan, with its trading center at Murzuq and with Tuareg roaming the region, had autonomous status under hereditary rulers of its own, but paid tribute to a suzerain Tripoli.

The greater entity of Tripolitania emerged from the early-fifteenth-century conflict between Christian Europe and Ottoman Islam for control of the North African ports. Tripoli itself fell to Spain in 1510, but was then conquered in 1551 by the Ottoman Empire and became the capital of an expanding state. Though designated a western province of the empire, Tripolitania was functionally autonomous, with power wielded by a Turkish pasha and a *dīwān*, or ruling assembly, drawn from among the resident Turkish officer class. Gradually, Tripolitania spread eastward, encompassing the whole of Cyrenaica, up to the desert border with Egypt.

The Turkish military rulers generally excluded indigenous Libyans from holding government office, discouraged social integration with them, and, in particular, preferred sexual relationships—and marriage—with slave girls to those with indigenous women. Such policies proved largely ineffectual, however, except in promoting resentment among the increasing numbers of the so-called *kulughlis*, the progeny of the relationships between local women and Turkish men, who were denied access to high office. In 1711, Aḥmad Qarāmānlī, one such kulughli, took advantage of a quarrel between the pasha and his admiral to mount a successful coup. Popular support for the ensuing regime led in 1722 to an Ottoman decree that recognized Qarāmānlī as the first in a hereditary line of pashas to govern Tripolitania.

The Qarāmānlī dynasty would survive until 1835, despite sometimes murderous feuding within the family, social unrest in periods of drought and pestilence, and a formidable but failed attempt in 1793 to restore the substance of Ottoman sovereignty where there was only the semblance of it. This turbulence did nothing to reduce the importance of the Libyan connection in the trans-Saharan slave trade.

Yūsuf Qarāmānlī, who ruled from 1796 to 1832, sought direct control of that trade and in 1810 dispatched a military expedition to Ghadames that secured for a while the submission of the Tuareg in the region. He followed this in 1811 by military backing for a Tripoli merchant, Muḥammed al-Mukani, to depose the five-hundred-year-old black ruling dynasty of the Fezzan and triple the tribute the autonomous Sultanate traditionally paid to Tripoli. Al-Mukani had the ruler and his nearest likely successors all strangled, and was appointed Bey of Fezzan, with the title of Sultan only to be used when in residence.

In 1818, Captain G. F. Lyon of the Royal Navy joined a British scientific expedition bound for the Fezzan. When he arrived in Tripoli, he recorded that al-Mukani (or "el-Mukni," in his version), having established himself in power, "waged war on all his defenceless neighbours and annually carried off 4000 or 5000 slaves. From one of these slave-hunts into Kanem he had just returned to Tripoli, with a numerous body of captives and many camels, and was, in consequence, in the highest favour with the Bashaw [Pasha]."[7]

The journey from Tripoli to Murzuq, capital of the Fezzan, by the Sultan and his caravan, to which Lyon was attached, took thirty-nine days, and "the road, with the exception of the immediate vicinity of the towns, was a dreary desert, having but few wells, and those of salt water. Nothing could have been more fortunate than our travelling with the Sultan; our difficulties must otherwise have been very great."[8] This says something of the risks that slave caravans, less well provisioned and more impatient in their progress, must have run in the journey from Murzuq to Tripoli.

In Murzuq (which he spells "Morzouk"), Lyon learned that the Sultan had in his establishment "about fifty young women, all black and very comely . . . guarded by five eunuchs, who keep up their authority by occasionally beating them."[9] To the town, "many parties of Tuarick [Tuareg] came with their slaves and goods."[10] And, Lyon reported, after describing their complexion, costume, and customs: "The Tuarick, or more properly tribes of them, are always at war with the Soudan states, and carry off from them incalculable numbers of slaves. They are so completely masters of their weapons, and so very courageous, that they are much dreaded, which enables them to traverse unmolested, and in very small bodies, countries full of armed people."[11] This report was clearly based on what Lyon had been told, but there is no reason to doubt its accuracy. Personal observation informed another report:

> At the end of this month [August 1819], a large Kafflé [caravan] of Arabs, Tripolines, and Tibboo, arrived from Bornou, bringing with them 1400 slaves of both sexes and of all ages, the greater part being females. Several smaller parties had preceded them, many of whom also brought slaves. We rode out to meet the great kafflé, and to see them enter the town—it was indeed a piteous spectacle! These poor oppressed beings were, many of them, so exhausted as to be scarcely able to walk; their legs and feet were much swelled, and by their enormous size, formed a striking contrast with their emaciated bodies. They were all borne down with loads of firewood; and even poor little children, worn to skeletons by fatigue and hardships, were obliged to bear their burthen, while many of their inhuman masters rode on camels, with the dreaded whip sus-

pended from their wrists, with which they, from time to time, enforced obedience from these wretched captives. Care was taken, however, that the hair of the females should be arranged in nice order, and that their bodies should be well oiled, whilst the males were closely shaven, to give them a good appearance on entering the town.[12]

Nor were the hardships by any means at an end:

All the traders speak of slaves as farmers do of cattle. Those recently brought from the interior were fattening, in order that they might be able to go on to Tripoli, Benghazi, or Egypt: thus a distance of 1600 or 1800 miles is to be traversed, from the time these poor creatures are taken from their homes, before they can be settled; whilst in the Interior they may, perhaps, be doomed to pass through the hands of eight or ten masters, who treat them well or ill, according to their pleasure. These devoted victims fondly hoping that each new purchaser may be the last, find perhaps that they have again to commence a journey equally long and dreary with the one they have just finished, under a burning sun, with new companions, but with the same miseries.[13]

Lyon was indignantly aware of how far the slaving activities that served the Libyan trade were conducted in breach of Islamic law: "It is expressly said that Moslems may take or destroy all those who do not believe in Islamism; but that they should first endeavour to instruct, and on their refusing to acknowledge the Koran, then make them slaves. The same law distinctly teaches that those who are already Moslems cannot be taken captive or sold. Nothing, however, is further from the idea of a Mohammedan, than to instruct the Negroes: for, instead of endeavouring to convert them in his faith, he appropriates and sells them for his own advantage. This is sufficiently unjust, but the conduct of Mukni and his men is infinitely more so; for they seize on the inhabitants of whole towns where the only religion is that of the Koran, and where there are Mosques; and this is without scruple or remorse."[14]

Lyon had no doubts about the Sultan's personal responsibility for such practices and worse, with the recruitment of Arabs, Bedouin, and "some of the Tibboo of Tibesty and Gatrone," drawn "in hopes of obtaining a share in the plunder," to conduct his warfare: "No Fezzaners are ever allowed to go on military excursions, being considered too pusillanimous to be trusted; but they pay deeply for their exemption from bearing arms, by being obliged to support those who do. There are no wars in which the Sultan is called upon to engage; but his love of gain, and the defenceless state of the Negro kingdoms to the southward, are temptations too strong to be resisted. A force is therefore annually sent, not to fight (for the Negroes cannot make any resistance against horsemen with fire-arms) but to pillage these defenceless people, to carry them off as slaves, burn their towns, kill the aged and infants, destroy their crops, and inflict on them every possible misery. These inroads have sometimes been conducted by Mukni in person, and in his absence, by some of his principal men."[15]

Nonetheless, as Lyon observed, slaves—once their masters rather than their captors and dealers were in possession of them—were treated relatively well in the Sultanate:

> The better class of the people, or those who have some property . . . have great power to oppress and ill treat their inferiors; yet are as free with their slaves as with each other, and associate as much with them. A slave will come and sit down with his master, though not on the same mat, and join in the conversation, amusement, or meal, even without a shirt on his back; when the master wears his best clothes, however, he is too dignified to permit such freedom.[16]

He also noted:

> In Morzouk about a tenth of the population are slaves, though many have been brought away from their countries so young as hardly to be considered in that light. With respect to the household slaves, little or no difference is to be perceived between them and freemen, and they are often

entrusted with the affairs of their master. These domestic slaves are rarely sold, and on the death of any of the family to which they belong, one or more of them receive their liberty, when, being accustomed to the country, and not having any recollection of their own, they marry, settle, and are consequently considered as naturalized. All slavery is for an unlimited time, unless when a religious feeling of the master induces him to set a bondsman free on any great festival, on the occasion of a death, or, which not unfrequently happens, from his wish to show approval of the slave's services.[17]

In marked contrast was the brutality of the dealers, which Lyon recorded among the last of his observations on returning to Tripoli in March 1820, one year after his departure from there:

None of the owners ever moved without their whips, which were in constant use; that of Hadje [sic] Mohammed more so than the rest: in fact, he was so perpetually flogging his poor slaves, that I was frequently obliged to disarm him. Drinking too much water, bringing too little wood, or falling asleep before the cooking was finished, were considered nearly capital crimes, and it was in vain for these poor creatures to plead the excuse of being tired; nothing could at all avert the application of the whip. No slave dares to be ill or unable to walk; but when the poor sufferer dies, the master suspects there must have been something 'wrong inside,' and regrets not having liberally applied the usual remedy of burning the belly with a red hot iron; thus reconciling to themselves their cruel treatment of these unfortunate creatures.[18]

In Tripoli itself, for dealing in slaves, Arab traders favored the Spanish piastre, a silver coin weighing nine drachmes, or a little over one ounce. The Swedish consul there from 1822 to 1828 recorded the prevailing local prices for slaves as 650 to 750 piastres for a black eunuch; 90 to 100 for an adult male; 70 to 80 for a youth; 40 to 50 for a boy under ten; 120

to 150 for a woman; 90 to 100 for a girl; and 50 to 60 for a girl under ten.[19]

Al-Mukani had clearly been serving the Libyan connection well with such supplies. Yet either these were still insufficient to satisfy the appetite of Tripoli or he was deemed to be taking too large a cut for himself, because Tripoli removed him in 1820 and appointed another subordinate Sultan. Moreover, in response to increasing French and British imperial ambitions in North Africa, Yūsuf Qarāmānlī sought a countervailing alliance and aggrandizement south of the Fezzan. In 1821, he sent an army to campaign along with the forces of Bornu, an expedition that brought Tripoli some six thousand slaves with a similar number of camels. Further such campaigns followed until 1824, but with unexpected consequences.

The very success of the campaigns promoted the repute and aspirations of 'Abd al-Jalil, commander of Tripoli's army in the south and leader of the powerful Awlad Sülayman Arab tribe. In 1830, he summoned his tribesmen to revolt and seized Murzuq in 1831, declaring an independent Sultanate of the Fezzan, and though driven out in 1832, he continued to campaign through southern Libya and still farther south to the region of Lake Chad.

Meanwhile, in 1830, French forces had attacked Algiers, initiating a war of conquest that would eventually take all of Algeria. A French squadron, dispatched to Tripoli, imposed humiliating treaties upon the Pasha, requiring a limit on the size of his fleet, the satisfaction of French creditors, and the payment of a war indemnity. In 1832, confronted by rebellion, disaffection, and intrigue, Yūsuf Qarāmānlī abdicated in favor of his son 'Alī.

While 'Alī had the support of local citizens, the religious and military authorities in Tripoli, and the French consul, the contending claim of Yūsuf's nephew Muḥammad was advanced by the British consul and by an important community of kulughlis. An Ottoman decree of 1834, appointing 'Alī as Pasha, did little to quell the opposition to him; and with its prestige dangerously at stake, in 1835, the Ottoman Empire dispatched ten warships and an equal number of troop carriers. A further imperial decree swept aside both contenders and reduced the status of Tripolitania to that of a mere province.

The Ottoman occupying force encountered such widespread armed opposition that it would take seven years before the region of Tripoli it-self was subdued, another year before Ghadames and the Fezzan were brought under control, and another fifteen years before the last of the re-sistance was crushed. 'Abd al-Jalil himself was captured and executed in 1842, but some of his tribal followers refused to submit. Under the com-mand of his son Muḥammad, a thousand warriors moved southward along the trans-Saharan trade route, pursuing the traditional predatory practices of this trade and eventually seizing control of Kanem in 1870.[20]

A more formidable challenge to Ottoman authority in the region came from the reformist Muslim movement founded by Muḥammad bin 'Alī al-Sanūsī (1787–1859). Born in an Algerian village, al-Sanūsī became a poet, mathematician, historian, theologian, and traveling preacher. His message of universal brotherhood was modeled on the Prophet's ideal community, but took into account a modern world whose challenges could be mastered only by the force of personal faith and in-dividual effort. He attracted disciples in Arabia and across North Africa. Then, in 1853, he finally settled at Jaghbub in eastern Cyrenaica, where the caravan route from the west and that from the south met on the way to Egypt.

Al-Sanūsī had wells dug, roads made, and a town built where Saharan nomads and caravan traders could stay and store their goods in its ware-houses. Tribal pacts were promoted or negotiated to secure the safe pas-sage of merchandise, and visitors were influenced by what they learned there, to stay and study, become holy men themselves, and carry the Sanūsī message to others. All this had a militant—even military—politi-cal dimension. Increasingly, the settlements of Sanūsī teachers and mis-sionaries developed into fortified monasteries. Jaghbub was reputed to have enough weapons to arm three thousand men.[21] Such preparations were supposedly directed at confronting Western imperial expansion, but the secrecy surrounding them suggested Al-Sanūsī's own mistrust of the Ottoman authorities.

By the time of al-Sanūsī's death in 1859, his influence had spread throughout the Sahara, engaging such tribal forces as the major Tuareg confederations. The fraternity continued to grow in numbers and sup-port under the command of al-Sanūsī's two sons, one a scholar and the other a warrior. By the 1880s, the Sanūsī order was believed to have almost three million followers and to be capable of deploying some twenty-five thousand armed tribesmen, including fifteen hundred horsemen.

By the early twentieth century, the value of the trade south from Benghazi on the Mediterranean, through the oases of Kufra, Jalu, and Awjila, to Wadai beyond the Sahara, was estimated at 200,000 pounds sterling, or just under $1 million at the contemporary exchange rate,[22] to the considerable profit of the Sanūsī order, which controlled the oases. Furthermore, this was only one among several trans-Saharan trade routes that relied on the protection provided by the Sanūsī. According to Philip Curtin: "Another from Tripoli through the Fezzan to Zinder (now in Niger) and on to northern Nigeria carried goods of even greater value."[23]

The Sanūsī attitude to slavery was scarcely ambivalent. Certainly, al-Sanūsī himself bought slaves from Arab traders, educated them in his community, and then freed them with the charge of returning as missionaries to their homelands. Yet neither he nor his sons in succession to his leadership intervened against the slave trade. Indeed, by promoting pacts between various tribes and even providing guardians for the safe passage of caravans, the Sanūsī order manifestly facilitated and fostered the trade. Moreover, there is evidence that slaves were employed as agricultural workers in the Saharan oases controlled by the order. Henri Duveyrier, a French traveler, estimated the slave population at its Cyrenaican headquarters alone at two thousand in 1883.[24] Clearly, with Sanūsī influence so strong, the slave trade continued to flourish.

On the pretext of spreading the faith, the Sultanate of Wadai in the Central Sudan preyed on the pagan peoples to the south for slaves. While other routes came under increasing surveillance and pressure by European and European-influenced Ottoman power, the Wadai-Benghazi route was partly protected by its very remoteness and hazards, but also by the facilities and peaceful transit through nomadic tribal areas that the Sanūsī provided.

This was a trade that took manufactured goods, mostly arms, to Wadai and brought back some raw materials but mainly slaves. The extent of the arms trade may be assessed by both the quantity and the quality of the guns that successive Sultans of Wadai accumulated. Sultan Muḥammad al-Sharif (died 1858) owned only three hundred; Sultan

'Alī (1858–1874), four thousand muskets; and Sultan Dudmurra (1902–1909), some ten thousand rifles, which included breech-loading Colts, Remingtons, and Winchesters. The average annual export in slaves through Benghazi was roughly 1,000 in the early nineteenth century, between 2,000 and 2,400 in mid-century, and declined toward the close of the century, not for lack of supplies, but because shipment through the Mediterranean was becoming increasingly difficult.[25]

This was by no means the end of the desert trade and its Libyan connection, however. The oasis of Jalu, a six-day journey south of Benghazi, was an important station along the trans-Saharan route, for traders from the states along the Niger bend, from Bornu and the Fezzan, as well as from Wadai. From Jalu, traders might move slaves either to northern Cyrenaica or to the oasis of Siwa, where they could deal illicitly, dispose of their stocks for local use, or restore them to a suitable condition for clandestine marketing in Egypt or beyond. A British traveler, visiting Siwa in 1898, found slaves working in the fields, living in the town, and passing through on the way to Alexandria and Istanbul.[26]

In 1858, the British Consul-General in Tripoli estimated that the slave trade constituted "more than two-thirds of all the caravan trade" across the Sahara.[27] The German physician Gustav Nachtigal, who traveled from Tripoli to the Fezzan, Bornu, and Wadai a decade later, estimated slave exports from Wadai at fifteen thousand.[28] In 1869, Nachtigal met daily small caravans en route from Murzuq to Tripoli.[29]

By the time of Nachtigal's travels, Ottoman edicts against the slave trade had been issued, but evidently to small effect in the Libyan region. The Governor of the Fezzan, he reported, had an income of up to forty thousand marks a year from the transit toll on slaves, which represented—at the rate of two Maria Theresa dollars, or one and a half ounces of silver, per slave—some five thousand slaves.[30] Since this was considerably more than the Governor's annual salary, it is easy to see why he treated the relevant edicts with less than due respect; and the same applied to officials lower down the line. In the Fezzan, during Nachtigal's travels there, directives against the slave trade were delayed whenever a caravan was due, until the slave tax had been paid.[31]

Indeed, connivance at and complicity with the slave trade extended to the highest level of Ottoman rule over Libya and beyond. The

Governor-General in Tripoli commissioned Bu Aischa, head of the caravan in which Nachtigal first crossed the Sahara, to collect a few eunuchs for the Ottoman Sultan. Bu Aischa acquired in Kuka, the capital of Bornu, a considerable number of slaves, for both the Governor-General and himself.[32] When Bu Aischa left Tripoli more than two years after setting out on his expedition, he took with him many slaves, including eunuchs and dwarfs.[33]

Despite these evasions of the law, the Islamic export trade in black slaves from Tripoli was declining as Britain in particular exerted pressure on the Ottoman government and French imperial power spread to major slave catchment areas in Africa. Edicts could not without risk be too blatantly disregarded. Nachtigal estimated that between five thousand and eight thousand slaves a year had previously been taken through the Fezzan, but by 1869 this number had fallen by at least two-thirds.[34] A caravan proceeding northward from Kuka with as many as fourteen hundred slaves in it and reaching the Fezzan after Nachtigal's own arrival there was greeted as a rare event.[35] But the event was itself evidence that decline was still not disappearance.

Ralph Austen, one of the few scholars undaunted by the difficulties of assessing the volume of black slaves in the Islamic Trade, is convinced that the Libyan connection was long of prime importance in the trans-Saharan sector: "For those periods in which we have richer documentation—the late sixteenth century onwards—it is clear that Libya was the major slave outlet. In fact, while the few pre-seventeenth century quantitative observations which cite areas are almost entirely limited to the western Maghrib and adjacent Saharan zones, we know from extensive non-quantitative evidence that even in medieval times the Fezzan was the principal Saharan entrepot for Sudanic slaves, many of whom must thus have exited Africa via Tripoli, the closest Mediterranean port."[36]

Austen distinguishes four periods in his estimates of traffic to Libya from the middle of the sixteenth century to the early twentieth century. For the first period (1550–1699), he suggests there was an annual average of 1,500, or 225,000 overall; for the second (1700–1799), an annual average of 2,700, or 270,000 overall; for the third (1800–1856), an annual average of 3,100, or 176,700 overall; and for the last (1857 on), an annual average of 2,000, or 113,000 overall. This represents a grand total, from 1550 to 1913, of 784,000. On his estimate of an overall 20 percent death rate during the transport of the slaves, about 942,000 were caught by the Libyan connection from the middle of the sixteenth century.[37]

Austen suggests that for the period from 1857, when the Ottoman *firman*, or decree, against the slave trade was formally in force throughout the empire except for the Ḥijāz, exports to and from Libya did decline, though it is difficult to know by how much, since the decree "suppressed the official record-keeping far more effectively than it affected the substance of the trade."[38] Given the widespread evasion of such record keeping, Austen's estimated annual average of two thousand for the ensuing period seems credible.

That such numbers did not lead to a comparable growth in the black slave population of Libya is easy enough to explain. Libya was a region of scarcely tapped natural resources—the rich reserves of oil were yet to be discovered and exploited—with relatively little agriculture and a comparatively small population. The domestic demand for slaves was correspondingly small, and most of the slaves imported were speedily dispatched to other markets in Islam. Even after Ottoman officials were ordered in 1848 to take no part in the slave trade, 1,474 slaves are known to have been exported from Tripoli to the Levant in 1849, another 2,733 in 1850, and, as Jamil M. Abun-Nasr writes: "slaves continued to reach other parts of the Ottoman empire from Tripoli, even after the abolition of slavery in Turkey itself in 1889."[39]

There were other reasons for the lack of growth in the black slave population. Traditionally, there was a high rate of manumission, often after only seven years of slavery. Black children fathered by the owners of their mothers were generally freed quickly. Black women, who constituted the majority of imported black slaves, had a low reproduction rate, largely because of a susceptibility to Mediterranean diseases. In 1891, the British consul in Benghazi estimated that there were only six thousand black slaves in the whole of Libya.[40]

Al-Sanūsī reportedly once predicted that Tripoli would fall to "the people of Naples."[41] In 1911, Italy pounced on a pretext for war with the Ottoman Empire and invaded Libya. By the following year, Italy had wrested recognition of her sovereignty there, but exercised control over only the coastal region. In large measure due to the strength of the

Sanūsī order, the further advance of effective Italian rule was slow and costly. It took a series of military campaigns from the mid-1920s to 1932 before the conquest of Libya was considered complete.

Meanwhile, the slave trade, less a flow now than a trickle, was finding its own course and outlets. At the start of the 1920s, Rosita Forbes, a British visitor, saw in Jalu "smuggled slave boys and girls of eight to ten years."[42] Prices still rose and fell with the pressure of demand and the availability of supplies. An Egyptian traveler, Hussanein Bey, had been offered a slave girl for the equivalent of £5 sterling ($24) in 1916. At Kufra in 1923, the price was the equivalent of between £30 ($137) and £40 ($183).[43] A Danish Muslim visitor to Libya in 1930 reported that a slave market was held every Thursday in Kufra and that a good slave there cost the equivalent of £15 ($73).[44]

TEN

THE TERRIBLE CENTURY

In all the many centuries of the Islamic trade, it was in the nineteenth century that the largest numbers of black men, women, and children were enslaved and the largest numbers of other blacks killed in the process. This was the case despite—or, arguably, because of—increasing Western pressures against the trade. Certainly, the raiding and warfare for slaves were conducted on a scale and with a ruthlessness that seemed at times to be frantic.

In 1808, Britain decided to withdraw from the Atlantic slave trade and directed her efforts to promoting the withdrawal of other Western states. While the Atlantic Trade was her prime preoccupation, Britain began early to exercise pressures against the Islamic one as well. Here, however, the campaign required more circumspection. Muslim susceptibilities and accordingly relations with Muslims everywhere were involved.

EAST AFRICA

Omani Arabs had been trading for slaves along the East African coast for centuries. An Italian physician, serving at the royal court in Muscat from

1809 to 1814, wrote that almost its entire revenue came from the tax on slave imports;[1] and of Oman's eight hundred thousand inhabitants around 1840, an estimated one in three was black.[2] At least two thousand slaves a year were absorbed internally by Oman, while those that re-mained from the imported numbers were dispatched elsewhere, many for sale along the Makran coast.

During the eighteenth century, Kilwa had become East Africa's prin-cipal port for the export of slaves, drawn initially from southeastern Tanganyika and then increasingly from the region of Lake Nyasa. The Omanis on the coast were based at Zanzibar and, after taking control of Kilwa in the mid-1780s, diverted to that island the bulk of the trade in slaves and ivory. By 1834, exports of slaves drawn from the mainland had reached an annual figure of 6,500. By the 1840s, the annual numbers had risen to between thirteen thousand and fifteen thousand. Some of these slaves were destined for markets in the Middle East. Most, however, were designated for Zanzibar, where the labor-intensive cultivation of cloves had begun soon after 1810 and was expanding rapidly in response to the growing world demand for cloves. By the 1850s, the island's population might have included no fewer than sixty thousand slaves.[3]

The ruler of Oman, Sayyid Said ibn Sultan, transferred his court to Zanzibar in 1840. The island had become, as a result of his policies, the most rewarding part of his realm: the paramount port on the western side of the Indian Ocean, the source of virtually the entire world supply of cloves as well as the main sales outlet for ivory, and the largest slave mar-ket in the East.[4] From that base of riches and power, Said greatly ex-tended his authority over the mainland coast. If one after another of the coastal towns formally lost its traditional independence, however, the benefits of increasing trade provided some consolation.

Bagamoyo, in particular, flourished. Its rich agricultural hinterland, its open beaches suitable for the arrival of dhows, and its proximity to Zanzibar made it the predominant mainland outlet for the slave trade. Coastal caravans to the interior relied on porters, and Bagamoyo alone contained an estimated thirty to forty thousand at peak season. Most of these ventures were financed by local Asians from India, a majority of them Muslims, who had settled in the coastal town but mainly in Zan-zibar and who provided trade goods on credit at high rates of return.

Those conducting the trade included Arabs; it was to the so-called northern Arabs, or Omanis, that the more ferocious aspects of slaving in the region came to be ascribed. In fact, perhaps most of the leading slavers were Afro-Arabs, or the progeny of inter-ethnic unions, and the trade itself became increasingly a Zanzibari rather than an Omani one. Certainly, many of the main slavers, along with many of the regional slave dealers, were as black as their victims.

In the last resort, Said relied on British power to protect him against Arab contenders for his rich realm (indeed, it was British power which forced the retreat of Egyptian armies in 1839) and the threat that other European imperial powers, principally the French, might seek to devour it. He was not inclined, however, to surrender the enormous tax revenues accruing to him from the slave trade. Along with members of his family, he was personally invested in the trade and was, besides, mindful of the revolt by powerful subjects that his agreement to suppress the trade might provoke. The British government, too, despite its commitment against the trade, was reluctant to antagonize an ally or so imperil that ally's position that it found itself having to deal with someone worse.

The result was a slow diplomatic dance of pressure, resistance, concession, subterfuge, and connivance until, in 1845, Said agreed to a treaty that outlawed the sea trade from the coast between the ports of Lamu in the north and Kilwa in the south, except for the transport of slaves from one to another part of the Sultan's African domains. The open export trade shifted to Kilwa, and slaves, brought to Zanzibar for its supposed domestic needs, were then exported through any gap in British naval surveillance to different markets in Islam.

Said's death in 1856, when Zanzibar became independent of Oman, brought to the throne his son Majid, who proved less amenable to British pressure. In 1859 alone, nineteen thousand slaves were recorded as arriving at Zanzibar, but this number was based on customs returns and therefore excluded those imported, free of duty, by the Sultan and members of his family, as well as the large number of slaves smuggled to the island. In 1868, the British consul reported that thirty thousand slaves, most from the region of Lake Nyasa, were annually arriving at Kilwa and that two-thirds of them were then shipped directly to Zanzibar, with the remainder sent to northern ports in Oman or smuggled elsewhere. The report also estimated that for every slave arriving at Kilwa, another had died in the course of procurement and transport.[5]

At Zanzibar, the slaves were unloaded hurriedly. The dead were thrown overboard to drift with the tide, until they rotted in their passage. The sick and weak were left to lie on the beach, to save the customs-house tax, in case they died before they could be sold. The remainder were made to wade ashore, given food and water outside the customs house, and dispatched to their temporary owners, who kept them for a few days of recuperation. Oiled and attractively clothed, they were then taken to the slave market for sale. Sometimes, however, greed or anxiety did not allow time for adequate recuperation.

Captain Colomb of the Royal Navy, assigned in 1868 to command of the *Dryad* for operations against slave traders in the Indian Ocean, recorded his visit one evening to the slave market, where upwards of three hundred slaves were being auctioned:

> There were perhaps twenty auctioneers, each attending a separate group, and selling away as hard as possible . . . One of these strongly attracted my attention . . .
>
> His "lot" appeared to be lately imported; they were all young boys and girls, some of them mere babies; and it was amongst them that the terribly painful part of the slave system was to be seen. I mean the miserable state, apparently of starvation, in which so many of the poor wretches are sometimes landed. The sight is simply horrible, and no amount of sophistry or sentiment will reconcile us to such a condition of things. Skeletons, with a diseased skin drawn tight over them, eyeballs left hideously prominent by the falling away of the surrounding flesh, chests shrunk and bent, joints unnaturally swelled and horribly knotty by contrast with the wretched limbs between them, voices dry and hard, and "distantly near" like those of a nightmare—these are the characteristics which mark too many of the negroes when imported. All, however, are by no means so. I have seen, in the same batch, some of these skeletons, and others as plump as possible. In this very group it was so.[6]

Along with other hostile observers of the Islamic slave trade—including David Livingstone, who was the most impassioned and influential of them—Colomb drew a distinction between the horrors involved in the supply of slaves and their subsequent treatment by their Arab owners. Indeed, he confessed that he was unable to discover if the free black in Zanzibar was in any respect better off than the slave:

> The owner of the country estate takes from his slave the labour of five days a week. In return he gives him as much land as he can cultivate. The owner of the town slave at least houses, feeds, and clothes him; but more generally he allows him besides, all that he can make by his labour over about fourpence a day.
>
> In all cases, the Arab noble is the feudal chief of his dependents, and offers them the protection we understand by the term.[7]

It is not certain that the lives of all—even perhaps most—slaves in Zanzibar were as congenial as Colomb considered them to be. Yet the weight of evidence elsewhere does support the view that the treatment of slaves by their owners was markedly more humane than the treatment accorded by those engaged in procuring and transporting them.

Traditionally in Islam, slave trading was not an honored occupation, despite the fact that even the morally fastidious seemed willing enough to pay for its products, and those who were engaged in it were not likely to be among the most honorable traders. Procurement was frequently conducted in the lawless, brutalizing conditions of raiding or warfare, and subsequent transport involved for the dealers the movement of merchandise rather than persons. Not least, as the trade came to be increasingly threatened by enactments and related enforcement measures against it, any remaining humanitarian restraints vanished. The Islamic trade had always involved violence and cruelties, suffering and loss of life. In this regard, the nineteenth century proved to be exceptional only in the extent of its horrors.

As the supply of white slaves from Circassia and Georgia sharply declined, the Egyptian market turned increasingly to the abundant source of black slaves from the region of the Upper Nile. Assembled at El Fasher and other oases, the slaves were then transported along the ancient and still often hazardous routes to the great market at Es Siout,

250 miles south of Cairo. Such traffic was estimated to bring between five and six thousand slaves, most of them females, annually into Egypt. Then, in 1820, the army of Muḥammad 'Alī, Egypt's Ottoman Viceroy and effectively independent ruler, conquered northern Sudan. Khartoum, at the junction of the White and the Blue Nile, grew from a fishing village to an administrative and commercial capital that was also the collection and distribution center for slaves, with a catchment area for raiding that reached to Gallabat on the Ethiopian frontier.[8]

The Egyptian government sought slaves for its army, and military officers from Arabia came to Khartoum for slaves. The Viceroy even paid his troops in slaves, and the troops subsequently often sold the slaves to dealers. By 1838, between ten and twelve thousand slaves were being imported into Egypt annually; the males mainly for military, and the females for domestic, service. Muḥammad 'Alī himself, not renowned for the delicacy of his feelings, visited Sudan in that year and was so disturbed by what he saw of slave raiding that he ordered an immediate stop to such activities by his soldiers and even freed five hundred recently captured slaves. Yet raiding not only continued but increased, reaching ever farther south and southwest. J. Petherick, the British consul and ivory trader, officially based at Khartoum in the late 1850s and early 1860s, reported on the thousands of slaves sold in the great market at El Obeid in Kordofan.

Increasingly beyond Egyptian government control, Afro-Arabs carved out their own spheres of slaving. Such were the Ja'aliyīn (or Ja'alūyyīn) of southern Nubia, who identified themselves as Arabs—even tracing their descent to 'Abbas, the Prophet's uncle, in Arabia—but who were ethnically more Nubian than Arab. By the early nineteenth century, the Ja'aliyīn were engaged in the trade along the southern route to the border of Ethiopia, eastward to Suakin at the Red Sea, and westward to Kordofan and the Sultanate of Darfur.

The Egyptian conquest of Nubia and the adjoining region of Sudan made little difference to the operations of the Ja'aliyīn merchants who, along with Egyptian Coptic and Levantine ones, relocated to Khartoum. Slave traders extended their reach into Bahr El-Ghazal and farther south into Equatorial Africa. Because the Egyptian government was unable or unwilling to extend its control that far, the traders established their own, from armed camps (*zariba*), protected by slave soldiers equipped with the latest rapid-fire guns. Since most of the traders were based in Khartoum and recruited associates or assistance from the Ja'aliyīn living there, they came to be widely known as "Khartoumers."

One Ja'alī, named al-Zubair Rahma Mansur, a merchant in the Bahr El-Ghazal region during the 1850s, asserted his political and military leadership over other Ja'aliyīn there in the following decade, and by 1874, he was powerful enough to conquer the Sultanate of Darfur. Provoked too far, the Egyptian government dispatched a military force to capture him and take control of his domain.

His son, Rabih Fadlallah, otherwise known as Rabih el-Zubair (al-Zubayr), became one of the most infamous slavers of all. He mobilized a force of Ja'alī followers with slave soldiers from his father's campaigns, moved west of Darfur into the slave catchment region south of Wadai, and there raided for slaves relentlessly until 1893. Wadai sent an army against him, only to be defeated, and Rabih then proceeded westward, to conquer the kingdom of Bornu. This brought him into conflict with French imperial expansion, and in 1900 he was captured by a French military force. His head was impaled on a pole, perhaps as a symbol of the fate facing all those who stood in the way of the new power thrusting its rule ever deeper into Africa.[9]

Meanwhile, the slave trade had long been taking multitudes of victims from across a vast area. Whatever repeated denials were issued from Cairo, the Egyptian government was so involved in the trade that it had established large barracoons (enclosures) for the collection of slaves, where the conditions caused many to die from smallpox and other diseases. Survivors faced additional trials. It was estimated that, for every ten slaves who reached Cairo, fifty had died along the way.[10] Some of the highest Egyptian officials in the area covered by the trade were profitably involved in it. The *mudir*, or governor, and his chief military officers at strategic points along the route were often parties to the transit and disposal arrangements, in return for a cut that commonly amounted to a fifth of the sale price.

The impact on the catchment areas could be calamitous. Samuel Baker, the British explorer, first journeyed through the region of Gondokoro in 1863, at which time he found it populous and prosperous, with large herds of cattle. Returning in 1872, he discovered that the people had all but disappeared. Egypt's developing economy had widened the classes and increased the numbers of Egyptians with the appetite and means to acquire slaves.

By 1869, the ruler and his family had two thousand household slaves, with many hundreds more who labored on his sugar plantations in Upper Egypt. The several wives of well-to-do men would each have black slaves, some of whom were wet nurses. Low-ranking civil servants on relatively meager salaries owned domestic slaves. Even small-scale farmers had slaves whom they could send in their place when they were summoned to provide the labor alternative to taxes. Large numbers of slaves were used on irrigation schemes. Nine out of every ten workers on the pumps in Isna Province, for instance, were slaves by 1884.[11]

Charles Gordon, appointed Governor of Egypt's Equatorial Province in 1873, arrived to find a disorderly administration there. The few Egyptian regular soldiers were in league with the Danaqli, Northern Arabs who had settled in the area, and together went everywhere accompanied by women slaves who had been captured as far south as the Acholi, in what would become Uganda. But the prime catchment area remained Bahr El-Ghazal, and Gordon estimated that from this region alone, in the period 1875 to 1879, at least eighty to a hundred thousand slaves had been exported to the north.[12]

Under intensified British pressure, the Egyptian government agreed to the Anglo-Egyptian Convention of 1877, which banned the import and export of Sudanese and Ethiopian slaves, and empowered British ships to stop and search all vessels suspected of carrying slaves in the Red Sea, the Gulf of Aden, and Egyptian waters. This and attendant measures proved largely ineffectual, however. Much of the Red Sea coast was under Ottoman control and beyond the compass of the Convention. Moreover, slavery itself survived in Egypt. Only in 1883, with the British occupation of Egypt, did the laws against the trade begin seriously to be applied. By 1886, thirty-two dealers, who had been openly conducting their business in 1883, were reduced to three. By 1889, a report claimed, somewhat prematurely, that both the import and sale of slaves in Egypt had ceased altogether.[13]

Matters were very different in Sudan. The followers of an Islamic fundamentalist movement under a self-proclaimed Mahdi captured El Obeid in early 1883, annihilated a British army later that year, and took control of the Bahr El-Ghazal slave catchment area. Under the Mahdi and even more so under his successor, the Khalifa, the slave trade thrived. Great numbers of captives, taken in the course of raiding or warfare, were sold to dealers for export, especially to Arabia. The onetime British consul in Jedda, A. B. Wylde, reported in 1887 that slaves — males, including eunuchs, and females alike — had never been so cheap or so numerous in the area of the Red Sea.[14]

When the British took control of Sudan after the Battle of Omdurman in 1898, they came across the consequences of such widespread warfare, disease, and starvation. Continual raiding for slaves in Bahr El-Ghazal had so depleted the Bari people that the effects would still be evident in the 1920s. Captain McMurdo, who became director of Egypt's Anti-Slave Trade Department in 1900 and extended its writ to Sudan, visited the district bordering Ethiopia in 1902 and estimated that, as a result of so much raiding mainly for female slaves, the male to female ratio there was now seven to one.[15]

The claim in 1889 that both the import and sale of slaves in Egypt had altogether ceased was at odds with reality. Slaves, again mainly female, had entered Egypt from Sudan, some of them as alleged refugees, in the time of the Khalifa, and the northward flow continued. The laws were not always strictly enforced, because many Muslims resented them as an abridgment of their rights and even an attack on their religion. The harem system facilitated the concealment of numerous female slaves in the towns and cities, while, in distant oases, slaves were held or traded well away from official eyes.

There were, however, countervailing factors. The risk of losing slaves through discovery and seizure, without compensation and with punishment of the owner, made slaves a diminishingly attractive investment. Western cultural influence, including its particular condemnation of slavery, had an impact, as did the development of a more extensive free labor market in an expanding urban economy. Not least, the British reconquest of Sudan cut traditional supplies. Accordingly, in 1904, when Lord Cromer reported that the systematic slave trade in Egypt no longer existed, this was virtually the case.

Slaving in Sudan itself was less easy to suppress. In Kordofan, raiding by the Baggara and Kababash tribes was a customary test of manliness; the price of a bride was often paid in the form of slaves to her parents. The recruitment of local Arabs to a mounted police patrol at El Obeid in 1902 had some impact, as did a leading slave dealer's sentence, in 1903, of five years' imprisonment. Also effective was the establishment in 1908 of military posts on the frontier between Bahr El-Ghazal and French Equatorial Africa, whose sparsely controlled neighboring region had been a major source of slaves. The trade from the eastern region of Sudan to the Red Sea coast, for the onward shipment of slaves to Arabian markets, proved more difficult to suppress. Even the arrest and sentencing of fifty-eight dealers, in the span of eighteen months from January 1905, succeeded only in somewhat reducing the trade.

Within the traditionally large market demand for Ethiopian slaves, particularly prized were the Oromo—widely known as the "Galla" (an offensive term, like "nigger" or "kaffir," given them by their Amhara overlords).[16] This was by no means exclusively because of their light complexion, since they came in varying shades to the darkest. They were sought for their commonly slim shape, regular features, celebrated gazelle-like eyes, and long, straight, or slightly curled, hair. Market convention ascribed peculiar beauty to Oromo girls and peculiar intelligence to Oromo boys.

By the nineteenth century, Oromo slaves predominated among those exported from the markets at Gondar and Gallabat in northwest Ethiopia. They were the favored prey of Egyptian raiders from Sudan, and were supplied to Muslim dealers even by Oromo chiefs in their own western areas. Although Theodore, the emperor of Ethiopia, issued directives against the slave trade, he himself reportedly informed slave caravans of the safest routes for transport. By 1866, thousands of Christians, mainly Oromo, were being sold each year, five hundred on some days at the market in Gallabat alone. Muslim dealers collected their supplies at Zeila and Tajurra for shipment to markets in Egypt, Arabia, and Turkey. And all of this was excused on the grounds that it involved only Christians or idolators.

In 1884, the London *Anti-Slavery Reporter* estimated that almost eight thousand slaves were still being exported each year from Ethiopia, and that King Menelik received, as the price of his connivance, one slave for every ten exported.[17] In 1903, Menelik at last decreed an end to the slave trade throughout Ethiopia. Informed opponents of the trade remained skeptical. They were right to be so. In 1910, a visitor to Tajurra found that the export trade was alive and well, with no stigma apparently attached to those responsible for it. Moreover, this included a small proportion of castrated boys.[18]

The Red Sea, whose principal ports were nominally under Ottoman sovereignty, provided the passageway for the majority of slaves exported from East Africa during much of the century. By the 1860s, dhows flying the Ottoman flag were carrying up to fifteen thousand slaves a year in the period of the pilgrimage. Many were then sold at auction in Jedda and Mecca, or exchanged privately for steel weapons from Damascus, carpets or turquoise from Persia, silks and jewelry from places farther east. Repeated Ottoman edicts against the trade, in response to British pressure, were of little avail. The Sultan's own prohibition, extended to the Ḥijāz in 1865, was widely disregarded. The trade actually increased, since its illegal status relieved it of the 25 percent duty previously imposed on dealers, who now simply smuggled their stocks, with the connivance of officials and the cooperation of a supportive population. The *Anti-Slavery Reporter* published an estimate from its correspondent at Alexandria in 1878 that twenty-five thousand slaves a year were being sold or exchanged in Mecca and Medina.[19]

The Ottoman Sultanate was unlikely to take decisive action against the trade when Anatolia, at the very heart of the empire, provided a prime market for black slaves. The Azizieh Company, a shipping line in which the Viceroy of Egypt himself was a major stockholder, transported black slaves from Alexandria to various Anatolian ports, and smaller ships carried slaves along with other cargo there. In 1869, some three thousand black slaves were imported into Anatolia alone, and the British consul at Smyrna reported that this traffic, by steamers from Egypt or by land via Baghdad, was notorious.[20] Other black slaves arrived with pilgrims returning from Mecca and Medina. After a series of ineffectual edicts that increasingly strained British patience, the Sultan finally issued, in December 1889, a "Law for the repression of the Negro Slave-Trade in the Ottoman Empire."

Twelve slave dealers were still openly conducting business at Jedda in 1902. And in 1910, young eunuchs were still being sold to Arab slave dealers at Tajurra, for resale in Arabia, where they were employed not only as supervisors at the holy places but as guardians of harems and managers of the grander households. Anatolia had long been a major market for eunuchs and continued to be so in the nineteenth century. There, as elsewhere in Islam, eunuchs commanded great esteem. The *Anti-Slavery Reporter* records: "When any eunuch, whether attached to the [Sultan's] Seraglio or to a private harem, enters one of the tramcars in Stamboul, all the Turks who may happen to be in the vehicle immediately rise, salaam profoundly, and remain standing till the great man has chosen a seat for himself."[21] This scarcely mollified Western opinion, which was well aware of the costs involved in the provision of eunuchs. A. B. Wylde, sometime British consul at Jedda and widely traveled in the Middle East, reported that every eunuch represented "at the very least, 200 Soudanese done to death . . . say there are 500 eunuchs in Cairo today: 100,000 Soudanese had died to produce these eunuchs."[22]

Muslim representations that slaves in Islam were in general humanely treated by their owners had equally little effect on Western opinion, as evidence mounted on the horrors attending their procurement and transport, with the devastating impact on much of the East African interior, during the nineteenth century. In 1871, a Select Committee of the British Parliament, appointed "to inquire into the whole question of the Slave Trade on the East Coast of Africa, into the increased and increasing amount of that traffic . . . and the possibility of putting an end entirely to the traffic in slaves by sea," was provided with appalling testimony.[23]

One account from 1860 reported: "Natives of India who have resided many years in Kilwa . . . state that districts near Kilwa, extending to ten or twelve days' journey, which a few years ago were thickly populated, are now entirely uninhabited; and an Arab who has lately returned from Lake Nyasa informed me that he has travelled for seventeen days through a country covered with ruined towns and villages which a few years ago were inhabited by the Mijana and Mijan tribes and where now no living soul is to be seen."[24]

Other accounts, contemporary and subsequent, from explorers, travelers, missionaries, diplomats confirmed the statement in the committee's report that the traffic had increased and was continuing to do so, with corresponding violence and desolation.

In the Unyamwezi region, between Lake Tanganyika and the coast, Arab or Afro-Arab traders had established small communities, with their two centers at Tabora and, on the east coast of the lake, at Ujiji. From there, in the 1880s, A. J. Swann wrote, "The Arab system extended to great distances, and octopus-like, grasped every small unprotected village community, making the whole country a vast battlefield wherein no one was safe outside the stockades."[25]

A Catholic missionary, visiting the slave market at Ujiji in 1888, found a large square, bordered by mud huts, that was crowded with slaves, joined by cords or chains in long lines, and with others, revealing signs of starvation, in the streets. Nearby was a cemetery where the dying as well as the dead were left for the hyenas.[26]

Among the most notorious of the Afro-Arab slavers was Tippu Tip, who had by the late 1860s established himself west of Lake Tanganyika. When H. M. Stanley reached, in 1883, what would come to be called Stanley Falls, he encountered the consequences of the raiders: "Every three or four miles we came in view of the black traces of the destroyers. The scarred stakes, poles of once populous settlements, scorched banana groves, and prostrate palms, all betokened ruthless ruin."[27]

Added to the multitude of slaves who died during the raiding were those who perished in the journey to the coast. The missionary A. J. Swann, on his way to Lake Tanganyika, encountered Tippu Tip's caravan, with slaves who had already journeyed 1,000 miles from the Upper Congo and had an additional 250 miles to go. They were chained by the neck in long files, some of them in six-foot forks, and with many of the women bearing babies on their backs. They were in a filthy condition, and many of them were scarred by the cuts of the hide whip.[28] In the two-hundred-mile crossing of Lake Tanganyika, slaves were so closely packed in canoes that some of them, already in a much enfeebled condition, died.

Frequently, slaves who could not keep up with the pace of the caravan were left to die of starvation or were summarily shot. Routes favored by slave traders could be easily identified by the skeletons that were visible at

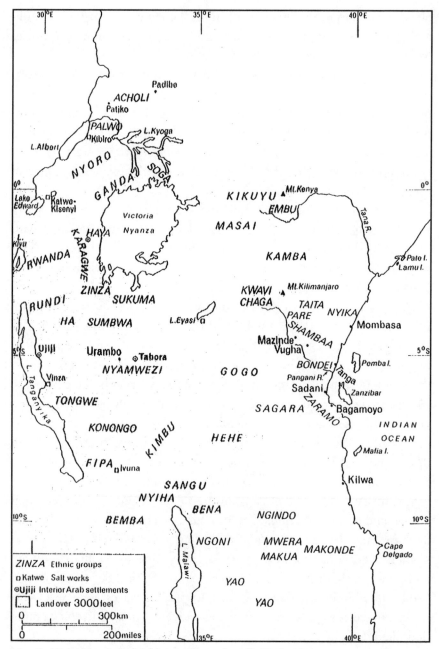

Map 5: East Africa. Lake Malawi was formerly called Lake Nyasa

intervals alongside the track. The Reverend Horace Waller, for a time Lay Superintendent of the Universities Mission to Central Africa, estimated that "four or five lives were lost for every slave delivered safe at Zanzibar."[29] He held to the view that the profit attainable at the coast for a slave was so great that it was almost immaterial if many died along the way. "It is like sending up to London for a large block of ice in the summer," he stated. "You know that a certain amount will melt away before it reaches you in the country, but that which remains will be quite sufficient for your wants."[30] Given the toll in procurement along with that in transport, Livingstone conjectured that the price paid for every living slave was at least ten dead.[31] These estimates were horrifyingly greater than the one-to-one ratio reported in 1868 by the British consul in Zanzibar.

The rewards of the slave trade overwhelmed any religious inhibitions that some of the traders and other beneficiaries might have had. For the slavers themselves, after all material costs had been subtracted, profits were estimated at over 60 percent, and substantially higher for any who traded at the same time in ivory, "sought as eagerly and bought as cheaply as slaves."[32] Indeed, the ivory and slave trades were closely connected. Slaves carried the ivory to the coast, though few in Victorian Britain or elsewhere in the West would have given much thought to the likelihood that the ivory of their piano keys, billiard balls, and knife handles had come to them in this way.

The Indian—mainly Muslim—merchants and bankers in East Africa, who provided credit in goods or cash for the caravans in expectation of a suitable return, certainly found the business profitable enough to continue risking their investment in it. The Sultan of Zanzibar himself, according to British Foreign Office calculations in 1871, derived £20,000 ($97,200), or roughly a quarter of his annual income, from the proceeds of the slave trade.[33]

The profit chain reached farther, of course—to the markets of the importing countries, and the shipments there often involved additional horrors and suffering. From Zanzibar, by way of Lamu, it was two thousand miles to the Red Sea, and to the Persian Gulf, twelve hundred miles. Many dhows carried inadequate supplies of food and water so as to cram more slaves into the available space. One large dhow, arrested by the British ship *Daphne* on the Somali coast, was found to hold 156 slaves:

On the bottom of the dhow was a pile of stones as ballast, and on these stones, without even a mat, were twenty-three women huddled together, one or two with infants in their arms. These women were literally doubled up, there being no room to sit erect. On a bamboo deck, about three feet above the keel, were forty-eight men, crowded together in the same way; and on another deck above this were fifty-three children. Some of the slaves were in the last stages of starvation and dysentry.[34]

Brutality in procurement and transport seemed to increase in proportion to the pressure exerted, chiefly by Britain, on land and sea, against the trade. This, in turn, only heightened such pressure, which conveniently provided imperial expansion with a moral pretext.

In Uganda, Arab or Afro-Arab traders reached the kingdoms of Buganda and Bunyoro in the second half of the nineteenth century. There, among captives taken by either kingdom from the other in raids or warfare, they found large supplies of slaves, and were soon transporting up to an estimated four thousand of them a year to the coast. Large, however, was never enough. Bishop Tucker encountered a fifteen-mile-wide area devastated by slavers who had bribed local chiefs to collaborate with them in raiding.[35] A British treaty with Buganda in 1892 prohibited raiding for slaves as well as trading in them, their import or export, and with the declaration of a protectorate in 1894, the status of slavery itself was abolished in the kingdom. Bunyoro, to the northwest, was meanwhile conducting an extensive trade in slaves for arms and ammunition with Arab or Afro-Arab dealers. Not even a British military expedition against the capital of the kingdom put an end to it.

In the more remote areas of Kenya near Lake Rudolph, slaving parties from the coast were active in the 1890s, engaging in expeditions that lasted a year at a time. A few traders would form a temporary partnership, each of them supplying a number of porters, themselves often slaves, and together they would acquire trade goods on credit from one or another Indian merchant. At the head of the caravan, a combined guide and supposed sorcerer would carry a white flag emblazoned with symbols and phrases from the Koran, which was believed to possess ex-

traordinary power. At the end of the expedition, the profits were distributed among the partners according to the number of porters each had
contributed.[36] The assumption of a British East African Protectorate in
1895 ended most of the slave trade in the region, though that from the
northeast to the Somali coast continued until well into the twentieth
century.

By the early 1880s, Arab or Afro-Arab raiders were operating from the
western shore of Lake Nyasa and extensively in the region of the Upper
Zambezi, capturing young girls in the vicinity of Blantyre, fomenting
African wars, and trading for slaves with local chiefs. The raiders had at
least twelve dhows on the northern half of the lake, and to the south, a
Baluchi slaver, with five dhows on the lake, had five hundred men who
ranged the country for slaves. Operating from villages with high stockades and protective embankments, this force was safe against all but a
considerable military commitment against it. In 1889, Britain's acting
consul, John Buchanan, reported that successive caravans of slaves were
moving from the southern shore of Lake Nyasa to the northern stretch of
the Portuguese coast, where the authorities were suborned to ignore
them.

One area in particular, northwest of Lake Nyasa, demonstrated how
much devastation was caused by the trade. A valley about twenty-five
miles long had once been the fertile home of the Nkonde, renowned for
their artistic ability, which was evident in their finely made and pat-
terned spearheads. The Ngoni, to the east of the lake, were the first to
raid and pillage the Nkonde for slaves, but slavers led by an Afro-Arab,
Mlozi, came close to eradicating them in the late 1880s and early 1890s.
Their villages were all burned, and the survivors fled to caves or remote
parts of the mountains. Mlozi then added insult to so much injury by
proclaiming himself "Sultan of Nkonde."

In early 1891, Harry Johnston was appointed Her Majesty's Commissioner and Consul General to the Territories that were under British influence to the north of the Zambezi. He was specifically charged, as the
first of his responsibilities, to end the slave trade by all legitimate means.
It took him several years to clear the slavers and their stockades from the
lake region, and it was only in December 1895 that his forces assaulted
the stronghold of Mlozi and captured him. Then, in the presence of

Nkonde chiefs and almost six hundred duly liberated slaves, Mlozi was hanged.

When Germany and Portugal, with strategically situated East African colonies, increasingly supported Britain in suppressing the slave trade, it gradually diminished to snatch operations and surreptitious export on those dhows that successfully evaded the naval patrols. In 1899, one Arab dhow carrying sixty slaves to Muscat was captured sixty miles south of Mombasa, and another, carrying twenty, in the harbor of Zanzibar.

The decree that ended the legal status of slavery in Zanzibar and Pemba was signed by the Sultan in 1897, and it was extended to the mainland ten years later. Slavers from Muscat and Arabia took to kidnapping children on the beaches of the islands and smuggling them in canoes onto dhows farther out to sea. As late as the 1960s, East African port authorities were still enforcing regulations limiting the numbers considered reasonable for crews on varying sizes of dhow: eight to ten for small vessels, fourteen to twenty for middle-sized ones, and twenty-one to thirty for large ones. In 1961, one large dhow was encountered that had a "crew" of fifty-three.[37]

THE SUDANIC STATES AND SAHARA

The expansion of Western power, with its commensurate impact on the temporal sway of Islam, led in the eighteenth century to a spread of Muslim religious fervor. This was most marked in the fundamentalist Whahhabi movement, which displaced Ottoman rule of Arabia around 1747 and established a puritanical regime that would last for sixty-five years. The same fervor stirred Muslims in India to rebellious resentment at British rule, and it ignited a series of holy wars in the Western and Central Sudan that changed the political map of Africa.

The Fulani, a pastoral people with linguistic links to the Tucolor in the lower Senegal region, had begun moving eastward in the fourteenth century. By the sixteenth century, they were strongly settled in Masina, upstream of the Niger River bend, and were still moving eastward, into Hausaland, or the northern region of what would become Nigeria.

Most Fulani remained a pastoral people, but increasing numbers,

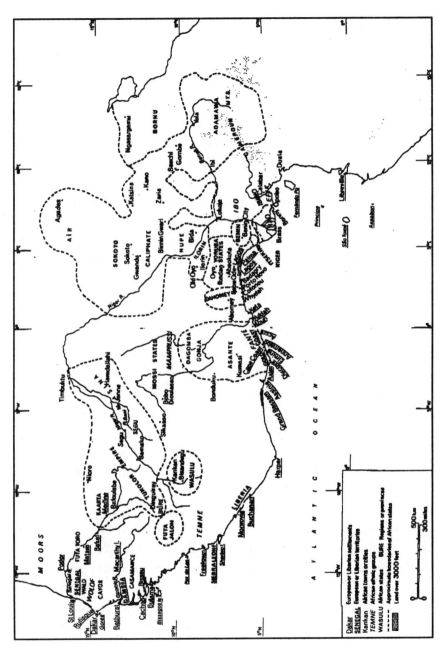

Map 6: West Africa in the nineteenth century

especially in Hausaland, took to urban life and became Muslims. Some were drawn to the strong tradition of Islamic scholarship in the Sudanic belt. Among them was Usmān dan Fodio, in the northern Hausa state of Gobir. During the last decade of the eighteenth century, he led a revolt directed not only at the rulers of Gobir but at all the Hausa kings, whom he denounced, despite their professed adherence to Islam, as virtual pagans. By 1810, this revolt had become a jihad, which swept across Hausaland to replace all the established Hausa ruling families with Fulani emirs.

Such extensive success was due to several factors. Two leading military commanders—Usmān's younger brother, Abdullahi dan Fodio, and second son, Muḥammad Bello—were literate and familiar with the large Islamic military literature in Arabic. Muḥammad Bello in particular proved to be a formidable tactician, coordinating the cavalry under his command with skilled Fulani archers. Yet, however adept and innovative the commanders were, they would not have made such headway without popular support for their cause and a decline in popular allegiance to the traditional rulers. The call of the jihad to confront despotism and corruption met a ready response, as did the issue of enslavement.

Many of the jihadists themselves owned slaves, and their military commanders had acquired combat experience and skills through slave raiding. The jihad, however, was expressly committed to observing the Koranic ban on enslaving fellow Muslims. This was in sharp contrast to the practice sanctioned by the Hausa rulers. For slave raiding had become so important to the Hausa economy that scant regard was paid to whether the victims were Muslims or not.

Promoting this indiscriminate enslavement, which strained the limits of social tolerance, was the mounting availability of muskets. These were sought not only because they conferred prestige and power on the kings and courtiers of Hausa rule. They also made raiding for slaves easier and the yield of captives greater, while providing a major motive for such raids, since slaves were the main payment required by traders for guns. Not surprisingly, Muslims rallied to a jihad whose success would offer them the security of Islamic law, while non-Muslims were attracted by the prospect of enjoying the same security by the simple expedient of converting to Islam.[38]

By 1812, the jihad had created a Fulani empire based on Islamic constitutional models and designated a Caliphate. Usmān became the first Caliph. In practice, however, he retreated into scholarship, and the empire was divided between Abdullahi dan Fodio, who ruled the western half from Gwandu (or Gando), and Muḥammad Bello, who ruled the eastern half from the walled city of Sokoto that he had founded. On Usmān's death in 1817, Bello succeeded him as Caliph and proceeded to consolidate the empire. Meanwhile, the momentum of expansion was not easily arrested. The Fulani armies moved southward into Yorubaland, where they captured the northern provinces of the Oyo empire and established the emirate of Ilorin, the base for the spread of Islam among the Yoruba.

Historically, the Fulani had moved eastward, and their empire was accordingly soon at war with the kingdom of Bornu. Fulani armies conquered the Bornu region of Adawama, but this proved to be the limit of their success. They had a formidable adversary in the ruler of Bornu, Muḥammad al-Amīn al-Kānamī, a devout Muslim. Like Usmān dan Fodio, al-Kānamī claimed to have been visited by the Prophet and was sufficiently versed in classic Islamic scholarship to invoke it for his own purposes. In contrast to the repressive fundamentalism of the Fulani jihad, he took the more pragmatic approach of defending what was known as "mixed Islam," or a Muslim rule tolerant of subjects who adhered to other beliefs. It was this that doubtless contributed to his success in promoting a defensive popular mobilization with a jihadist fervor of its own.

To the west, in the extensive region that encompassed the upper reaches of both the Senegal and Niger rivers, Fulani pastoralists had long since settled. In Masina their traditional chiefs, who paid tribute to the animist Bambara kings, were nominally Muslims, practicing a version of "mixed Islam." Then, in the second decade of the nineteenth century, Aḥmad b. Muḥammad, a Fulani who had reportedly studied under Usmān dan Fodio and might even have fought in Usmān's jihad, launched a jihad of his own.

This was initially directed against the Fulani chiefs, whom he denounced as idolators. His success was so great, however, that it soon overwhelmed the Bambara and other animist or partly Islamized peoples in the region. The result was an empire, with its capital city of Hamdallahi, which lasted under Aḥmad b. Muḥammad's son and grandson until 1862. In that year, another jihad, led by 'Umar b. Sa'id, submerged the region in an even more extensive empire, dominated by the Muslim Tukulor people, and this would survive until 1893, when it fell to French imperial expansion.

The initial idealism of the jihad had time and again in Islamic history given way to the priority of prey in the course of conquest and its aftermath. The nineteenth-century jihads in the west of Africa were no exception. The prospect of booty, particularly slaves, was a prime motivation for some of those involved in advancing the jihads, and this became more dominant in the warfare, both offensive and defensive, that followed the establishment of empire. One factor was the development of large-scale, slave-worked estates, as an alternative form of exploitation to the exacting taxes on peasant agriculture that Usmān himself had expressly condemned. Along with the Caliph, emirs, and the higher state officials, others, especially the merchants (including Tuareg and Arabs), profited from this practice, with large slave-worked estates of their own. Furthermore, slaves could generate income for their owners by engaging in various occupations, such as house building, ironwork, and weaving.

As elsewhere in Islam, slaves were used in the army, often for the same sort of warfare and raiding by which they had been procured. Here, however, there was at least a distinct prospect of a promotion that might bring freedom. Indeed, many of the army generals were of slave origin. Slaves were employed in the civil service, especially at the palaces and courts of rule, as well as for less elevated work in the stables and as domestic menials. They were also employed to entertain the rulers, nobility, and the rich, though not always in such dignified roles as musicians and storytellers. At the royal court of Bornu, festivals were celebrated with wrestling matches between slaves from different peoples, which often ended in serious injury or death.[39]

Individual members of the Sudanic ruling elites might each own as many as two to three thousand slaves, and slave markets as well as slave depots became common in the region. One British explorer reported an estimate he had been given that there were thirty slaves for every free man in the city of Kano.[40] This was almost certainly an exaggeration, but other evidence suggests that slaves were the largest component of the population there.

With the mounting demand for slaves in the Muslim-ruled Sudanic kingdoms and empires, non-Muslim communities or peoples within or bordering the states created by the jihads were relentlessly raided. Even al-Kānamī, who had confronted jihad with the alternative of "mixed Islam," to promote popular resistance and preserve the kingdom of Bornu, came to sanction slaving raids against the Bade people in the west of his kingdom, on the grounds that they were infidels—"not saying their prayers, the dogs."[41] Indeed, in Bornu, as widely elsewhere in the region, rulers did not encourage their non-Muslim subjects to convert, since this would present doctrinal difficulties in enslaving them. Moreover, in some Muslim areas, such as Kano, the rulers interpreted any resistance to injustice, or to any other abuses, as rebellion, tantamount to apostasy, and accordingly a sanction for the enslavement of those responsible.

An especially impelling factor was the extensive development of the export trade in slaves. One scholar, Abdullahi Mahadi, citing the estimated ten thousand slaves transported annually across the Sahara during the nineteenth century—a total volume of one million—commented that this "must be low indeed." By the 1840s, he elaborated, the trans-Saharan trade from Hausaland and Bornu would hardly have existed without the exports of slaves. By the late 1850s, the slave trade was responsible for two-thirds the value of all caravans, and this continued throughout the rest of the century. "The problem, therefore, was not that of supply but of demand. While there were buyers, the market would ever be abundantly supplied."[42]

The mounting demand was evident in the enthusiasm of the traders, who made slaves the main currency for purchasing horses, sought by Sudanic rulers for purposes of prestige as well as warfare. Indeed, most North African merchants would accept only slaves for horses and sometimes for other goods, too, including salt. Soon, North Africans themselves came to be directly involved in raiding for slaves. Al-Kānamī, seeking allies to help him promote the power of Bornu and his own command of it, offered Yūsuf Pasha of Tripoli the inducement of such raiding, in particular against the rival Muslim-ruled state of Baghirmi to the southeast of Lake Chad. In 1821, a single expedition by the Pasha's forces carried off more than ten thousand captives from only four towns; and countless males were slaughtered not only in the process of raiding but subsequently because too many had been captured for the order and security of transport.[43] Al-Kānamī himself, in his wars against the Sultanate of Baghirmi, enslaved more than thirty thousand of its people.

The collaboration of al-Kānamī with Yūsuf Pasha and with merchants, mainly from North Africa, proved so successful that it promoted raiding far beyond Baghirmi, which declined into a vassal state of Bornu. It was the merchants who frequently took the initiative, inciting al-Kānamī and other rulers to joint ventures, or providing inducements for permission to organize their own raids against particular towns or villages. From the Fezzan, which extended across major Saharan trade routes, raiders came to prey on the northern Central Sudan. The Tuareg, among others, directed their attention farther westward, targeting the Fulani empire of the Sokoto Caliphate, for combined slave-raiding operations with the military forces of the states to the north.

So profitable did the trade become that North African merchants were reputed to grow rich from a single short stay in the Central Sudan. They were soon scattered throughout the vast region, some settling in areas as remote as the valley of the Upper Benue River, while their communities in the cities and larger towns increased markedly in size. Many of them, bankers as well as merchants, were based at Ghadames, south of Tunis and southwest of Tripoli, which was the financial center of the trans-Saharan trade. Along with merchants from other towns in the central Sahara who invested and participated in the trade, they had associates and agents, including members of their own families, across the Central Sudan.

As the British traveler Alexander Gordon Laing remarked of these merchants in 1825: "They calculate with profound nicety the expense of carriage to distant countries, duties, customs, risk, trouble, the percentage that the goods will bear, and even do business by means of bills and unwritten agreements and promises."[44]

Many of them traveled to the Central Sudan for extended stays, participating in raids or accompanying the raiders, and establishing themselves at the courts of the various rulers, where they were accorded high status and enjoyed corresponding privileges. Some were even appointed to the councils of state and held such crucial posts as that of treasurer. In this, they were not beyond advancing their influence by claiming to be *sharifs* (direct descendants of the Prophet), entitled to give judicial advice, which was generally directed to the purpose of acquiring still more slaves. They were at best indifferent to the wrongs perpetrated by the ruler against his subjects. Indeed, insofar as it served their interests, they were likely to have encouraged abuses. Accordingly, they were neither liked nor trusted by the populace.[45] At the royal courts, their very presence in often sumptuous dress, along with the luxury goods they brought with them, promoted an imitative consumption, adding yet another demand to the existing ones for horses and muskets.

Not only were horses expensive — costing as much as twenty slaves apiece — but increasingly they needed to be replaced. Those peoples subjected to being raided for slaves came to recognize how effective the use of poisoned arrows against horses could be. Furthermore, horses became such a status symbol that even a lowly official considered it necessary to own as many as his means or credit allowed. Not least, a very rage developed for accumulating weapons and other imports, as much, it would seem, for the pride of possessing them as for their function.

One official in Bornu, who died in the early 1870s, left an estate of several thousand slaves, one thousand stallions and many mares, twenty-seven storerooms of cloth and other goods bought from traders, an armory of several hundred muskets and carbines, along with a thousand swords and five hundred shields, twenty thousand Maria Theresa dollars in coin, and a thousand or so head of cattle.[46]

The North African merchants were well aware of the temptation provided by future settlement for present possession. They offered ready credit for periods of repayment that might reach to three years, at correspondingly inflated prices for the goods they supplied. Not only rulers but their provincial officials, and even the subordinates of such officials, were lured into deepening debt. This had a predictable impact in increasing the scope and intensity of raiding for slaves. The Sarki of Zinder, an independent emirate north of the Fulani Caliphate, owed so much by the 1840s that he was virtually compelled to order a series of raids as the only way of settling his account. The rulers of Zinder might have depopulated the entire region by their raids, had they not deliberately adopted the policy of leaving enough survivors to breed new victims.[47]

When, for one reason or another, the limits on raiding other peoples had been reached, rulers and officials preyed on their own populations, increasingly by adjustments to the law, in total disregard of Islamic doctrine. In Zinder, for instance, a boy who stole some trifling article might, along with all the members of his family, be enslaved and sold as punishment. Insubordination or some other offense—real or merely alleged—by a minor official might be punished by fines, payable in slaves, on the towns or territories connected with the office, or even by raiding them for slaves. One vassal ruler, alerted to a likely raid on his territory, entreated the king of Bornu to impose any punishment on him except a raid and was forthwith fined fifteen hundred slaves.[48]

Rulers also took to increasing taxes, payable in slaves, on provincial or vassal governments, which in response intensified their raiding. Local communities, fearful of being targeted, took to raiding one another for enough slaves to bribe or appease the officials who threatened them. Parents gave up one of their children in the hope of safeguarding the rest. Few were ever able to feel safe. State officials, on tours of duty, were known to ignore the law and simply seize people for slavery, while provincial governors did not intervene, for fear that the officials were acting on the orders or with the sanction of the ruler.

The demand for slaves, to feed both domestic and foreign appetites, grew more and more difficult to satisfy. Dealers often had to wait months and even years for the supplies they wanted. One obvious reason was the loss of population, existing and potential, that resulted from the incessant raids. The targeted seldom accepted their fate without some resistance, and this might mean the deaths of double the number taken captive. Even then, it was prevailing practice to kill many of the surviving adult males who had been injured or were insufficiently submissive for safe transport, while females, especially young ones, and boys were all seized, as these were the ones most in demand by the markets.[49]

Young boys, in particular, continued to be sought so that they might be turned into eunuchs. And given the account of how the operation was performed in Bornu, it is surprising that any at all should have survived. Gustav Nachtigal recorded that a member of the ruling elite there, a certain Laminu, "appears to have been sufficiently devoid of conscience to collect from time to time hundreds of boys, and to subject them to castration, condemned though this is by Islam. Under the pretext of wanting to circumcise the boys, the barbers who performed the operation are accustomed with a quick grip to grasp the whole of their external genitals in the left hand, and with the right to amputate them with a sharp knife. Boiling butter is kept in readiness and poured on the flesh wound to staunch the bleeding of the unfortunate boys."[50]

Furthermore, supplies of new slaves were depleted before they ever reached their export markets. The desert crossing had always been difficult and hazardous. During the nineteenth century, it came to cost more lives, as traders grew increasingly anxious to realize profits. The relentless advance of European, primarily British and French, imperial expansion in Africa closed certain catchment areas and transport routes to the trade, while threatening others. Increasingly, too, traditional markets, such as those in the Ottoman Empire, were vulnerable to diplomatic and financial pressures, from European governments to undertake official action against the trade. All this added an element of urgency to greed among the traders.

Greater risks were taken in preparing for the conveyance of slaves and in dictating the pace of the journey. Supplies of food and water were all too often inadequate; haste or ruthlessness forced women and children to cover long distances on foot, their progress encouraged by beatings; greater numbers succumbed to the changes in climate and temperature or to sheer misery and despair. The death rate was high. According to Abdullahi Mahadi: "Estimates indicate that it was as high as twenty per cent; an estimate grimly attested by the thousands of skeletons stretched between the central Sudan and North Africa."[51] It is small wonder that market demand was not satisfied by the supplies that reached it.

In the Western Sudan, so long a catchment area for the Atlantic Trade, the decline and eventual extinction of that trade was not accompanied by a fall in the rate of enslavement. On the contrary, the rate increased, to supply Islamic domestic as well as foreign demand. Slave villages came to surround the capitals of Muslim African states, to provide food for the rulers and their officials, retinues, and armies. In cities along the Saharan fringe, slave labor produced grain and textiles for

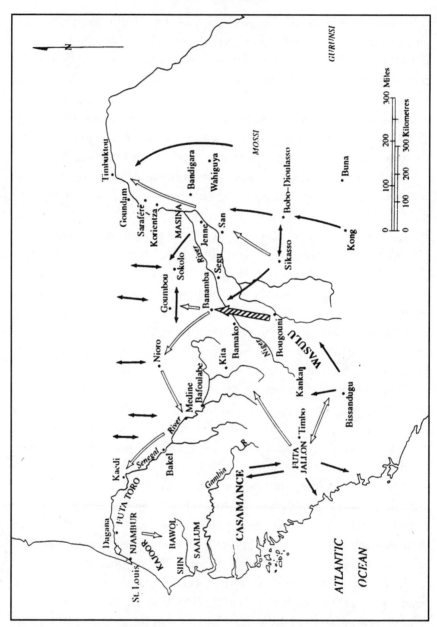

Map 7: West African trade routes

trade with Moors and the Tuareg. The development of commodity production for European markets led to a corresponding demand for slave
labor, especially in the coastal areas. Even the marabouts, Muslim
monks or hermits, renowned for their personal austerity and influential
in the promotion of various jihads, relied on slave labor to sustain them
in their rural retreats. Indeed, as in the Central Sudan, jihads that began
partly in protest at abuses connected with the slave trade ended in a reliance on a slavery that would be still more extensive and productive of
abuses.

New rapid-firing rifles, used by cavalry to sweepingly fatal effect,
made slave raids easier. The rifles also made such raiding all the more
necessary, since slaves were the main means of paying for them. Furthermore, the very possession of these weapons promoted expansionist
designs, so that states which did not have them sought to acquire as
many as possible in order to defend themselves. Against such pressures,
Muslim piety was an inadequate guardian of compassion and rights. Ma
Ba, for instance, the great Senegalese leader in Muslim reform during
the 1860s, was simply outflanked by his principal lieutenants, who took
to raiding for slaves with unreformed zeal.

These raids had a devastating impact. Wasulu, in the south of the region, had been visited by European explorers who reported as late as
1879 that the area was both prosperous and densely populated. By 1888,
a visiting explorer described it as desolate, with thirty-six abandoned villages, or half the number that he saw in a journey of four hundred kilometers. Six years later, when the French established a post at Bougouni,
they conducted a census in the area and found fewer than five thousand
people, many of them living, doubtless for safety, in the immediate vicinity of the post.[52] Primarily responsible for this desolation was the empire
building of Samori, who would subsequently be viewed by the nationalist movement in Guinea as its progenitor. To the east was Sikasso, whose
rulers were scarcely less ravenous in raiding for slaves across the vast area
under their control, especially in the 1890s. The ravages of the Afro-Arab
slaver Rabih al-Zubayr reached from East and Central Africa to northern
Cameroon.

Slaves needed to be moved with speed from the places where they
had been seized, so as to reduce the risks of their escaping, and many

were taken directly to where they could be sold or traded. The center for such commerce in the Western Sudan was the region of the Maraka people. They had traditionally traded—millet and cloth for hides and livestock—with Moors migrating south in the dry season, and they now specialized not only in supplying surplus grain from slave-worked plantations but in providing markets where the Moors could trade salt and horses for grain and slaves.[53] Chief among their towns for this trade was Banamba, which, founded only in the 1840s, became the chief slave market in the Western Sudan.

Samori's caravans and officials or agents from Sikasso brought slaves to Banamba, where they traded for horses. Many slaves stayed in the vicinity of the town itself, which, by the end of the century, came to be surrounded by slave-worked plantations for a radius of fifty kilometers. Many others were taken north to Mauritania, which supplied salt as part of the payment for them. But the predominant line of trade was roughly horizontal: eastward, supplying weapons to states such as Segu; westward, supplying slaves for plantation labor, mainly in the peanut-growing coastal basin of Senegal and Gambia. Commercial reports for the traffic through Médine on the Senegal River from December 1888 to November 1889 suggest that there were twelve to thirteen thousand slaves transported in that twelve-month period alone.[54]

South of the Gambia River was another large, if lesser, slave-trading center in the region of the Futa Jallon, where the Futa people exchanged their surplus cattle for slaves from Samori's supplies or those of traders in the forest areas and along the coast. Still other centers lay in the east, among the Mossi, who had little domestic use for slaves but were major suppliers to the trade, and in Masina, where all but perpetual warfare provided captives for the trade. Most of this traffic went north, to the Niger bend and especially to Timbuktu, for buyers at the southern fringe of the Sahara and beyond.

As in the Central Sudan, slaving undoubtedly took a high toll in lives, as did the transport of slaves. Indeed, slaves might be sold several times before reaching a more lasting destination and be made to travel long distances. Some caravans, like those dispatched by Samori, could be large, at times containing six hundred slaves. Small-scale traders might have traveled with no more than two or three. There developed a proliferation of markets, big and small, with brokers who specialized in the trade and usually kept stocks of a few slaves at least.

Despite official claims to the contrary, the army of the advancing French empire came to be involved well beyond merely taxing the trade. In successful military campaigns, France's indigenous troops and allied forces were permitted to take as many captives as they could; and most of these, if not all, soon became new supplies for the trade. At the capture of Sikasso in 1898, large numbers were taken northward by way of the important Niger market at Segu, and French agents, rewarded with up to twenty slaves each, doubtless disposed of these profitably. It was only in 1901 that French government directives were issued for the suppression of the trade. Even then, slaves continued to reach the market, a result of raids along the southern edge of the Sahara and of illicit trading, mainly of children either kidnapped or sold during the distressful times of famine.

For many centuries, merchants—mainly Moors from Morocco and Mauritania, but also Tuareg and Tadjakan ones—traded Saharan salt and other goods in Timbuktu for gold dust, ivory, pepper, and, above all, slaves. One early-nineteenth-century writer reported that a 50 percent profit was possible from this trade in salt, purchased along the way.[55] In 1816, one caravan from Wadi Nun, in Morocco, contained fifteen hundred to two thousand camels, had acquired a "considerable amount of salt" at Ijil, and was making for Timbuktu to buy "a great number of Negroes." Near the end of the century, caravans of the Tadjakant tribe in the Sahara were setting out with two to three thousand camels, to trade salt for slaves in Banamba.[56]

The French conquest of Timbuktu in 1894 reduced its role in the trade, which came increasingly to be controlled by the Saharans and directed to new market centers such as Bassikunu and Sokolo along with the still dominant Banamba. French traders, seeking to compete with the use of European merchandise in developing their own trade, were unsuccessful. The salt-for-slave equation remained the crucial one. French intervention against the slave trade, most successfully with the defeat and capture of Samori, the greatest slaver in the Western Sudan, reduced the volume of trade but did not end it. Instead of relying on Western Sudanic slavers, Moors from Mauritania, along with Kinta and

Tuareg, acquired slaves for desert and desert-fringe markets by doing their own raiding and kidnapping. In 1899, for instance, the Kinta, "a respected clerical clan," enslaved the entire population of one village.[57]

Many of the slaves brought to the desert markets as a result of raids or trade were kept there, for both social and economic reasons. Domestic work was deemed to be beneath the dignity of Tuareg and other Saharan tribal women, who left to slaves such chores as fetching water, collecting firewood or dung, preparing and serving food, cleaning, caring for children, weaving cloth. The very numbers available also promoted their increasing use in the cultivation of grain, the expansion of existing date-palm groves or the establishment of new ones, the collection and transport of gum, and the augmented production of salt.

Estimates of the slave population in the desert region during the last decade of the nineteenth century are necessarily rough, since they are extrapolated backward from returns and studies made during the twentieth century. Scholar Ann McDougall suggests, on such evidence, "a very conservative estimate" of a hundred thousand "employed in the Sahara or settled by Saharan masters along the desert-edge."[58]

ELEVEN

COLONIAL TRANSLATIONS

It was intermittently by conquest but more lastingly by the diffusion of ideas that Islam had spread through large areas of black Africa, extending the reach of an Islamic commitment to slavery and the slave trade. European imperial conquest brought new masters, with a professed commitment not only against the slave trade but against slavery itself. Profession was not, however, the same as practice. The metropolitan governments looked for economic benefits from their colonies, with the reduction of costs in consolidating and administering their conquests.

Colonial administrations feared that too radical and rapid an interference with slavery might disastrously damage economies so reliant on slave labor and might also provoke a militant reaction from the traditional leadership, whose collaboration was considered crucial to the pacifying and cost-saving policies of indirect rule. The suppression of the slave trade, a priority of metropolitan public opinion, was pursued with relative, if irregular, dispatch. The suppression of slavery would be a more protracted process.

NORTHERN NIGERIA

The British had acquired the bulk of territory in what had been the vast Sokoto Caliphate. The first British high commissioner of the region, which would become Northern Nigeria, was Sir Frederick (later Lord) Lugard. By 1906, he was ready to issue, with the assertion of assistance from the Sultan of Sokoto himself, a policy directed effectively at starving slavery to death, while emphatically rejecting outright abolition. As Lugard formulated the arguments: "To prematurely abolish the almost universal form of labour contract, before a better system has been developed to take its place, would not only be an act of administrative folly, but would be an injustice to the masters, since Domestic Slavery is an institution sanctioned by the law of Islam, and property in slaves was as real as any other form of property among the Mohammedan population at the time that the British assumed the Government, a nullification of which would amount to nothing less than wholesale confiscation."[1]

The policy pursued under his influence involved a more or less insidious assault on the system. The suppression of the slave trade, with an end to all raiding, was one way of denying the institution of slavery its main nourishment. Another was the freeing by law of all children born to slave parents after the end of March 1901, which deprived the institution of any natural increase or replenishment. In dealing with the current population of slaves, Lugard simply adapted the Islamic practice of *murgu*, by which slaves might purchase their freedom from the earnings of their labor. From a system based on the willingness of masters to offer and honor a contract of sale, it became one based on the legal entitlement of slaves to such a contract, with their freedom then duly established by a decree of the courts.

Tens of thousands obtained their official freedom in this way, which neither violated Islamic tradition nor alienated masters, who were effectively compensated for the loss of their property. There was a further impulse to the widespread acceptance of this reform, in a self-enfranchisement that the colonial government did little to confront. In the early years that followed the British conquest, many slaves—"the total could easily have reached a hundred thousand or more"—simply absconded, sometimes in large groups, from their masters.[2]

This promoted among many masters a disposition to adapt rather than resist. Freeing slaves in return for contractual payments was plainly preferable to their freeing themselves without any payment at all. More preferable still was the willingness of slaves to accept their condition on alleviated terms. Labor requirements came to be widely reduced from five or six days a week to three or four. Further incentives were provided in the form of "presents"—food, clothing, tobacco, salt—on major Muslim festivals or such family occasions as weddings and funerals.

Most of those who absconded in the wake of the British conquest were laborers on the plantations of rulers, aristocrats, and leading merchants. A number of concubines, too, fled to their former homes. In these cases, colonial officials considered it necessary to intervene. Effectively drawing no distinction between concubines and wives, they maintained that these women had no right to desert their husbands. The concubines themselves, protected in their defiance by armed resistance from kith and kin against efforts to secure their return, impelled the officials and individual masters alike to think again. One effect was to promote the marriage of concubines, whose freedom was purchased by their proposed husbands through the courts. Another was to increase the incidence of *purdah*, or female seclusion, which tended to reduce the use of many concubines as menial labor.

A further factor in eroding the institution of slavery came from the tax policies introduced by the British colonial administration, mainly directed at raising immediate government revenues and at promoting economic development that would increase taxable resources. The system that was devised was complex, not least because it incorporated and adapted various traditional forms of taxation.[3] The impact was relatively simple.

A proportional tax was levied on crops, on the assessed values of landholdings, and on the size of households. This last involved the taxation of slaves for the first time, with the householders themselves responsible for the payments. Since receipts from contractual manumission were explicitly exempt from the tax, masters found the arrangement acceptable, since it would supply them with the means to meet their tax liabilities. Slaves taking advantage of the arrangement found it easier to meet their own ransom payments. In 1912, the railway between Kano in the north and Lagos at the coast was completed. The ensuing boom from the production of peanuts and cotton for export provided new opportunities for paid employment not only in agriculture but in trade and transport.

In addition, colonial policy toward the ownership and use of land promoted the growth of a productive peasantry from among former slaves. The British claim to ownership of the land by right of conquest could scarcely be contested on legal grounds by Muslim rulers and aristocrats who had operated on the same principle. The right of use to the land—previously controlled, at least in theory, by the emirs—was extended by the colonial administration to encompass freed slaves and those in the process of purchasing their freedom. Many traditional landlords simply acquiesced, since land that lost its labor force no longer had any productive value.

With its economic function so rapidly contracting, slavery in Northern Nigeria survived increasingly in forms of domestic service, mainly concubinage, and these vestiges gradually came under increasing pressure as well. Yet the attitudes of command and deference, patronage and dependency lasted much longer. The emirs and other beneficiaries of the old regime, redeployed by the colonial authorities as their agents, continued to use their power and prestige to their own benefit. Furthermore, freedom from slavery was not freedom as the British applied the term to themselves.

FRENCH SOUDAN

In 1848, the National Assembly of France had abolished slavery in all her colonies. Vast French conquests in Africa led to practices which attenuated this decision. In the French Soudan in West Africa, the army effectively sanctioned slavery by recruiting slaves along the Middle Niger River and diverting to their masters a share of their military pay. The colonial administration also settled fugitive slaves, along with homeless women and children, in special so-called liberty villages. These people were treated mainly as a source of forced labor for military recruitment, the movement of goods along the routes of campaigning, and work on the construction of the railway to Bamako. Not surprisingly, the villagers came to be known as "the slaves of the whites."[4]

French conquest of the vast region was actually accompanied by a marked increase in enslavement and the connected trade. Slave-based economies, especially that of the Maraka in the area of the Middle Niger, responded to the development of colonial markets in Bamako not just by buying yet more slaves but by increasing the surplus value they extracted from those they owned, prolonging the working day, decreasing rations, and disregarding customary labor practices.[5]

Under pressure from public opinion in France, aroused by reports of sanctioned slavery in her African possessions, the Minister of Colonies appointed a civilian governor of the French Soudan. In 1894, the new administration issued decrees against slave caravans and markets, along with a provision for a fine on every slave brought into French territory. The publication of the decrees, posted at central markets, set off a flight of slaves.

Meanwhile, with the advance of French conquest in West and Equatorial Africa, the supply of new slaves from indigenous warfare was sharply reduced. Labor shortages resulted, and the slaves who had not fled were emboldened to resist—by strikes and even violence—increasing demands on their labor. Driven by these events, the Governor-General of French West Africa, as part of a reformed judicial system announced in 1903, issued express instructions that slavery was no longer to enjoy legal status, and that masters accordingly would have no right to apply, through colonial and indigenous courts or military tribunals, for the repossession of fugitive slaves.

Still larger numbers of slaves began abandoning their Maraka masters, making for their original homes or settling at places along the route. By May 1905, armed confrontations between slaves determined to leave and masters determined to keep them were widespread. To deal with the threat of economic as well as civil disorder at its center in Banamba, the colonial authorities declared that all slaves who left their masters without permission were to be regarded as vagabonds and arrested. In addition, a military detachment was sent to assist in securing a "reconciliation by reciprocal concessions."[6] Efforts at reconciliation soon failed, however, and recognizing the inevitable, the Governor-General in December 1905 decreed an end to the slave trade and to the alienation of any person's liberty in French West Africa. By April 1906, the departure of slaves from Banamba had accelerated sharply.

Almost certainly influenced by what had happened in Banamba, this exodus soon occurred in numerous places across the colony. Some idea of the overall scale may be suggested, from the rare comparative data, by the rise in the population of certain *cercles,* or administrative districts, to which the departing slaves migrated. Between 1905 and 1913, the population of Bougouni increased from 95,592 to 162,343; of Ouahigouya, from 92,566 to 310,000; of Sikasso, from 164,410 to 223,719; and of Koury, from 224,266 to 322,083.[7]

In short, slaves effectively freed themselves, while the colonial authorities vacillated between the commitment to abolish slavery and alarm at the consequences of doing so. However, not all slaves returning to their areas of origin were welcomed in villages whose current chiefs had acquired their dignities by collaborating with the conquerors, and from which their families had fled. Many of those who experienced hostility reacted by establishing new villages of their own. Still others, mainly those who had been born into slavery, asserted their freedom by staying with their former masters only after negotiating with them such new terms of service as more food and better working conditions.

Attitudes of deference survived nonetheless. Some of the newly freed continued to pay their former masters the zakāt, or traditional tithe, originally collected by Islamic authorities for social welfare, thus implicitly recognizing them as owners of the land. Furthermore, with French military conscription during the First World War, many of the freed accepted recruitment as substitutes for the sons of their former masters, though this in itself would lead to the erosion of deference. With their outlook affected by their experiences in military service, often abroad, they renegotiated their terms of employment on their return.

The end of slavery had various other social consequences. Despite certain economic dislocations, there was a rapid adaptation to changing circumstances. Maraka owners who had lost their slaves maintained agricultural production either by working on the land themselves, along with their previously secluded women and their children, or by hiring laborers. Some areas, notably those on the fringe of the Sahara, lost population. Others, notably the Middle Niger Valley, prospered from their closeness to the colonial commodity markets. Former slaves earned and saved enough to buy their own farms or moved into other occupations such as cloth making, commerce, and transport. Since slaves were now no longer an available investment, capital moved into other sectors, such as livestock and trade goods.[8]

MAURITANIA

French policy in Mauritania followed a distinctive route from the outset and continued in that direction long after the conquest of the interior between 1905 and 1910. The colonial administration maintained that the "nature and law of slavery" were distinctive in Mauritania and that freeing the slaves would be a "revolutionary" intervention, productive of much political discontent and social distress.[9]

The slave-owning tribes, known as Moors, encompassed pastoral nomads, settled cultivators, merchants, clerics, and warriors, whose differences were submerged in a formidable adherence to their customs, values, religion, and property. The French had promised to respect these in return for submission, and, as the notables of Adrar—the interior region with the greatest potential for protracted resistance—made clear in negotiating surrender, this involved the ownership of slaves. French agreement to such an accommodation was excused as strategic pragmatism. The tribes in Adrar had a close kinship, as well as religious and commercial relations, with powerful and pugnacious tribes to the north (in Morocco and Spanish Sahara) who paid little regard to lines drawn on the map. The French military authorities wished above all else to avoid a hostile alliance between such northern forces and those in Adrar itself.

The social structure of Mauritania was more complex, however, than a mere division into masters and slaves. There also existed a peculiarly important component of *haratin*, or freed slaves, who legally could own property, bequeathable to their children, and could marry by choice. Yet, far from being the social equals of their former masters, the haratin owed them a continuing obligation in the form of a tribute usually provided through annual payments in cash or presents in kind. And this obligation, with its associated status, passed from one generation to the next in endless succession. There was accordingly an earthly recompense, as well as the possibility of heavenly reward, for masters who freed their male slaves. No earthly recompense applied, however, to the freeing of their female slaves, whose labor, sexual use, and progeny would thereby pass to their own control or to that of the free men they might marry. As a result, female haratin were more likely to have been born to such status than given it by their masters.[10]

For the female slave, one hope of escape from her condition glimmered in marriage to a *tirailleur*, one of the low-rank—generally black—soldiers in the French army who were overwhelmingly recruited from outside Mauritania but were currently based at camps in Mauritanian towns. However, from reluctance to antagonize the owners of female slaves, and on the pretext that a tirailleur might marry a slave only to continue treating her as such after returning with her to his home village, the French administration introduced regulations to discourage these unions. No slave woman might be taken in marriage unless she had first been freed and a formal bride-price paid for her; she was not allowed to follow her husband out of the country; and should he leave the country himself, both bride-price and any children of the marriage were to stay behind with the wife.

In practice, the unwillingness of masters to free female slaves not only ignored Koranic calls to compassion but flouted the law. All too often, for instance, a master might accept the bride-price, permit the marriage of a female slave, and then refuse to free her. Further, when rights to the children came to be disputed, local custom or the decision of a local Muslim court to the same effect prevailed, and the child was awarded to the father. The slave woman who sought her freedom through marriage risked finding herself deprived both of her freedom and her children.

French conquest was attended by no policy of financial investment in Mauritania, but it had a disproportionate impact nonetheless on a relatively small and mainly nomadic population, from the commercial and agricultural boost generated by the military and the administrative colonial presence. An expanding market for wage labor and goods provided the haratin with new economic opportunities, including the accumulation of means with which to acquire their own slaves. One consequence was a reinforced association of the haratin with the traditional slave-owning "nobles" rather than with the slaves whose ethnic origin and color they so often shared. Another was that masters, no longer able to acquire new slaves from a south under French rule, more resolutely resisted losing their existing female ones.

Committed to the policy of accommodating slavery as the price of political peace, the French administrators exercised the remaining serious option of outlawing the slave trade, but with conciliatory interpretations of how the trade should be defined. As the colonial governor advised in 1918: "It can happen that in certain contracts between Moors, for the constitution of a bride price for example, it is specified that a slave be given by the spouse. This is not, in my opinion, an act of slave trading—a slave whose condition we have already recognized, remains in the family and does not leave the country. This is not a loss for the masters."[11] In effect, this constituted, and would long continue to do so, official connivance at an internal slave trade in virtually all of its customary forms.

Some male slaves fled from their masters to seek paid employment and enjoy freedom across the border in the south. They found instead that even when paid employment was available, working conditions were often harsh, and freedom amounted in all but name to slave labor. Slave women also fled, so that leading Moors in 1922 protested to the administration that large numbers were being drawn to Atar, the capital of Adrar, and demanded measures against it. The administration expressed concern and enacted measures, but evidently to little effect, since the protests were still being made twenty years later.

The survival of slavery was due to more than the tightening control exercised by masters over their slaves. The sheer force of tradition and of religious duty, as communicated to the slaves by the masters, was a factor. So was the knowledge that both the colonial officials and the Muslim courts favored the rights of masters over the freedom of slaves. Not least, slaves were unwilling to lose the sustenance provided by their masters for a freedom that might well bring greater hardships along with it. Periods of economic distress both made the escape to freedom easier and demonstrated the ensuing difficulties.

The years 1930–33 saw severe drought in Adrar. Many nomadic Moors left the region in search of pasture elsewhere, and often left their slaves behind, who then drifted into the towns and joined the swelling population of the unemployed. Female slaves, unable to get domestic work, found their only means of survival in prostitution. To the south, the region of Trarza, dependent for its prosperity on the markets of Senegal across the border, was correspondingly stricken by their virtual collapse in the spreading economic depression. There was even a resurgence of slave trading in the country, as some owners sold their slaves to Adrar merchants, who either kept them or sold them to merchants north of the border.

The colonial government, alarmed at the contraction of the agricultural economy, took to threatening landowners among the Moors with fines or the alienation of their holdings if they did not make efficient use of their existing palm-tree groves, extend them with new plantings, and devote more land to growing grain. By the mid-1930s, adequately skilled slave labor, for date-palm agriculture in particular, was growing scarce. Landowners were forced to hire haratin, some of whom, having successfully bargained for better pay, accumulated enough capital to invest in farms or become petty traders.

World War II hit hard the markets both to the south and the north, while the worst drought on record augmented the economic distress. According to Ann McDougall: "The era is most vividly remembered today as 'the time of nakedness.' The complete absence of cloth in the Adrar actually confined people to their homes, and sent desperate men rummaging through army rubbish bins for scraps which could be sewn together. In the midst of such misery, haratin and slaves who could not be absorbed as manual laborers were 'reduced to vagabondage and theft.' Once again, as in the crisis of 1930–1933, slave-trading revived, particularly in 1946–1947, and women turned to prostitution."[12]

Difficult times provided peculiar opportunities for those with the means to exploit hardship. A few haratin bought animals, date palms, and other property from landowners forced to sell by the pressure of debt or the sheer need of money to feed their families, and like their noble patrons before them, they invested some of their enhanced resources in the purchase of slaves. Hammody of Atar, for instance, having laid the foundations of his fortune as a dealer in meat and skins, controlled most of the property in Atar by the end of the war. He also bought slaves, for labor on his lands and as concubines, one of whom, a woman from Mali, he married. When he died in 1961, the legacy to his thirteen children included some two hundred slaves.[13]

SOMALIA

In 1892, the Sultan of Zanzibar ceded to Italian commercial interests control over the Benadir Coast of southern Somalia. The Sultanate had, from 1873, issued successive decrees against the slave trade and slavery itself along the Somali coast. Yet so slight had been the impact that in 1903, Italy's Benadir Company was openly collaborating with local slave dealers, and a household census found that almost a third of Mogadishu's 6,700 inhabitants were slaves, with several thousand more in other towns. They worked in the textile and sesame oil industries, as porters, dockers, and domestics, and most of them were owned by rich Arab and Somali merchants. In 1906, when the Italian government took direct control, its first governor estimated the total slave population of the colony at somewhere between twenty-five and thirty thousand.[14]

The government had already been driven, by the pressure of an Italian public aroused by reports of the Benadir Company's connection with slave trading, to issue a series of ordinances in 1903 and 1904 outlawing the slave trade and providing for the immediate freedom of all slaves born before 1890. In the towns, where the administration supplied funds for the reimbursement of masters to make the process more acceptable, freed slaves moved into domestic service with their former owners; into poorly paid employment as porters, sweepers, waiters; or into destitution and crime. Away from the coast, in the agricultural areas along the rivers, the pursuit of official policy was more protracted and troubled.

The colonial authorities, confronting the problems produced by emancipation in the towns, were in no mind to extend them elsewhere. But slaves in the interior had minds of their own. Reports of what was happening on the coast led to a higher rate of desertions, initially among plantation slaves along the Shabelle River, but spread rapidly from there. Masters responded by exercising closer control and inflicting harsher punishments on those caught trying to escape. The effect was to accelerate rather than arrest the flight, especially in areas with relatively large concentrations of recently imported and less conditioned slaves.

The Italian authorities grew increasingly alarmed. They had yet to extend their control over much of the interior and were particularly concerned to conciliate Somali slave-owning clans, stirred by smuggled guns and rebellious exhortations from across the border in British Somaliland, where a dervish movement of armed resistance was confronting colonial rule. The Italians accordingly took a conciliatory approach toward slave owners in the interior. Judicial tribunals urged slaves to reach some accommodation with their masters, as the price of their freedom. This policy persuaded many to remain with their masters as client laborers rather than as slaves. There were also those who acquired their freedom in other ways. Abandoning their masters, they settled either in one of the villages inhabited by client cultivators, working for wages on the land of some Somali "noble" clan, or among freed slaves already working their own farms in the Shabelle Valley.

Such laborers and cultivators, however, were in the front line for conscription to work on government projects. Understandingly, therefore, many freed slaves moved to settle in the remote villages that had been founded by runaways during the nineteenth century, mainly in the brush-and-forest region of Gosha along the lower Juba River. There were some sixty of these villages, with a total population of twenty to thirty thousand; still others in the vicinity of Avai; and all of them exchanged their agricultural surpluses for pastoral products and craft goods with nearby Somali "noble" clans, in a political and economic accommodation of mutual benefit.

Finally, there were the religious settlements, connected with one or another of the three main Islamic orders, or *tarīqat*. The earliest of these settlements had been founded in the mid-nineteenth century by *tarīqah* sheikhs, and subsequently grew in both number and size, especially in the early twentieth century. They attracted, as M. Colucci writes, "individuals without kin, small groups forced out of their clans, slaves without masters and clients without protectors,"[15] as well as refugees from drought, warfare, and other misfortunes. The colonial government treated them with special consideration, so as to divert them from allying themselves with hostile slave-owning clans or with the dervish movement across the border. It gave stipends to their sheikhs, took their side in disputes over land rights or the harboring of fugitives from clan law, and, not least, exempted them from labor exactions.

The religious settlements came to contain between fifteen and thirty thousand farmers, while an additional twenty thousand lived in the villages founded along the Juba by runaway slaves. Together, these accounted for probably a third of the entire agricultural population, with the rest composed of client cultivators and part-time herders.[16] In consequence, Italian colonists and concession-holding companies experienced increasing difficulty in attracting adequate labor for their agricultural enterprises. Then, in 1922, the Fascists took power in Italy and provided their own solution to the labor problem.

The new regime introduced an annual hut tax, designed to drive many Somalis into wage labor as the only means of paying it, expanded the scope of direct labor conscription, and extended economic control not only throughout the colony but, in a prefigurement of subsequent imperial aggression, beyond it into Ethiopia. From 4 agricultural concessions in 1920, the number grew to 119 by 1933. Incentives provided by Italian companies—mainly the giant SAIS (*Società agricola italo-somala*)—in housing, land-for-food production, tools, seed, and medical care for agricultural workers, did not make the forced nature of the labor any more widely acceptable. Decades later, elderly Somalis would recall the various forms of conscription: from so-called recruitment on renewable four-year contracts for agricultural labor, to government schemes for labor on public works, which disrupted families and resulted in fatal accidents to numbers of those engaged in digging canals. Even the religious settlements lost their exemption from providing labor, a change in policy that might well have been responsible for two rebellions mounted by Somali religious leaders in 1924–25.

The "noble" Somalis, while using the term *habash* for clients of slave ancestry, distinguished further the *jerir*, literally those with "curly hair," or the evidently "Negroid." The Italian authorities lumped the two categories together in the term *liberti*, or the "freed." Yet it was the jerir who seem to have been the prime targets of Fascist labor conscription.[17]

The defeat of Italian forces across the region of the Horn in 1941, during World War II, brought an end to Fascist rule over Somalia, which was consigned first to British and then to democratic Italian trusteeship, until an independent Somalia emerged. The impact of historical divisions in society was to prove more lasting. Slaves and client cultivators had provided labor in the precolonial era. Freed slaves and client cultivators provided, through duress of one sort or another, menial and dangerous labor during the era of colonial rule. In general, their relatedly low social status ensured that they would continue to do so for long afterward.

ZANZIBAR AND THE KENYAN COAST

Along the coast of Kenya, and on the islands of Zanzibar and Pemba, the Sultanate of Zanzibar had a prosperous plantation economy reliant on slave labor. When, in 1890, the British government declared the Sultanate a Protectorate, it had to deal directly with the challenge of slavery. It certainly did not act with heedless dispatch. It was only in 1897 that slaves on the islands were given the right to claim their freedom, and even then, concubines were exempted and would remain so until 1909.

The prime objective of British policy on the islands was to preserve the productive—predominantly clove export—economy by ensuring that the planter class was supplied with an adequate labor force. In consequence, abolition came with claws. Freed slaves were liable to taxes or labor exactions. They needed to show possession of a regular domicile and means of subsistence, or be designated vagrants with concomitant penalties. Where their domiciles were situated on the property of another person, they had to pay the owner rent, or its equivalent in labor or produce, as was agreed before the district court.

Some slaves, arriving at court to claim their freedom, abandoned their cases when informed that they would lose their customary homes and productive plots if they did not pay rent for them. Many, however, did claim and obtain their freedom, while others freed themselves without bothering about the courts or official certificates. There were alternatives to plantation work: casual labor at the port, domestic service, or, by migration to Kenya, employment on the railway there. Some freed slaves simply took to squatting on some corner of a local field where they could raise subsistence crops, in the hope of being ignored or at least not forcibly removed.

The resultant labor shortage led the planters to adapt their attitudes. The work week of five days, current at the height of slavery, became a work week of three. Those laborers who were still slaves were given wages for working on their free days. Former slaves, paid on a piecework basis and coming to exercise their bargaining power at the critical harvest time, were conciliated with increases in rates of pay. Colonial officials blamed the planters for exercising inadequate discipline. They introduced a contract system with penal sanctions, but to little avail.

Planters wanted willing workers. Picking cloves required delicacy and skill, so the trees would not be seriously damaged. Resentful or inattentive workers could prove costly. Planters began circumventing the system and the courts to make their own productive arrangements. This came increasingly to involve acceptance of squatters, who settled on the land to grow their own crops rent-free in return for some agreed amount of wage labor. By 1917, the British Resident described squatting as "universal."[18]

There were further sources of colonial frustration. The liberated slaves seemed unwilling to adopt the values of a social order that criminalized vagrancy, adultery, drunkenness, and dancing. Frederick Cooper states: "The crime figures—a rate of over one conviction per twenty people in Zanzibar town in 1906, about one per fifty 'natives' (let alone exslaves) overall—suggest a turbulent population that the almost total absence of less ambiguously defined crimes, like murder, would seem to belie."[19]

The flogging of offenders became standard practice. A report to the Colonial Office recorded 365 floggings in 1914, for such offenses as theft, drunkenness, fighting, disorder, and refusal to work. Many of the offenders bore characteristic slave names. The Colonial Office itself complained that the government of Zanzibar "was overdoing things,"[20] and by the 1920s, the administration had become less intrusively repressive.

Even on its own terms, British rule over the islands proved to be an economic failure. At the time of its inception, its officials and associated merchants had generally agreed that the islands were too reliant on the export of cloves. Yet, from 65 percent of export income in the 1890s, cloves were, by the 1920s, accounting for 70 percent—a degree of dependence on a single crop whose dangers were intermittently evident with sharp falls in the international price of cloves. This dependence had serious ethnic implications, in the disproportionate ownership by Arabs of the clove trees.

On Pemba, an island with significant clove cultivation by peasants, Arabs represented 12 percent of the population but owned 46 percent of all the clove trees, and though Swahili overall owned 47 percent of all the trees, the majority of Swahili owned not one. In Zanzibar itself, Arabs represented only 5 percent of the population but owned 68 percent of all the clove trees.[21]

Britain's commitment to maintaining the dominance of the Arab planter class as a source of social stability went further. State schooling was primarily provided for Arabs, serving few Africans, and then very rarely beyond the lower grades. It was predominantly Arabs who were recruited to posts in the administration. The resultant popular resentment would take some time to surface and, as will be seen, would do so with a vengeance.

British policies toward the Kenyan coastal strip, acquired as part of the Zanzibar Sultanate, were somewhat different from those pursued on the islands. The strip had a distinctive identity, a position that was formalized in 1920, when it remained a Protectorate while the rest of Kenya became a Crown Colony.[22] For all that, the very designation of the territory as the Kenya Colony and Protectorate implied and involved some correlation of policies toward both.

Relatedly, British rule of the coastal strip was directed more at encouraging European settlers and satisfying their need for labor than at protecting the interests of the Arab and Swahili plantation owners on the coast. When slavery was abolished there in October 1907, courts were instructed to inform slaves that they might leave their owners, who needed to prove any corresponding loss if they were to qualify for compensation. In the event, many slaves simply abandoned their owners or remained only after negotiating new conditions of labor. Significantly, the total paid in compensation amounted to less than the government spent in a single year to provide white settlers with agricultural services.

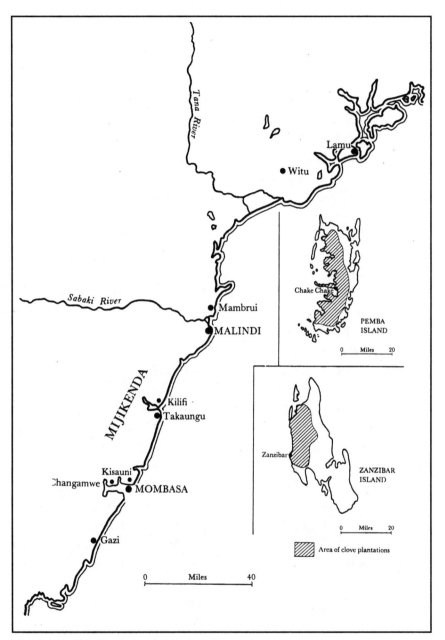

Map 8: Zanzibar, Pemba, and the coast of Kenya

Some former slaves gravitated to the fast-growing town of Mombasa, where they found work as dockers, local porters, or police, and as domestic servants for officials, merchants, or European settlers. Others followed the railway into the interior and worked for wages or engaged in petty trade. Still others made a living by *tembo* tapping, or extracting the sap of the coconut tree to make palm wine, by fishing, and by engaging in the crafts and services that their independent access to local markets sustained. Many, however, became crop-raising squatters on Arab- or Swahili-owned land, paying rent, in cash or kind, or working for wages when the landowners needed their labor. In this, they were joined by such coastal peoples as the Mijikenda, who much preferred squatting to receiving higher wages but having to accept the contract-labor conditions and tight discipline on the plantations of European settlers.

The colonial authorities regarded squatting as inimical to the capitalist values and objectives they were dedicated to instilling, and all the more dangerous for the effect that these practices on the coast might have on the interior. They reacted with a form of direct action that they had avoided on the islands.

With the end of slavery, squatters from the Giriama subgroup of the Mijikenda people had turned land on both sides of the Sabaki River into highly productive grain-growing areas. Shortly before the outbreak of World War I in 1914, the colonial authorities began expelling these squatters to the designated Giriama Native Reserve. Armed patrols arrived to remove them forcibly, burning the huts and household possessions of Giriama and former slaves alike. The transfer of some fifteen thousand people from fertile to inferior land resulted in famine, and the government found itself having to supply grain to an area that formerly exported it. The Colonial Office was not pleased, and a new Governor would report that there had been "very grave mistakes" made.[23] By 1917, the Giriama were returning as squatters on land from Kalifi to Malindi along the coast, where they were welcomed by Arab and Swahili landowners, as well as north of the Sabaki River.

During World War I, the military demand for porters led to the extensive conscription of Swahili and Mijikenda. Not surprisingly, it evoked disturbing memories. Cooper writes: "To some, the passage of officials and chiefs through villages searching for able-bodied men must have resembled a slave raid: in remote areas behind the coast entire villages sometimes fled into the bush and lost their crops."[24] Even women arriving at Malindi might be seized and only released when their menfolk enlisted. To further resentment, officials redirected labor from Arab and Swahili employers to European-owned estates.

The end of the war brought a boost to coastal agriculture and especially to the commercial development of Mombasa. Increasing numbers of migrants were drawn there to a market for casual labor that offered relatively good wages and a desirable measure of independence. One result was the outbreak of rioting in 1923 between migrants from the interior and coastal workers, many of them former slaves, competing for such jobs. The onset of the Depression made Mombasa an even stronger magnet, since casual labor, if only for one day in five, was the sole alternative to destitution for the landless and unwanted in agricultural employment. During World War II and its aftermath, colonial commodities were in rising demand, but the benefits went predominantly to the proprietors of production. Any increases in wage rates lagged behind the pace of inflation in Mombasa and its vicinity. The result was a rash of strikes and civil turbulence that pointed to the more widespread growth in hostility to colonial rule.

Squatter agriculture on the coast had long been accepted by the colonial authorities as an intractable fact. Colonial tax and land policies, however, made it difficult for squatting to become the basis of a thriving peasant production for export. Far from being able to accumulate capital to extend their operations or even to buy the land they worked, many squatters survived by borrowing at high rates of interest on the collateral of their crops.

In the 1950s, militant resistance to colonial rule in Kenya was advanced rather than arrested by a state of emergency repression, conducted to deal with the so-called Mau-Mau rebellion. The related repression, often indiscriminate in its impact, alienated many Africans who had not been "rebels" themselves. Then, as the pace of British decolonization quickened, Arab landowners led a movement for the autonomy of the ten-mile Coastal Strip, "technically still on lease from the Sultan of Zanzibar," on the grant of independence to Kenya.[25] Yet regional autonomy was never a serious option, and any doubt evaporated in December 1963, when Kenya, including the coast, achieved independence.

The new regime proved, however, no more committed to resolving the squatter issue than its predecessor had been. Its policy of resettling some squatters on government land effectively amounted to exchanging one landlord for another. At the end of the 1970s, a smoldering resentment at their plight still existed among people on the coast. As Frederick Cooper recorded in his historical account, *From Slaves to Squatters*:

> Giriama and the descendants of slaves both express a deep bitterness against the grabbing of land and the exploitation of labor by Arabs. This bitterness embodies an acute sensitivity to history, to the slave labor that the ancestors of some experienced, to the slave raids that ancestors of others endured, and to the control of rich coastal lands by Arabs and Swahili that has forced all to enter into relations of subordination in order to farm and to eat. One Giriama squatter referred to squatters as '*watumwa wa siri*,' secret slaves.[26]

On the islands, as the colonial government moved during the 1950s to the phased development of elected representation, politics assumed an increasingly divisive, interconnectedly ethnic and economic cast. Planter, predominantly Arab, interests promoted the Zanzibar National Party (ZNP), while squatters and casual laborers rallied to an alliance of groups, representative of the long-indigenous coastal culture and the interests of more recent migrants from the mainland, in the Afro-Shirazi Party (ASP).

By 1958, landowners were evicting squatters who refused to support the ZNP and were seeking to infiltrate their own supporters in port employment. Squatters reacted by refusing to fulfill their labor commitments and by planting crops that damaged clove trees; a further backlash involved the boycott of Arab- and Indian-owned shops. In the elections of 1961, Arabs and Africans attacked each other at polling stations on Zanzibar and ignited rioting in the plantation areas that left 68 dead and 381 injured. On Pemba, with previously less polarized politics, resentment at Arab domination now gathered force as well.

In 1963, with the impending withdrawal of British rule, elections demonstrated a popular majority behind the ASP on both Zanzibar and Pemba. It was the planter-dominated coalition of the ZNP, however, that won a majority of seats as a result of "flagrant gerrymandering."[27] The ZNP's command of the newly independent state was short-lived. An armed revolt by recently dismissed police of mainland origin became a proclaimed revolutionary regime whose leaders identified themselves as African and radical, with most of them calling themselves sheikhs and remaining firmly in the fold of Islam.

The Sultan and senior officials were permitted to flee. In fact, thousands of ZNP supporters, including many Arabs, left the islands. An unknown but certainly sizable number of others lost their lives in a rampage of retribution for past wrongs. Large estates were expropriated, mainly for redistribution to peasants. Large businesses were transferred to state control. Julius Nyerere, President of Tanganyika, who was disturbed by a dangerously volatile situation nearby, in which Cold War rivalries had begun to intervene, offered the offshore islands a union, and in April 1964, Tanzania came into being.

There seems little doubt that memories of slavery, or at least their recall in oral tradition, were an element in the ethnic violence that swept the islands. Yet economic frustrations and resentments were clearly the dominant factors, and British rule bore much of the responsibility. Here, as in other parts of Africa where it assailed first the Islamic slave trade and then the institution of slavery, European colonialism preserved the force if not the face of old subjugations and introduced new ones, with costs and consequences that have outlived its own formal departure from the continent.

TWELVE

SURVIVALS OF SLAVERY

On December 10, 1948, the United Nations General Assembly adopted the Universal Declaration of Human Rights with a specific provision prohibiting slavery. In 1953, the French ambassador to Saudi Arabia reported to his government that in Jedda a male slave under the age of forty was fetching £150 ($420) in private sales and a girl under fifteen as much as £400 ($1,124).[1] In the same year, the Sheikhs of Qatar, visiting Britain for the coronation of Queen Elizabeth II, included slaves in their retinues, and they would do so again for a visit in 1958.[2]

Visiting Djibouti in 1956, John Laffin observed a slave auction outside a large warehouse near the docks, during which "perhaps 200 slaves" were sold in his presence. These were Africans from the area around Lake Chad (then part of French West Africa) who had been brought to Djibouti by Arab slavers, "some of whom were said locally to be directed by a Frenchman." The buyers at the auction were dealers from Arabia, who would be transporting their merchandise across the Red Sea for the markets in Jedda and Medina:

> Men, women and children were brought from the warehouse and paraded on a raised platform so that all dealers could clearly see them. A trader would nudge a slave's jaw

with a stick and the man would open his mouth to display
his teeth. Another probe with the stick and he would flex
his arm muscles. Young women were forced to expose their
breasts and buttocks. A dispute developed over the virginity
of a tall young ebony woman, and during the hour-long argument she was forced to squat while one of the most
prominent buyers examined her with his fingers. She was
terrified; her trembling was visible fifty yards away.

Occasionally children were sold in batches. They did
not cry, mainly, I think, because they had no tears left, but
they held tightly to one another and kept looking around as
if for help. Boys of about ten or twelve had their anuses examined; homosexual buyers are fussy about disease.[3]

In 1956, James Morris, a journalist working for *The Times* of London,
visited Saudi Arabia and subsequently wrote: "As an industry and social
institution, slavery is still important to the Saudis, unlikely though it may
seem sometimes amidst the hygiene of the oil towns or the grand office
blocks of Jedda. Among rich men a young slave girl is an acceptable gift.
Among merchants, a stout negro is a useful piece of equipment."[4]

In 1961, at a high political level, came corroboration of reports that
slavers were tricking Muslim blacks into accompanying them on the pilgrimage to Mecca, where these were then marketed as slaves. Muḥammad Heikal, editor of the Egyptian newspaper *Al-Ahram*, was also an
influential adviser to President Nasser. Attending a conference at Casablanca, Heikal was present at an exchange between Libya's Minister of
Foreign Affairs and Sheikh Muḥammad Mehdi, a member of the Mali
delegation, who was pressing for the extradition of a Malian citizen then
living in Libya. Heikal reported the Sheikh's remarks:

The man in question is wanted by my country. He was the
chief of a Mali tribe. A little before my country's independence [in 1960], he called upon the members of his tribe
to undertake the pilgrimage to Mecca. Many listened
to him. Among them were men and a large number of
women accompanied by their children. After much excite-

ment they arrived at Mecca, and there they were sold to
many slave traders. After having gained money by selling
his own people this man left Mecca, and instead of returning to Mali, he went to Libya where he opened a business.[5]

In 1962, there came further corroboration of slavery in Saudi Arabia.
Marzouk, a worker there, had been freed by his master, who demanded
fifty thousand rials as the price of freeing Marzouk's wife and children.
Marzouk made a public appeal to his fellow workers for contributions to
this cost. His cause was taken up by a leading Saudi trade unionist,
Nasires Said, who sent a telegram, subsequently published in the Egyptian newspaper Al-Goumhouriya, to King Ibn Saud. It read: "The slave
merchants claim that the slave-trade is permitted by Islam, but Islam and
every other divine religion rejects this. We ask that the farce of one human being selling another should cease, because it is a disgrace which
ridicules Saudi Arabia before other nations."[6]

Nasires Said fled to Cairo from the rage of the Saudi authorities.
Marzouk's wife and children were reportedly sold to another master in
Riyadh.

Also in 1962, twenty Saudi princes fled to Egypt after an abortive attempt at a pro-Nasser coup. On Egyptian radio they denounced the
Saudi involvement in slavery:

> We consider it our sacred duty to make the international
> public aware of the question of negro and white slavery in
> Saudi Arabia . . . . All humanitarian organizations must in-
> tensify their campaigns and their protests to denounce and
> put an end to the evil of negro and white slave traffic.
> Agents go as far afield as Africa, Iraq and Iran to find their
> human merchandise, which they bring back to Saudi Ara-
> bia. The slave is often put to work for oil companies and his
> wages paid to his master.[7]

It was clearly in the political interest of Nasserist Egypt to diffuse accusations of slavery in Saudi Arabia. But hostile propaganda did not necessarily invalidate charges for which there was corroborative evidence.

Such evidence was provided by Laffin on the particular tribes, routes, and merchants engaged in the slave trade. He named "the el Dowasir tribe, operating in the northern part of the desert and the region of Qatar; the al Mourra tribe operating around the Buraimi Oasis; as well as the al Dohm, al Nabit and al Habbar tribes." He then listed the main slave traders "who made seasonal trips to Dubai and Muscat and brought back slaves in groups of fifty or sixty at a time."[8] Slaves were being imported from Ethiopia, Somalia, and other parts of Africa as well as from Asia and Europe.

In 1970, Britain's Anti-Slavery Society cited "an expatriate administrator employed by the government of a Middle East country" as the source for information that, in the previous decade, there had been an average annual surplus of fifteen thousand people entering southern Arabia over those leaving the region. Nor, according to the same source, would deaths, unrecorded departures, intended settlement, and clerical errors have accounted for the extent of the difference. The same source disclosed that in 1966, for instance, at least three hundred Somali women had been imported into southern Arabia as slaves.[9]

In 1971, Dr. Oliver Ransom, who had worked in Africa for thirty years, claimed that black children were still being auctioned in the Red Sea ports, and in 1973 Lord Wilberforce—a descendant of William Wilberforce, the great abolitionist—cited regions where slavery survived, including the Sultanates of Muscat and Oman, which had enjoyed the protection of British arms until 1970.[10]

Laffin's indictment, published in 1982, claimed that Africans were still being tricked into visiting Mecca as pilgrims and being enslaved there. Air transport had made such traffic easier, since the victims could be brought from source to market in a single hop. And Saudi Arabia was probably still "the principal importer of slaves."[11]

It is doubtful that such preeminence can reasonably be asserted for Saudi Arabia today. This is scarcely because there has been a corresponding modernization of attitudes and practices in the government. The reach and rigor of religious law in many respects would have been regarded by Islamic Spain a thousand years ago as intolerably repressive. But a multitude of imported temporary settlers, mainly from Asia, for use as contract laborers or domestic servants, often involving in practice a form of servitude distinguishable from slavery only in the absence of ownership, has made traditional slavery somewhat superfluous. Moreover, the international opprobrium attached to slavery, in an age of ceaseless global newsgathering, is likely to have discouraged even the Saudi regime from supporting or conniving at the slave trade.

Nonetheless, where destitution thrived and there were those ready to exploit it, slavery continued to find a market in Islam. In the late 1970s, a Muslim member of the Lebanese commercial community in Freetown, Sierra Leone, was combining the sale of clothes, radios, jewelry, cameras, Islamic texts, and copies of the Koran with the supply of slaves to his compatriots in Beirut. One slave, called Jennifer, perhaps nine years old at the time, was sold to him by her widowed mother and sent to Beirut. Jennifer would later claim that she knew of ten other girls who had been sent there by the same dealer. This was by no means a unique instance of Lebanese slave trading. Already in 1973, the Anti-Slavery Society had reported to the United Nations the prosecution of nine Ghanaians and a Lebanese, at Accra in March of that year, for having sold 20 fourteen-year-old Ghanaian girls to buyers in Lebanon.

Jennifer's Lebanese owner, a certain Nasser, was a police officer who became, according to her, "a general." She was made to work seven days a week, often from 5:30 in the morning until 1:30 the next morning, and was beaten by her owner as a matter of course. "I was often so tired I fell asleep over my food," she would later tell an interviewer. "I was not allowed to eat until they had finished and then I was only allowed to eat what they left. If I did not work fast enough they shouted at me and called me slave and dog, and said my father was a dog. Always they threatened to kill me if something went wrong."[12]

Her status as a *sana*, or slave, was stressed in various ways apart from such abuse. She was made to sleep in a cubbyhole, to sit on the floor and never on a chair, to wear only cast-off clothes, to eat only with her own knife and fork from her own plate, and to drink only from her own cup, which was supplied to her so that she did not contaminate the household utensils. When the Nassers entertained many people, members of the extended family brought in other slaves to help her, and there were at least another half dozen female slaves in the apartment block where the Nassers lived. The slaves were not permitted to join their owners in the building's basement shelter during the bombings and street fighting of Lebanon's long civil war.

Islam has not been impervious to ideas and pressures from without, nor unresponsive within to those in favor of reform. Even most of the self-avowed fundamentalist regimes have repudiated slavery, in practice as well as precept. There are, however, two states, Mauritania and Sudan, with rogue regimes that accommodate not only the widespread practice of slavery but also policies amounting to racism in the treatment of blacks.

MAURITANIA

The "Islamic Republic of Mauritania," extending eastward from the Atlantic, lies between the Arab-Berber Maghrib to the north and the black African states of Senegal and Mali to the south. The size of its population is uncertain. The government has refused to publish the results of the census it undertook in 1988; nor, given the nature of the regime, would publication of the data command any credit in the absence of evidence that the census had been independently conducted. The *World Bank Atlas, 1997* listed the population in 1995 at a little over 2.25 million.[13]

According to Human Rights Watch/Africa, roughly a third of the inhabitants are *beydanes* (literally "white men") of Arab-Berber descent, otherwise known as Moors (or white Moors). Another third, called *haratin* (derived from the Arabic word for freedom) and otherwise known as black Moors, are former black slaves or their descendants "who remain politically and culturally tied to their former masters." The final third, generally blacks (sometimes known as Afro-Mauritanians) from various ethnic groups of which the largest is the Halpulaar, encompasses an untold number of people still held in slavery.[14]

The persistence of the practice is not persuasively denied by repeated enactments against it. Slavery was abolished in the independence constitution of 1961, and abolished yet again, by presidential decree, in July 1980. In November 1981, a government ordinance asserted that slavery had been definitely abolished throughout the national territory. All slaves were held to have become haratin. But if many existing haratin, jealous of their dignity, found this offensive, it was merely a fiction that did nothing to change the facts. A representative from the Anti-Slavery Society in London, who visited Mauritania in 1981, estimated that "the country probably holds a minimum of 100,000 total slaves with a further 300,000 part slaves and ex-slaves."[15] In its 1993 annual report, the International Labor Organization cited the continuing problem of slavery in Mauritantia.[16]

Kevin Bales, in a recent study of "new slavery," such as various kinds of bonded labor in the global economy, deals also with the survival of Mauritania's "old slavery": "In Mauritania today there is no slavery, and yet everywhere you look, on every street corner and shop, in every field and pasture, you see slaves. Slaves are sweeping and cleaning, they are cooking and caring for children, they are building houses and tending sheep, and they are hauling water and bricks."[17]

Moustapha, a shepherd who escaped from his master in March 1990 and was interviewed three months later in Senegal, reported that slaves were still being openly sold: "The last sale I remember happened during the last winter season [November 1989 to February 1990] when a boy of two was sold by his master, Mohamed ould Mbarak, to Naji ould Rouej. The mother had just stopped suckling the boy. The sale took place in a village called Dranji in the region of Trarza."[18]

These sales, however, run the risk of attracting disagreeable publicity. Therefore, other methods are used to disguise the transactions or otherwise perpetuate the system. One black health worker recounted some of them: "Nowadays beydane tribes make discreet arrangements among themselves. A slave is given in exchange for something else. Then there are the 'presents.' I recall the case of a young woman who had a child. The child, who was eight months, was given to a cousin of the master, as a 'present' for life. It was agreed not to transfer the child to his new owner until the mother had stopped breast-feeding him."[19]

Devices such as these, if brought—albeit rarely—to the attention of the courts, are usually countenanced by them. In 1992, a fourteen-year-old slave girl, Salkha Bint m'Bareck, was given to her master in part payment for a car and taken to the capital, Nouakchott, where she escaped to the house of a cousin. There she was arrested, and a lawyer was hired to fight her case in court. It was ruled that she be returned to her master, since she was a minor, and there was no one else legally responsible for her.[20]

The law itself leaves ample room for evasion. The presidential edict of 1980 abolished slavery, but not slave ownership. It recognized the rights of owners by stipulating that they should be compensated for their loss of property. And since no financial payment has been provided by the state, the abolition of slavery has been little more than propaganda for foreign consumption, Indeed, religious authorities within Mauritania have assailed the act of abolition itself.

"This 'abolition,' " according to El Hassan Ould Benyamine, imam of a mosque in Tayarat, "is not only illegal because it is contrary to the teachings of the fundamental text of Islamic law, the Koran. The abolition also amounts to the expropriation from Muslims of their goods, goods that were acquired legally. The state, if it is Islamic, does not have the right to seize my house, my wife or my slave."[21]

Furthermore, the children of slave women are considered to be the property of their masters, and in instances where a freed slave woman has appealed to the courts for custody of her children, she has gotten short shrift. The master maintains that the children are his own, and that the mother is his wife. Kevin Bales states: "Judges, and the ulemas of the Islamic courts, can be counted on to accept this argument; after all, they normally have slaves in their households as well."[22]

As these two cases demonstrate, there are slaves who run away. But many accept their condition. Boubacar Ould Messaoud, born a slave in 1944, has founded *SOS-Esclaves* (SOS-Slaves), which helps runaways. He is aware that there are slaves as well as masters who consider slavery the normal lot of life: "You have people like my mother, who thinks that there is nothing wrong with slavery. They have no other universe. After 15 or 20 generations, people become totally submissive."[23]

Submissiveness is often a consequence of ignorance. The vast majority of slaves are illiterate, not least because it is so rare for any of them to get any schooling at all. Few are even aware that there have been enactments against slavery. Certainly their masters have not informed them.

As Moustapha the shepherd reported: "I never heard the abolition discussed in my master's house. I learned of it from some Halpulaar villagers living near us. I don't know of any slave who got to know about the abolition in his master's home. All the ones I have met who have heard of it learned from other black communities, which is why masters are so sensitive to any contact between slaves on the one hand, and free haratines [haratin] or other blacks, on the other hand."[24]

Even suspicion of a little knowledge can produce punishment. Moustapha at first did not believe what he had been told of abolition and visited the villagers again to talk about it further: "My master became suspicious when I came back late and he found out that I had seen our Halpulaar neighbours. In order to show his displeasure, I was undressed, my hands and feet tied up and I was made to lie flat on my stomach in the burning sun. I was then whipped with a whip made of cowhide and during the night, when the temperature was cold, they kept pouring water all over my body."[25]

Not the least of the discouragements to widespread absconding or revolt among slaves is the fear of how else they would survive in a poor economy of high unemployment. Bales met a "White Moor" businessman, some of whose slaves raised produce in his home village; others, who were more trusted, traveled to Senegal for the purchase of vegetables; and still others staffed his four shops, selling food and household goods, in the capital.[26] Evidently, the inducements to absconding and the apparent opportunities to do so were outweighed by the provision of food and shelter, however mean, alongside the alternative of destitution.

Moreover, the difficulties of finding paid employment are compounded for absconders by informal policing. As Bales has written: "In a country organized into extended families, the escaped slave is an outcast. Immediately identifiable by color, clothing, and speech, an escaped slave would be asked, 'Who do you belong to?' by any potential employer. From the perspective of those in control of jobs and resources, escaped slaves have already proved their untrustworthiness by turning their backs on their 'families.' "[27]

Fear of abandoning traditional relationships grips many haratin, too. If they do find some paid work, it is often in the spaces deliberately left by the beydanes, the men employed in such socially disparaged activities as rubbish disposal, the women in selling cooked couscous, sometimes operating mini-restaurants, or drifting into prostitution.[28]

A few haratin do well in business and the professions or in government service, including the police and army. Comprising as they do only
a third of the population, the beydanes are not blind to the advantages of
incorporating some haratin in the mechanism of rule. In this they are as-
sisted by the deference, even submissiveness, which many haratin continue to feel toward beydanes. There are descendants from freed slaves
who still pay financial tribute to families of onetime masters, even when
they themselves are educated and have become successful in business or
the professions.

Not all of them by any means have proved to be so subservient. In
1974, a number of them founded a movement, which they named *El
Hor* (Arabic for "the free"), to advance the interests of their community
as well as of other blacks. They set out to encourage the establishment of
agricultural cooperatives by haratin and pressed not only for measures to
enforce the law against slavery but for land reform that would provide
the freed slaves with the means of gaining economic independence. The
peaceful methods pursued by the movement—mainly the distribution of
tracts and the holding of demonstrations—did not save it from an increasingly repressive response. Both leaders and ordinary members were
arrested, some of them tortured during their detention, in the crackdown
of 1979–80. And while haratin continued to be used in conducting the
repression, some of them, too, would be swept up as victims in a campaign against blacks that increasingly assumed a dimension of "ethnic
cleansing."

From the first, the regime seemed determined to promote and secure
beydane domination of the state. Ignoring the essential doctrine of Islam
that all Muslims are members of a single community, without distinction
of nationality, race, or color, and the adherence of virtually all blacks in
the country to Islam, the government effectively equated Islam with Arab-
ism. Arabic became the official language, the only one in which the
business of government and of the courts was conducted, as well as the
only medium of instruction in the schools. This was an effective while
oblique method of marginalizing blacks, since many of them knew, apart
from their respective vernaculars, only French, from the time when that
had been the official language.

More direct was the denial of loans to blacks by bank officials, all of whom were beydanes, and the expropriation of land in the south, long held overwhelmingly by blacks, for beydane ownership. This process of alienation took a massive leap with the Land Reform enactment of 1983, which began with the declaration "Land belongs to the nation and every Mauritanian, without discrimination of any kind, can own land in conformity with the law." The devil was in the tail.

Article 7 made collective lawsuits concerning property "legally inadmissible," a provision designed to exclude the assertion of customary tenure rights from consideration by the courts. Article 9 declared "dead lands" the property of the state, defining them as lands that had never been developed or whose prior development left no trace. Most black agriculturalists in the south traditionally relied on the annual floods rather than on irrigation ditches; and the rotation of crops left many fields fallow each year. The provision thus provided ample opportunity for local officials, whose powers were then made virtually unlimited by various decrees in 1984–85, to expropriate large tracts of land on the pretext that they were "dead." The prime beneficiaries were either beydanes in high-ranking government posts or their relatives, who were duly invested with ownership. A Mauritanian sociologist, interviewed at Dakar in March 1991, gave one measure of the results: "More than half the land in the Trarza region is owned by fifty-six people, all of whom have between 100 and 600 hectares. Of these fifty-six, fifty-five are Moors, one is black."[29]

Black resistance to these policies led in the mid-1980s to the formation by black intellectuals of a necessarily clandestine movement. Calling themselves the African Liberation Forces of Mauritania (FLAM), they issued, in 1986, "The Manifesto of the Oppressed Black Mauritanian," which attacked in detail the policies and acts of beydane domination. Twenty-one blacks were arrested as leaders of the movement, then tortured and sentenced to long prison terms. The government was making it clear that it would brook no opposition. But what followed five years later was beyond anything that the most fearful among the blacks might have imagined.

During the French colonial period, Senegal and Mauritania had both been administered from St. Louis in Senegal, as though they were two regions of a single state. Mauritanians had pursued their studies or

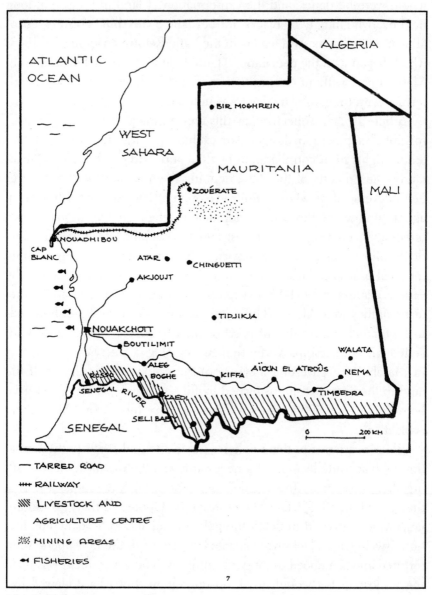

Map 9: Mauritania

had established businesses in Senegalese towns and cities, just as Senegalese had settled in Mauritanian ones. The Senegal River, which became the border between two independent states in 1960, continued to be regarded, by peasants and traders on both sides, as a street rather than a frontier.

Then, on April 9, 1989, in a village called Diawara on an island in the river, a dispute between Mauritanian herders and Senegalese farmers led to the death of two Senegalese. The looting of Mauritanian-owned shops in the nearest Senegalese town of Bakel began almost as soon as reports of the incident reached it. On April 22–23, looting struck the capital, Dakar, where much of the violence was committed by unemployed and domestically disaffected young Senegalese.

What developed on April 24–25 in Nouakchott, the capital, and in Nouadhibou, the second city and main port of Mauritania, was of a different order. Armed haratin were conveyed by military trucks into the districts where most Senegalese lived. There were reports that they brought with them the names and addresses of Senegalese, provided from the returns of the census conducted a few months before. In a frenzy of violence, Mauritanian as well as Senegalese blacks were clubbed and killed. Unofficial estimates put the number of dead at 150 to 200 or more.

When news of this spread to Senegal, rioting broke out in Dakar and elsewhere, directed mainly at "white Moors." The final tally of the dead, as Mark Doyle records, "appeared to be between 50 and 60," though "the figure could not be definitive."[30] The two states were now close to war, averted only by intense international pressure, with the pledge of planes from France, Spain, Algeria, and Morocco, for an immediate repatriation of Mauritanians and Senegalese to their respective countries. This involved airlifting some hundred thousand Mauritanians from Senegal and eighty-five thousand blacks, by no means all of them Senegalese, from Mauritania. There seems no reasonable doubt that the Mauritanian government exploited the occasion to expel Mauritanian blacks.

Many more were expelled across the river. Military forces arrived in the south and rounded up blacks. They beat some of the men and raped some of the women. They seized their possessions—sometimes even the clothes they were wearing—and, in particular, confiscated their identity cards and other documents that might prove their Mauritanian origin. Then they hauled their captives to the riverbank and ordered them at gunpoint to leave on the boats provided, or, if there were no more boats available, to swim or drown. During these deportations, 276 villages were burned or otherwise destroyed, according to the main legal opposition party, the Union of Democratic Forces (UFD).

In the cities and towns, similar treatment was meted out to blacks, especially civil servants and business employees, but including some army officers and police. They, too, were stripped of their possessions and all documents, before being trucked to the river and put onto boats. Moḥamed El Faso, an imam in Aleg, was among a number of eminent Muslim figures who were deported for being black:

> On May 10, a group of beydanes leading haratin came to our house. The haratin directed by the beydanes took everything they could lay their hands on. What they could not take, they destroyed. I had two large trunks full of Islamic books, including many copies of the Koran. They burned everything in front of my eyes. That of course hurt me the most and they knew that. They came beating wardrums. For them it was a war. On May 10, my house was burned to the ground. Aleg is a regional capital and there are rows of houses next to each other. But they were selective about choosing only black houses. My house was only 200 meters from the office and home of the governor of the region, which made it easy to see the extent of government complicity in these operations.[31]

The war had yet to be taken one stage further. For despite dismissals and deportations, there were, in the view of the regime, still too many blacks in disquietingly influential positions. In October 1990, on the pretext of a Senegal-based staging of a coup for which no credible evidence was ever adduced, the regime initiated a campaign of terror that lasted for several months. About three thousand blacks,[32] mainly in military service, others in civil service posts, were arrested. Five hundred to six hundred blacks, almost all from the armed forces and all belonging to the

Halpulaar ethnic group, were summarily executed or tortured to death in detention. Many of the survivors were maimed or paralyzed by the torture inflicted on them, and others later died from the effects. Some agreed under torture to sign confessions they were not permitted to read.

On April 10, 1991, fifty eminent Mauritanians, including former ministers of government, signed an open letter to the President, citing several hundred specific instances of extrajudicial execution and other atrocities that violated "the noble ideals of Islam, especially religious tolerance, brotherhood and the respect of the human being." The letter called on the government to set up an independent commission of inquiry that would determine responsibility for the crimes and to introduce immediately measures guaranteeing the rule of law.[33] In June 1993, the government gave its revealing response: amnesty for all crimes committed by the armed and security forces between April 1989 and April 1992.

Any dissent or embarrassing disclosure continued to be met with repression. In January 1998, the government detained Boubacar Ould Messaoud (President of SOS-Slaves), Brahim Ould Ebery (a senior member of the Bar Association), and Professor Cheikh Saad Bouth Kamara (President of the Mauritanian Human Rights Association). In early February, all three were put on trial, along with Fāṭima Mbaye, a lawyer and Vice-President of the Mauritanian Human Rights Association, for belonging to unlawful organizations, a term applied to organizations the government had not formally recognized. A fifth person, the representative of SOS-Slaves in France, was tried *in absentia*. All five were sentenced to imprisonment. Boubacar Ould Messaoud was also charged and convicted for having presented and distributed an unauthorized film. He had given an interview to French television news about slavery in Mauritania.[34]

SUDAN

Sudan, a country of twenty-seven million people,[35] has been torn by civil war for most of the past forty years. It is a war that has been fought all the more ferociously for involving both religious and racial conflicts. And it has led to a resurgence in slavery and the slave trade.

Even before the state became independent in 1956, there was grow-

ing apprehension among the majority black, Christian, or animist inhabitants of the South at the prospect of domination by the majority Arab
and Muslim inhabitants of the North. That such fears were well founded
became clear when the new government declared that Sudan was an
Arab state committed to Islam, and the military regime of General
Ibrahim Abboud (1958–64) aggressively pursued corresponding policies,
including the restriction of Christian missions. Furthermore, ethnic attitudes from the era of slavery remained a factor. The word *abd* for slave
"was still in common use to designate all black non-Arab Sudanese."[36]

Already in 1955, Southern army units had risen in armed revolt, and
growing popular support in the region turned the mutiny into civil war.
An estimated half a million lives were lost before a peace agreement in
1972 conceded regional autonomy to the South, while retaining the
Nuba Mountains and their mainly black inhabitants administratively
within the North.

From the late 1970s, increasing numbers of Sudanese with mar-
ketable skills, mainly Arabs, left the country to work abroad, especially in
the Gulf States. By 1983, there were three hundred thousand expatriates,
whose total remittances, of $2 to $3 billion a year, were ten times the
value of all Sudan's agricultural exports.[37] Sent by expatriates to their
families living in Khartoum and other cities of the North, most of this
money was spent on land speculation, residential building, and consumer goods. *Sudan's Invisible Citizens* reported: "Huge new suburbs
sprang up around Khartoum—one of the most opulent appropriately
called Riyadh. This was crucial to the Moslem Brothers' establishment
of a powerful economic base built upon the import of goods to feed the
consumer boom generated by the remittances."[38]

The boom in urban residential building attracted unskilled labor
from the depressed agricultural sector, and conspicuous consumption
opened employment opportunities in domestic service. Rural migrants
poured into the urban areas of the North, especially Khartoum, in search
of work, often to find that they were surplus to requirements. Their numbers increased enormously because of the famine that struck western Sudan in the early 1980s. The government of President Numeiri ordered
the refugees to return home, providing trucks, army, and police units to
persuade them. Such measures were both unpopular and ineffectual.

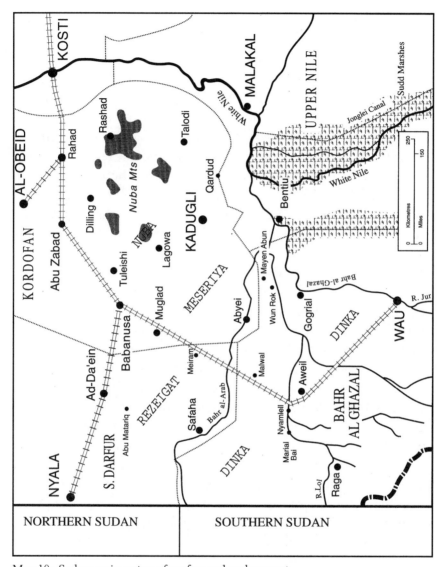

Map 10: Sudan: main sectors of warfare and enslavement

The migrants were allowed to stay, but only outside the cities, in squalid conditions.

There was another reason for the ceaseless flow of migrants. In 1978, oil had been discovered in the marshland area of the Upper Nile, and many in the South suspected that this prospective bonanza would be exploited mainly for the benefit of the North. Rising unrest in the region provoked a predictable response. In 1980, the government in Khartoum imposed military rule on the South, and in 1981, beset by mounting political discontent in the North as well, it arrested hundreds of its opponents. In May 1983, an army mutiny followed the government's decision to divide the autonomous southern region into three parts. The mutineers established the Sudan People's Liberation Army (SPLA) before the end of the year, and civil war resumed.

Although marked by widespread disregard for human rights in the South and in other areas where the civil war was being fought, multi-party democracy of a sort continued to function in the North. Then, in parliamentary elections, a candidate of Nuba origin was elected for a constituency in greater Khartoum. The implications were not lost on those who equated Islam with Arab dominance. In June 1989, a military coup brought to power the National Islamic Front (NIF). Its leader, Dr. Hassan al-Turabi, became the ideological guide of a fundamentalist regime; and though the NIF was soon formally abolished, it continued to control the state through the command its leaders and adherents exercised over the machinery of government. A so-called political system avowedly enshrining the Islamic principle of *shura*, or consultation, provided a semblance of popular bodies, though without parties or anything approaching what is generally understood as democratic elections. A commitment to free enterprise, avowedly based on Islamic economic principles, informed the sale of "state assets, at derisory prices to a favored few."[39]

From the first, the new regime made it clear that its view of an Islamic state would rely on repression. It declared a state of emergency, suspended the constitution, banned political parties and trade unions, and provided for detention without charge or trial. According to Amnesty International, it "ushered in a new era of human rights violations characterized by a range and scale of abuse unprecedented in Sudan's history."[40]

Associated with these abuses was the imposition in 1991 of a penal code based on *Sharī'ah*, or Islamic law. While the South was expressly excluded from its application, the code nonetheless confirmed for Southerners, including many who now lived in the North, that the regime was committed to an increasingly oppressive Muslim domination. And such a view was supported by a declaration from the regime in 1992 that it was engaged in a jihad against unbelievers. Amnesty International's summary indictment in 1995 was damning:

> Anyone suspected of opposition to the government or its policies is at risk of arrest. This is as true in the major cities and rural areas of northern Sudan as it is in the war zones. Displaced southerners, refugees, members of Muslim religious orders that do not conform to the government's interpretation of Islam, lawyers, members of the military, women protesting at the cost of living, students protesting at changes in their allowances, trade unionists, political activists, journalists, foreign nationals, musicians, artists, and many others have been detained.[41]

Not least among the areas hardest hit by such policies—in warfare and the famine attending it—was the region surrounding the Nuba Mountains in central Sudan, which was reported to have lost almost half its population. According to John Vidal in *The Guardian*: "Nuba is in the forefront of Khartoum's policies of extreme Islamisation. Churches and mosques are being destroyed, the latter on the grounds that they are not practising the fundamentalist religion favoured by the government." And the Nuba rebel commander, Ismail Khamis, was cited as saying: "The policy is to isolate the Nuba tribes, wear us down, politically neuter and then Arabise us. Khartoum does not want blacks like us to have any sort of power, but to remain fourth-class citizens."[42]

In this context, atrocities had no single home. Neither those defending the regime nor those confronting it have shrunk from attacking civilians, taking hostages, and seizing children for enlistment and training as soldiers. Rebellion does not extenuate, let alone exonerate, such abuses. Yet it is reasonable to argue that those who command the powers and resources of the state are commensurately the more culpable for misusing them. The nature of the regime, the policies it pursued, and the conduct of its officials overwhelmingly supported the charges of an interconnected religious and racial persecution.

One aspect of this persecution involved a campaign ostensibly to clean up the city streets by removing the so-called street children from them. Many—perhaps most—of the children, however, were not runaways or homeless. They lived with their families and were at the time on some errand or walking between home and work. Such information was never sought and, if offered, was ignored. The captives were transported for indeterminate stays in closed camps, generally far away from the place of capture. In Abu Doum, north of Omdurman, about 650 boys were held at a secret camp in June 1995, and at times the number reached as many as 1,000. Moreover, there were at least seven such secret camps for abducted children.[43]

One boy, a Christian whose family had moved to Khartoum from the South in 1983, was ten years old and had been sent by his father on an errand to the market when he was seized in 1990. It took his father three years to find him and secure his release. The boy reported that all in the camp, whatever their religion, were required to participate in the prayers and rites of Islam, that all the boys were black, and that the camp officials used to lash the boys or force some of them to lash others.[44]

The NIF regime did not reintroduce slavery in the Sudan. During the three previous years of elected government, for instance, Arab militias enjoyed official license to confiscate cattle, burn property, and capture civilians, as part of a policy to erode the supposed main social base of the SPLA rebellion among the Dinka and Nuba peoples. The civilian captives, most of them women and children, were then transported far from their villages of origin and kept as slaves, forced to do unpaid domestic work, to herd animals, and sometimes to perform sexual services for their masters. Not only militias engaged in such practices. Regular army troops and officers also took captives for use as slaves and sometimes sold them, even openly at village markets.

The authorities could hardly plead ignorance of the 1926 Slavery Convention as amended in 1953, to which Sudan was a signatory and which required the state to pursue the abolition of slavery in all its forms. In 1987, a study published in Arabic by two Sudanese university professors and human rights activists drew attention to the capture of Dinka civilians by militias, for enslavement and subsequent sale or ransom.[45] In 1988, the Anti-Slavery Society brought this and other evidence to the notice of the United Nations Working Group on Contemporary Forms of Slavery. The government of Sudan, while denying that slavery or forced labor existed in the country, agreed to allow a fact-finding visit by representatives of the Anti-Slavery Society. The coup of June 1989 intervened, and the new NIF regime refused to cooperate further.

Evidence of slavery, even of public auctions, continued to accumulate. At Manyeil in May 1994, an auction was held at which 150 children were sold. One child, a girl captured in the late 1980s at the age of seven, had been beaten and forced by her master in Darfur to work seven days a week. A Dinka bought her for a rifle and a cow, in order to obtain her freedom. In March 1995, more than three hundred women and children were abducted in a raid on the Nuba village of Dere; many were then taken to market in El Lagowa, elsewhere in the Nuba Mountains. In the same month, a joint army and militia raid in Bahr El-Ghazal, the southwest region neighboring the Central African Republic, enslaved 282 Dinka, of whom 48 were children. Some of the children, put up for sale at three different markets, were bought back by their families, and some others managed to escape and return home.[46]

The Dinka people in the northeast of Bahr El-Ghazal have been the primary target of slaving, and the main slavers have been government-armed militias, drawn from among the cattle-raising, Arabic-speaking Baggara people, who live in the neighboring regions of Kordofan and Darfur. The racial and religious prejudices that have long sustained such raiding continue, although they are now "clearly manipulated by the central government for its own ends."[47]

Journalists from the *Baltimore Sun*, who visited Sudan in 1996 to investigate slavery there, reported that "the masters themselves are mainly poor subsistence herders or farmers, scratching a living from a harsh land, using slaves for sexual or domestic purposes if they are girls, or the lowliest tasks if they are boys."[48] The slaves are regarded as property and may be sold, bartered, or given away; they are treated to frequent beatings, and sexual exploitation, of males as well as females, is "commonplace."[49]

Three years later, *The New York Times* published an article by A. M. Rosenthal that reported the continuing engagement to slavery and a slave trade: "The train pulls in and the refugees are herded out. Then they are sold to waiting merchants, into slavery. Slavery, not forced labor or some such euphemism . . . They were captured and sold in Sudan by government soldiers and militias . . . The number in Sudan can roughly be estimated—tens of thousands. Only owners take precise slave-counts."[50]

In December 1999, the Swiss-based aid organization Christian Solidarity International (CSI) "redeemed" 5,514 slaves during an eight-day visit by its representatives to Sudan, at an average payment of $50 a slave. These redemptions brought to more than twenty thousand the number of slaves freed by CSI since it commenced its purchase program in 1995.[51]

At the time of the military coup in 1989, more than one million people from areas of conflict or famine in southern and western Sudan had taken refuge mainly in Khartoum and in other northern cities. Many of them were not Muslims; most were women, children, and the elderly. Some had managed to build mud-brick dwellings on the fringes of the capital. Others lived in shacks made of cardboard and sacking, in squatter camps on wasteland or rubbish dumps. In August 1989, the government launched a campaign to clear the capital of this social and economic problem. The Minister of Housing for Khartoum State described the people involved as "an environmental hazard."[52] However, if some form of urban ethnic cleansing was a factor, and probably the dominant one—most of the refugees were black—there were other political and economic purposes behind the government's action. According to *Sudan's Invisible Citizens*:

> The present government of Sudan has regularly distributed land to the members of the NFL and its supporters, army officers, businessmen and professionals such as doctors, lawyers, engineers and agriculturalists at nominal prices. It has also distributed land to trade unionists, helping to buy their quiescence. All Sudanese who are in employment aspire to build their own house, and obtaining a plot of land

is the essential first step. Manipulating the land issue has proved to be a political master stroke by the government.[53]

While proclaiming that resettlement would only be undertaken on a voluntary basis, the authorities resorted to methods resembling those used in South Africa against blacks during the era of apartheid. Police and security forces, accompanied by bulldozers, irrupted into the squatter camps, sometimes at night, to demolish shelters and crush any resistance. So-called transit camps, at Jebel Aulia forty kilometers south of Khartoum, and on "a dry and wind-swept site" twelve kilometers west of Omdurman, held the removed squatters. Both camps were reportedly "ill-prepared and grossly inadequate." By late 1992, more than 700,000 people had been expelled from the capital for resettlement, and a further 160,000 had their shelters demolished between August 1993 and July 1994. Some 60,000 were forcibly resettled in the month of July alone.[54]

The majority of these transported refugees were blacks, as were the Nuba people, some of them Muslims, who were forcibly displaced from their homes in the south of Kordofan to "peace villages" in the north of the region. This was essentially a campaign, conducted by both the army and the Popular Defence Force militia, to deny popular support for the rebellion by moving the people themselves to areas under more secure government control. In the process, thousands of Nuba civilians were killed, women raped, women and children abducted, homes burned or demolished, stores of crops and livestock destroyed, to create famine conditions.

In February 1993, the U.N. Commission on Human Rights appointed as Special Rapporteur on Sudan a Hungarian lawyer, Gaspar Biró, who issued his report a year later, in which he cited continuing abuses by rebel forces in zones under their control. The main targets of his indictment, however, were the violations perpetrated by "government agents and officials," including summary executions, systematic torture, and the widespread arbitrary arrest of opponents. He also cited abuses against women and children such as abduction, enslavement, and rape, "carried out by persons acting as agents of the Government or affiliated with the Government."[55] The Sudanese government responded immediately by rejecting the report, attacking the competence, impartiality, and motivation of its author, and denouncing the U.N.'s criticism of Sudan's human rights record as an attempt to manipulate "the noble issue of human rights [to] wage war on Islam."[56]

As the twentieth century drew to a close, the end of the religiously fueled political and racial despotism was not in sight. A peace accord, signed in April 1997 between the government and five southern factions, pledged a referendum on Southern self-determination. But the leading Sudan People's Liberation Movement was not a party to it, and disaffected northern Muslims in the National Democratic Alliance joined the movement confronting the Khartoum regime.

Moreover, leadership of the regime itself moved increasingly from Dr. Hassan al-Turabi, blamed for its failures and unpopularity, to the previously mere figurehead President, Omar Hasan al-Bashir, who dissolved parliament and declared a state of emergency. According to Al Tayib Zain al Abdin, a professor of political science at Khartoum University: "Now, all the senior officers [of the army] are in Bashir's camp. None of them are siding with Tourabi [sic] . . . The people that criticize him are far more conservative than him on the issues of women, and on the rights of non-Muslims."[57]

Issues of racism and "ethnic cleansing" aside, the survival of state-sanctioned black slavery in Mauritania and Sudan today presents a series of crucial challenges. It is a challenge to Islam, in whose name and values the regimes of both states presume or pretend to act. It is a challenge to democratic governments which recognize and assert that their own values are neither safe nor sound in isolation from the rest of humanity. It is a challenge to the authority of the United Nations, whose Universal Declaration of Human Rights is so blatantly being breached. And ultimately, it is a challenge to the redemptive force of experience and memory, without which we may as well not bother with history at all.

Similar challenges came in the last century from a regime in South Africa that based its own version of racism on a deformed religious doctrine. Criticisms and protests by the United Nations and individual governments were ignored, since they were seen as little more than masks for indifference, cynicism, and collaboration. Then, under mounting popular pressure around the world for enforcement measures, the introduction of cumulative international bans on arms, oil, and, decisively, financial credits promoted the retreat of apartheid and, in 1994, the arrival of a nonracial democracy in South Africa. A corresponding movement of popular pressure for enforcement measures to eradicate slavery can scarcely come too soon. It can trace its beginnings back more than two hundred years, to the mobilizing demand for the abolition of the slave trade.

AMERICA'S BLACK MUSLIM BACKLASH

There were undoubtedly Muslim blacks in the United States long before the Black Muslim movement known as the Nation of Islam appeared in the 1930s. Michael Gomez writes: "Given that between 400,000 and 523,000 Africans came to North America during the slave trade, at least 200,000 came from areas influenced by Islam in varying degrees. Muslims may have come to America by the thousands, if not the tens of thousands."[1] A few are known by name and character, such as a certain Balali (Ben Ali), who managed a plantation with some five hundred slaves on the Georgia island of Sapelo, wore a fez and kaftan, observed Muslim feast days, prayed daily facing the east, and led eighty armed slaves in successfully defending the island against a British attack in the War of 1812. But increasing numbers of blacks, both slave and free, came to adopt Christianity, in all its various sects the dominant religion of American society, as they found material in the Bible relevant to their plight, and there seems to be no record of an assertive Muslim presence until 1913.

Islam emerged in a strange new form in Newark, New Jersey, that year, when a black migrant from the South called Timothy Drew founded the "Moorish Holy Science Temple." Black male adherents, redesignated "Moors," were required to have beards, wear the red fez, and were each given an identity card from "Noble Drew Ali, the Prophet." Each card was imprinted with the star and crescent of Islam and the magic number seven. It stated that the bearer worshipped the four prophets—Jesus, Muḥammad, Buddha, and Confucius—and was "a Moslem under the Divine Laws of the Holy Koran of Mecca, Love, Truth, Peace, Freedom, and Justice," with the concluding declaration "I am a citizen of the United States."[2]

The new prophet's inclusion of Jesus among his holy predecessors was doubtless directed to the overwhelming numbers of blacks in the Christian fold, but the essential call was expressly to Islam, whose summons to a community of belief beyond race seems to have had a particular influence on Drew. Indeed, it is likely that Drew's preaching of this message accounted for the success that he had in attracting followers. There was no such demonization of whites as would come to characterize the Nation of Islam, but among the estimated thirty thousand active adherents at "Moorish" temples in the black ghettos of the North, a racial militancy took reactive form. Just as whites, especially in the South, had traditionally forced blacks off the pavement to walk around them in the road, so some "Moors," especially in Chicago, brandished their identity cards and jostled whites off the pavement.

Then, in 1927, Drew mysteriously disappeared. Gilles Kepel writes: "It seems that the sect's leaders became involved in various lucrative activities, making their disciples buy potions, 'pure' foodstuffs, and talismans. The disputes over the control of this business appear to have led to a settling of scores, in the process of which the prophet was murdered. Unless, that is, he died in police custody."[3]

On July 4, 1930, a traveling salesman in silks made his first recorded appearance in the black ghetto of Detroit. He called himself Wallace Fard, and by the end of June 1934, when he, too, mysteriously disappeared, he had attracted some eight thousand local black followers, for a cult known as the Nation of Islam, which accepted him initially as Prophet and subsequently as Savior, or Allah incarnate. Press disclosures, based on FBI files, that he had been born of a white English father and a Maori mother in Hawaii and had spent three years in prison for having dealt in heroin, were to make little impact on the faithful. The Messiah was the message.

Fard called on American blacks to turn from their "Caucasian slave-masters" and accept their descent from blacks of the Arabian Shabazz tribe, with Islam as their true religion and Arabic as their true language. They were to abandon their "slave names" for Muslim equivalents; entrust the education of their children to a "University of Islam"—in practice, a primary school—where they would acquire their own knowledge rather than that of "the Caucasian devils"; abandon the "poisoned food" given them by whites for the food eaten in Africa; and practice marital fidelity. Not least, in rejecting American nationality, they were to have their own flag, a white crescent and star on a red background, bearing the words "Equality, Justice, Liberty, Islam."

In 1932, a member of the movement, influenced by one of Fard's prophecies that each adherent needed to sacrifice four "Caucasian devils" in order to "go home to Mecca," stabbed a co-tenant during a voodoo-type rite.[4] This attracted the attention of the authorities to the movement itself, and Fard vanished from public view. Subsequent claims of sightings were uncorroborated. Leadership of the Nation then passed to an unemployed black migrant from Georgia to Detroit called Elijah Poole.

Poole had met Fard in 1931 and would subsequently state: "I recognized him to be God in person and that is what he said he was, but he forbade me to tell anyone else. I was a student of the Bible. I recognized in him the person the Bible predicted would come two thousand years after Jesus' death."[5] Even though he changed his "slave name" of Poole to that of Muhammad and was appointed by Fard as "Minister of the Nation of Islam," the new leader found that his succession was disputed, and he was arrested in May 1942 for dodging the wartime draft. In prison until 1946, he used his time there to recruit black fellow prisoners to the movement.

Elijah Muhammad espoused various doctrines, from demonology to diet—published in 1965 as *Message to the Blackman in America*—whose authority derived from his proclaimed status as "Messenger of Allah." The whole body of accumulated scientific knowledge might deny some of his teachings, such as the descent of blacks from the tribe of Shabazz, which had arrived with the creation of the earth sixty-six trillion years ago. However, those to whom the message was directed, essentially the deprived and disparaged blacks in the ghettos, could find solace and pride in the assurance that it was whites who had walked on four legs and climbed trees at a time when blacks were highly civilized. Similarly, the assertion that the characteristic sexual promiscuity of whites had led to the rape of black slave women in America involved an intellectually indefensible demonization, but nonetheless evoked acceptance by expressing a historical black grievance.

This inversion of primitive attributes ascribed by racist whites to blacks was accompanied by an appropriation of the Biblical clothes in which black Christianity had for so long dressed its agony and hope. Elijah Muhammad declared: "Separation of the so-called Negroes from their slavemasters' children is a must. It is the only solution to our problem. It was the only solution, according to the Bible, for Israel and the Egyptians, and it will prove to be the only solution for America and her slaves, whom she mockingly calls her citizens without granting citizenship."[6] The Universal Negro Improvement Association, which had been founded in 1914 by Marcus Garvey and attracted close to six million paid-up members in the United States, had called for a return to Africa. Elijah Muhammad called for the eventual establishment of a separate black state in North America. This ultimately segregationist project was in direct conflict with the traditional objective of integration for which the established black leadership, including the influential black Christian preachers, spoke and worked.

Not surprisingly, the Nation of Islam remained a relatively insignificant sect. And then it acquired a young convert in Malcolm Little. He had been six years old when his militant father was killed, possibly lynched, in Lansing, Michigan, and fourteen years old when his mother was committed to a state mental hospital in Kalamazoo. Sharply intelligent, he had done well at school but had been discouraged there in his declared ambition to become a lawyer. His teacher, mindful of racial confinements in the land of the free, suggested that he would be better advised to become apprenticed to a carpenter. Malcolm would subsequently see in this the guiding hand of Allah, without which "I would probably be among the city's professional black bourgeoisie, sipping cocktails, and passing myself off as a community spokesman for and leader of the suffering black masses, while my primary concern would be to grab a few more crumbs from the groaning board of the two-faced whites with whom they're begging to 'integrate.' "[7]

Instead, he drifted into the ghetto hustler culture of robbery, pimping, and drugs, first in the Roxbury area of metropolitan Boston and then in Harlem, in New York City. In 1946, at the age of twenty, he was arrested and subsequently convicted of theft and receiving stolen property. He was sentenced to seven years in prison, and while there he learned from a fellow prisoner about Elijah Muhammad and the Nation of Islam. He marked his new life by refusing to eat pork in the canteen and by reading whatever came his way in a search for understanding. Released after six years for good conduct, he applied to Elijah Muhammad for a new name to replace his slave one. He was given an "X" until deemed worthy to have a Muslim name; and when he was finally deemed worthy, he decided to keep the X as symbolic both of his "ex"-slave descent and of the anonymous condition in which the ghetto blacks were reduced by white racism.

Personable, eloquent, and angry, Malcolm X made a powerful preacher, attracting tens of thousands of new followers to the Nation of Islam.[8] He was also important to the Nation in developing its paramilitary sector, the Fruit of Islam, whose members acted as stewards at rallies. In April 1957, when a Black Muslim follower was hit on the head by police and taken unconscious to the police station in Harlem, Malcolm X and Fruit of Islam members besieged the building until the follower was released and given medical treatment. In the same year, he was rewarded for his achievements by being made Elijah's national representative.

The time was right for his rise to national prominence. In December 1955, a black boycott against segregation on local buses had begun in Montgomery, Alabama, and this developed rapidly into a civil rights movement that confronted racial segregation in various forms across the South. Essential features of the movement were the militant engagement of young blacks, especially students; the active involvement of radical young whites, again especially students, from the North; a coalition leadership, mainly drawn from the Southern black churches, which came to be dominated by Montgomery's Martin Luther King, Jr.; and, crucially, an express commitment to nonviolence.

Malcolm X attacked this commitment, with its "mealy-mouth, beg-in, wait-in, plead-in kind of action."[9] And he did not spare those who commanded it: "Anytime a shepherd, a pastor, teaches you and me not to run from the white man, and, at the same time, teaches us not to fight the white man, he's a traitor to you and me."[10] The violence of his language, often deliberately employed to reflect the violent nature of American society, increased both his appeal to urban blacks, in particular the young, and the national attention he received.

Pressed by some black leaders to speak less emotionally, he replied: "When a man is hanging on a tree and he cries out, should he cry out unemotionally? When a man is sitting on a hot stove and he tells you how it feels to be there, is he supposed to speak without emotion? . . . But when a man is on a hot stove, he says, 'I'm coming up. I'm getting up.' Violently or nonviolently doesn't even enter into the picture—I'm coming up, do you understand?"[11]

Such language did not go down well with the Southern pastors, who rebuffed his suggestion that he join the mass demonstrations of 1963 in Birmingham, Alabama. Asked his views on the campaign and its leadership, he replied: "Martin Luther King is a chump, not a champ."[12]

Yet there were growing strains with Elijah Muhammad, whose lavish style of living and virtual harem of women struck the more ascetic Malcolm X as incompatible with the moral mission of the prophet. In turn, Elijah was increasingly disturbed by Malcolm's propensity to speak in such confrontational terms as to threaten a repressive response. Indeed, almost certainly with Malcolm in mind, he ordered Nation of Islam ministers to make no comment when President Kennedy was assassinated on November 22, 1963. At the beginning of December, approached by a reporter to comment on the assassination, Malcolm X responded: "[I] never foresaw that the chickens would come home to roost so soon. Being an old farm boy myself, chickens coming home to roost never did make me sad. They've always made me glad."[13]

When Elijah ordered him to make no public comment on anything, Malcolm X ignored the ban, and in late January 1964 he was dismissed as Elijah's national representative and minister of the Harlem temple. By early March, with reports of plots inside the Nation of Islam to kill him, Malcolm had decided on an outright break from the movement. While still expressing his support for Elijah's policy of separatism, he resigned from the Nation of Islam and formed a new group, the Muslim Mosque, Inc. Meanwhile, as discontent with Elijah's conduct and leadership, involving even members of his own family, fueled substantial numbers of resignations, the climate of reactive violence in the Nation was such that some dissenting members, including Elijah's own grandson, Hasan Harrieff, sought protection by the FBI.

Malcolm X went on two trips to Africa. The first involved a pilgrimage to Mecca, where he was profoundly impressed by the sight of Muslim pilgrims with white complexions and blue eyes. Converted to "the brotherhood of man," he denounced Elijah as a "faker" whose "distorted religious concoction" and "racist philosophy" in the name of authentic Islam had been used to fool the gullible.[14]

Louis Farrakhan, Nation of Islam minister at the Boston temple, wrote in the Nation's newspaper, *Muhammad Speaks*, of December 4, 1964: "Only those who wish to be led to hell, or to their doom, will follow Malcolm. The die is set, and Malcolm shall not escape . . . Such a man as Malcolm is worthy of death, and would have met death if it had not been for Muhammad's confidence in Allah for victory over his enemies." On February 21, 1965, at a meeting in Harlem of the Organization of Afro-American Unity which he had recently founded, Malcolm was shot and died soon afterward. Three members of the Nation were arrested and subsequently convicted of the murder.

Louis Eugene Walcott, the future Louis Farrakhan, was born in 1933 in the Bronx to a black mother, Sarah Mae Manning, who had immigrated from St. Kitts, and a light-skinned, possibly white, Jamaican immigrant father whom she had married but who had abandoned her once and would do so again. (The boy was conceived during a brief return by her husband and was named after Mae's lover, Louis Walcott, rather than his real father, Percival Clarke.) Paradoxically so proud of his light skin that she would scrub the boy vigorously when bathing him, in the belief that this would whiten him further, Mae was also a follower of Marcus Garvey, and might have communicated some awareness of American black nationalism to her son.

Gene, as he came to be called, was a gifted child. He went to one of Boston's leading public secondary schools, Boston Latin School, where entry depended on grades, and showed musical as well as athletic abilities. However, color imposed limits, and the family was poor. By the age of sixteen, he was earning money, under the name of "The Charmer," by singing Caribbean songs, mainly calypsos, in Boston's black nightclubs. Offered a scholarship, Gene went in September 1950 to the all-black Winston-Salem Teachers' College in North Carolina, where he soon experienced the cruder affronts of segregation. Three years later, having fallen in love with a Roxbury woman, Betsy Ross, whom he had made pregnant, he married her, abandoned college, and was soon successful again as an entertainer, now named "Calypso Gene."

Then, in February 1955, on tour in Chicago, he heard Elijah Muhammad speak at a Nation of Islam rally. He and Betsy both enrolled as members on the spot, though it was only when he heard Malcolm X speak, a few months later, that he decided to devote his life accordingly. As he would later declare, he had been repelled by the "hypocrisy" of organized Christianity, with its failure to confront the injustices suffered by blacks: "I went looking not for a new religion, but for new leadership that would address the concerns of black people. And I found Malcolm X and Elijah Muhammad. I was not interested in changing my religion, but they were Muslims and they spoke a truth I could identify with."[15]

Louis "Gene" Walcott, now Louis X, was assigned to Boston as a captain in the Fruit of Islam, but within a few months was made a minister. After working from various makeshift premises, by May 1957 he had acquired a permanent home for Temple No. 11 and was soon, with the help of speaking visits from Malcolm X, attracting numerous followers. He also cut a record with a calypso beat entitled "A White Man's Heaven Is A Black Man's Hell," which became the Nation's anthem and did much to advance his own reputation.

His loyalty to Elijah Muhammad remained absolute, even when, in 1963, Malcolm informed him of Elijah's widespread infidelities, reports of which were already circulating among blacks in Chicago. In May 1965, some three months after Malcolm's murder, he was appointed minister of Temple No. 7 in New York City and given the Muslim name of Abdul Haleem Farrakhan, though it was as Louis Farrakhan that he chose to be known. Two years later, he became Elijah's national representative. Meanwhile, violent acts of retribution from Nation of Islam loyalists continued. In 1973, three infants and a ten-year-old child were among the seven killed in the Washington, D.C., home of a Hanafi Muslim who had led a breakaway group from the Nation.

Far from discouraging such violence, Farrakhan seemed to stoke it. The day before one of those arraigned for the Hanafi Muslim murders was due to testify against his fellow conspirators, Farrakhan warned on the radio: "In the ranks of the black people today there are younger men and women who have no forgiveness in them for traitors and stool pigeons. And they will execute you, as soon as your identity is known."[16] The targeted "stool pigeon" reportedly heard the broadcast, refused to testify, and was found the next day hanging in his jail cell.

On February 26, 1975, Elijah Muhammad died. Farrakhan apparently expected to become the new leader of the Nation, but it was Elijah's son Wallace who succeeded instead. What followed was a full-blown reformation. Seeking to end the corrupt practices with which the Nation had become associated, Wallace ordered ministers to abstain from business operations. He canceled the dress code of jacket and tie for men and neck-to-ankle dresses for women. He renamed the Harlem temple after Malcolm X. He scrapped the demand for a separate black state. He opened membership in the Nation to whites and, on October 18, 1976, renamed the Nation of Islam the World Community of al-Islam in the West. "We're a . . . community that encompasses everybody. We have Caucasians and Orientals who are members and we are all just Muslims."[17]

Wallace was clearly seeking to bring the Black Muslim movement into the Islamic mainstream. It all proved too much for Farrakhan, who formally left the World Community in December 1977. Three months later, he announced that he would resurrect the Nation of Islam. If blacks continue "singing the lullaby of integration," he declared, "we will find ourselves dead under the heels of racism in the United States."[18] He took to lecturing around the country, establishing study groups as the basis for new temples, and by 1981 had drawn six thousand people to his Nation of Islam rally on Savior Day (February 26, the day usually chosen to mark the anniversary of Fard's birth).

Fard was restored to his status as Allah incarnate, after Wallace's disposal of that doctrine. Elijah Muhammad was translated from Messenger to Messiah, already resurrected, alive, and well, and ready for an imminent return. Indeed, according to Farrakhan, Elijah did not die naturally but was murdered, in a conspiracy that involved the U.S. government, unnamed members of his family, and Arabs who opposed him for not being an orthodox Muslim. Farrakhan himself was now Apostle and Prophet.[19]

Whatever the attraction of this theology, Farrakhan made his main impact with his rhetoric. He continued forcefully to attack white racism, but lashed out, too, at a growing black middle class that had abandoned the social decay and crime of the inner cities for the insulated suburbs. In 1979, addressing a conference of the National Black United Fund, he denounced those "bourgeois blacks" who had become "house niggers" in industry or government, more concerned with their proximity to power than with the many millions in America's black ghettos: "Come down from your false mountain that makes you unjustly proud of your little accomplishments and know that until all have gotten out of the valley, you have not reached the mountain."[20]

It was not so much this that brought him to national prominence as his particular targeting of Jews. Prime victims of religious and racial persecution through the ages, Jews had long been disproportionately represented among American whites opposed to racism, providing financial assistance to the National Association for the Advancement of Colored People (NAACP), and rallying as students to the civil rights movement. This had not protected them from the traditional charges that Jews exploited and deepened black poverty through the shops or apartments that some of them owned and then leased in the ghettos.[21]

The dynamic of Black Muslim anti-Semitism was more complex, and owed much to traditional religious and secular scapegoating in white Western culture. This involved, first, the charge against the Jews of having killed Christ and, then, of their being social parasites as practitioners of usury. On this widely disreputable base, Black Muslim leaders had elaborated old charges and provided new ones.

Elijah Muhammad, while claiming to sympathize with Jews for having been "roasted like peanuts" in the Holocaust, added that they were draining money from black ghettos with their stores and roach-infested slum buildings. A single Jew was "smarter than a roomful of white men. He can spend a quarter and make a million dollars. Or he can rob you blind while he's telling you a . . . joke." And Malcolm X attacked the skill of Jews in being able to sap "the very life-blood of the so-called Negro to maintain . . . Israel, its armies and its continued aggression against our brothers in the East."[22]

It was under the leadership of Farrakhan, however, that the Nation of Islam took to demonizing the Jews with inventive fervor. Jews were accused of having injected black babies with the AIDS virus.[23] They were held responsible for having masterminded the slave trade in blacks. Indeed, the Nation of Islam peddled *The Secret Relationship between Blacks and Jews*, a 330-page revision of history produced by its own Historical Research Department, to support the accusation. It even peddled copies of *The Protocols of the Elders of Zion*, a notorious forgery from Czarist Russia purporting to prove a Jewish conspiracy for taking command of the world. That this had been a mainstay of Nazi propaganda was apparently no discouragement.

Then in November 1993, Khallid Abdul Muhammad, the Nation of Islam's national spokesman and a favorite of Farrakhan's, went on the rampage in a speech at Kean College, New Jersey. Jews, he claimed, already controlled the world. Their supposed compassion for blacks in the civil rights movement had merely been a way of using them as "cannon fodder." And if six million of them had been exterminated by Hitler, it was because they had taken over Germany and "undermined the very fabric of society." Addressing the survivors, he declared: "You are a European strain of people who crawled around on all fours, . . . eatin' juniper roots and eatin' each other." Finally, in a tirade against whites, he looked forward to the slaughter of every one of them in South Africa.[24]

On February 2, 1994, the U.S. Senate, by 97–0, voted for the first time in its history to condemn a speech as "false, anti-Semitic, racist, divisive, repugnant, and a disservice to all Americans." On the same day, the Congressional Black Caucus repudiated its covenant with the Nation of Islam.[25] Farrakhan responded by condemning the manner of the speech rather than the matter, and deprived Khallid of his titles without expelling him from the Nation of Islam. Sixteen months later he would reinstate Khallid as a minister.

The more outrageous his remarks, the greater the publicity Farrakhan attracted, from denunciations in the press to interviews on television. What was seen as white hostility only commended him to many blacks, resentful at the record and residual force of white racism. Shortly after the press conference at which he had repudiated Khallid's remarks while repeating some of the charges they carried, a poll of blacks found that 70 percent of them believed that Farrakhan was saying what the country needed to hear; 63 percent believed that he had spoken the truth. More than half—53 percent—considered him a model for black youth, compared with 34 percent who considered him a racist or bigot.[26]

Yet for all the following that Farrakhan could attract and mobilize by demonizing whites—in particular, Jews—he was more rational and productive in recognizing and declaring that the black victims of white racism also victimized themselves. Like other Black Muslim leaders before him, he denounced the drug taking and dealing, the violence of crime and gang warfare, and the sexual promiscuity that poverty and rejection, rage and despair, promoted. The demand that blacks should reform themselves, in a commitment to regaining a sense of their own value and asserting their dignity, had been part of the message from the Nation of Islam. Farrakhan now sought to express and advance this message in spectacular form.

He called for a Million Man March by blacks to Washington, D.C., on October 16, 1995, for a Day of Atonement at which they would repent their shortcomings and commit themselves to a new future. The civil rights March on Washington in 1963, when Martin Luther King, Jr., made his celebrated "I Have a Dream" speech, had attracted an estimated quarter of a million blacks and whites. The Million Man March drew an estimated 400,000 blacks. Many, probably most of them, came not for the Nation of Islam, but to affirm their collective dignity. It said much for the failure of American society to deliver on its promise of inclusion in the thirty-two years separating the marches.

Farrakhan did not rise to the occasion. In contrast to King, whose speech in 1963 had been eloquent and short, he spoke for two and a half hours. He lost so many of his listeners in a labyrinth of historical references and numerological predictions that barely a third remained till the end to join in the pledge of black men to abstain from violence, drugs, sexual and verbal abuse, in helping to restore their community. Nonetheless, the March had been of his making, and the very success of its numbers augmented his credit among many blacks.

In the first two months of 1996, Farrakhan went on a so-called World Friendship Tour to countries in Africa and the Middle East. The reported pledge of $1 billion to him from Libya's ruler, Muammar Khadafi, to mobilize "oppressed . . . blacks, Arabs, Muslims, and red Indians" for influencing the outcome of the U.S. presidential election later that year, and Farrakhan's declaration in Iran that God would destroy America by the hands of Muslims, led the State Department to accuse him of "cavorting with dictators" in Libya and Iran.[27] One black journalist, Clarence Page, pointedly asked why Farrakhan had paid no heed to Arab enslavement of blacks in Sudan and the reported trucking of such women and children to Libya in 1993.[28]

It is certainly curious that the Black Muslim leadership in America ignores the continuing commitment to black slavery and oppression in Mauritania and Sudan. Instead, it targets Jews for their historical role in having masterminded the slave trade. In fact, there is no evidence whatsoever for this charge.

Reliable records on the Islamic trade are relatively sparse, but there is one rich exception. In 1890, a treasure trove of documents was discovered in a Cairo *geniza*, or storeroom attached to a synagogue. There, documents of various kinds had been placed, on the assumption that any of them might contain the name of God and accordingly should not be destroyed but be left to the course of nature. In the climate of Cairo, this course was one of preservation rather than decay.

Among the writings were letters, court records, contracts, accounts, dating from the tenth to the thirteenth century inclusive and emanating generally from Jews then living in the Islamic countries of the Mediterranean region. The documents were dispersed among libraries in various parts of the world, but in 1954 a scholar, S. D. Goitein, conceived the idea of drawing on them for a study of Jewish social history and Islamic civilization in the relevant area and period. The documents essentially reflected the lives and dealings of the Jewish middle class, and some of the material involved the ownership and treatment of slaves, mainly from black Africa. As Goitein, in his study of the documents, reports:

> It should be noted that none of the persons involved in the many transactions mentioned . . . seems to have been a

professional slave-trader. The term nowhere appears in the
relevant documents. The first proprietor of 'Musk' [a slave
girl recorded in the documents as having been sold three
times] . . . was a perfumer, the second a wax-maker and the
third a housewife. The same holds true of all other Geniza
documents dealing with the subject. In the thousands of
letters, accounts, and other papers dealing with business
(with one possible exception) I have not found any reference to the sale of slaves (in the plural) by Jews. Thus, I
can only confirm the opinion expressed by David Neustadt
(now: Ayalon) thirty years ago, that, during the classical Geniza period the Jews had no share in the slave trade.[29]

Goitein accepts that the Geniza period, for all its reach across four
centuries, does not contain the whole story. This is clear from his remark
that "the slave trade, in the ninth century still partly in Jewish hands, is
not represented in the 'classical' Geniza at all."[30] It would not be surprising if Jewish merchants had, at some periods in some places, been involved in a lawful activity of such economic and social importance.
What is surprising is that during such a long period of commercial prosperity and in such a central part of Islam as the Geniza documents
record, Jewish merchants were apparently not traders in slaves. It does
tend to suggest that Jewish involvement in the Islamic black slave trade
was relatively minor as well as intermittent.

Nor is there evidence that it was a very different case in the Atlantic
slave trade. Certainly, Jews were involved as traders, perhaps mainly in
the commercial connections between the Netherlands and South America. But anyone who has studied the Atlantic slave trade and slavery in
the Americas knows that it was overwhelmingly dominated by Christian
merchants.[31] To the Nation of Islam's anti-Semitic tirade in *The Secret
Relationship between Blacks and Jews*, the American scholar Henry Louis
Gates, Jr., head of the African-American Studies Department at Harvard
University, has given this reply: "American Jewish merchants accounted
for less than two per cent of all the African slaves imported into the New
World . . . all the Jewish slave traders combined bought and sold fewer
slaves than the single gentile firm of Franklin and Armfield."[32]

Nor is there evidence in any of Islam's sacred writings to support the grotesque racist anthropology propagated by the Black Muslims. Again, the overwhelming evidence is to the contrary. Jews as well as Christians were conceded a special relationship with Islam. Furthermore, the collective demonization of races or colors is wholly alien to Islamic doctrines as expressed in the Koran itself. The demonization of the Jews has its closest relative in the doctrines of Nazism. And that the Nation of Islam should be associated with those doctrines is not merely disreputable. In the shadow of the Holocaust, it is an abomination.

Such rampaging bigotry is to be regretted as well as denounced. For the Black Muslim movement has also been constructive. Black children, with a record of poor achievement at other ghetto schools, have performed markedly better at schools run or influenced by the movement, where they have been taught to take pride in their black cultural heritage.[33] By challenging the deprivation and disparagement in the decay of the ghettos with an assertion of dignity and purpose, Black Muslims have been more successful than the penal system in confronting drugs and gang warfare. In the aftermath of the Los Angeles riots in May 1992, for instance, the leaders of two young black gangs signed a truce at a local mosque and subsequently explained in an interview for a radio program: "The Muslims come and talk to you as a person. They respect you as you are. They don't look down on you."[34] The one known positive effect of American prisons on black crime, real or presumed, has been their role as recruitment grounds for the Nation of Islam.

Furthermore, the Black Muslims, for all their excesses, have been most effective in drawing attention to the continuing plight of many black Americans, victims of a racial discrimination that survives not only in the functioning of inherited social inequalities but also in the continuing impact of social prejudice. It is challenging, by any standards, that while blacks constituted 9.7 percent of the total population in 1930 and 12.1 percent in 1990, their share of the population in prison rose from 22.4 percent in 1930 to 45.3 percent in 1986.[35]

Deprivation as a cause of crime has remained all too relevant. In the wake of Lyndon Johnson's War on Poverty, which provided new opportunities, especially in government service, for blacks to enter the middle class, economic changes hit hardest the blue-collar jobs in the cities on which black male employment had traditionally relied.

According to Elliot Currie: "Between 1970 and 1980, New York City gained almost 275,000 managerial, professional, technical, and administrative jobs, but lost over 360,000 in blue-collar manufacturing, clerical work, and sales—a net loss of over 95,000 jobs in the central city." Between 1950 and 1970, there was a considerable growth in the urban employment of blacks who had not completed twelve years of education. After 1970, the urban industrial demand for poorly educated blacks all but disappeared. Currie adds: "In Philadelphia, for example, the number of jobs lost in the seventies for blacks without a high-school diploma almost equaled the number added in the previous *two* decades."[36]

The statistics also suggest that the judicial system and the conduct of police reveal a functionally racial bias. Black men and women account for 47 percent of all those who await trial in local jails or are serving short terms. They comprise 40.1 percent of the prisoners under sentence of death.[37] As Andrew Hacker records: "A study prepared in 1987 for a Supreme Court appeal found that murderers who killed white people faced a ten times greater chance of a death sentence compared with murderers who had black victims. When circumstances such as the ferocity of the crime and the social status of the victim were held constant, the prospect for the death penalty was still four times higher when the victim was white."[38] In the so-called tragic mistakes, when law-abiding people are killed in error by law-enforcement officers, the victims are almost always blacks.[39]

In April 2000, a report entitled *And Justice for Some*, prepared by the National Council on Crime and Delinquency and partly funded by the U.S. Department of Justice, found damning evidence of effective discrimination in the treatment of young blacks by the judicial system. Black teenagers are six times more likely to be jailed for their first offense than are white teenagers. In cases of violent crime, young blacks are nine times more likely to be jailed; and in the case of drug-related offenses, *forty-eight* times more likely. Black youths represent 15 percent of the under-eighteen population, but 26 percent of all under-eighteens arrested and 58 percent of the youth population in adult prisons. White youths convicted of violent offenses are jailed for an average of 193 days; black youths jailed for an average of 254 days. Julian Borger of *The Guardian* writes: "Proponents of tough juvenile sentencing have argued in the past that this imbalance is due to a higher crime rate among minority communities, but the new report suggests that an unequal treatment by the justice system is the more important factor."[40]

When Farrakhan denounces the reality of racism behind the ritual tributes that white politicians pay to the greatest society on earth, he reaches beyond the ghettos to blacks who have not changed their color on settling in the suburbs. And when he chides the black middle class with the reminder "know that until all have gotten out of the valley, you have not reached the mountain," the rest of America would do well to listen, too.

But there is a great deal more to the Black Muslim movement than that. In her recent book *The Battle for God*, Karen Armstrong, writing of Jewish, Christian, and Muslim fundamentalists, remarks that they "have neglected the more tolerant, inclusive, and compassionate teachings and have cultivated theologies of rage, resentment, and revenge."[41]

It is this that explains two curious features of the Black Muslim backlash. First, the survival of black slavery in parts of Islam is not condemned or even recognized, because it is outside the historical confines of the Atlantic Trade and the survival of racism in American society. Second, the memorialization of the Jewish holocaust, which should be welcomed since it promotes an awareness of the hell to which racism can lead, is belittled or scorned because there is no comparable memorialization of the black holocaust in the history of slavery.

What rage, resentment, and revenge have developed in the Black Muslim movement is a racism to confront racism. This defies the Koran, which expressly condemns racism without qualification. It dishonors the history of an Islam that, for all the engagement to slavery, the existence of color prejudice, and the conduct of rogue regimes, has overall avoided the institutionalized racism of the Christian West. And it betrays the longing and struggle of blacks, in their diaspora of slavery and prejudice, not for the freedom to practice their own racism, but for the redemption of freedom itself.

∩OTES

Monetary Values. I gladly express my gratitude here to Spink & Son, of London, for sharing their knowledge of coinage at all times and places, and to Kath Begley at the Bank of England, who has provided me with pound–dollar exchange rates and the current equivalent in purchasing power for a pound at any year that the book required.

ONE: CONTRASTS
1. Isma'īl R. al Fārūqī and Lois Lamyā' al Fārūqī, *The Cultural Atlas of Islam* (New York: Macmillan, 1986), p. 210.
2. Elie Kedourie, *Politics in the Middle East* (Oxford and New York: Oxford University Press, 1992), p. 26.

TWO: OUT OF ARABIA
1. Patricia Crone, *Meccan Trade and the Rise of Islam* (Oxford: Basil Blackwell, 1987).
2. *ibid.*, p. 170.
3. *ibid.*, p. 194.
4. *ibid.*, p. 241.
5. *ibid.*, p. 236.
6. Fārūqī and Fārūqī, *op. cit.*, pp. 112–16.
7. The Koran, trans. Arthur J. Arberry, The World's Classics, Oxford University Press, 1983, p. 413.
8. *ibid.*, p. 538.
9. Philip. K. Hitti, *The Arabs* (Chicago: Henry Regnery Co., A Gateway Edition, 1967), p. 40.
10. Fārūqī and Fārūqī, *op. cit.*, pp. 107–8.

11. Mark Huband, *Warriors of the Prophet* (Boulder, Colo.: Westview Press, 1998), p. 187, note 21.
12. Ira M. Lapidus, *A History of Islamic Societies* (Cambridge: Cambridge University Press, 1988), p. 38.
13. Robert Irwin, *Night and Horses and the Desert* (London: Allen Lane, The Penguin Press, 1999), p. 65.

THREE: IMPERIAL ISLAM

1. Maurice Lombard, *The Golden Age of Islam* (Amsterdam and Oxford: North Holland Publishing Co., 1975), pp. 105–14.
2. *ibid.*, pp. 115–16.
3. S. D. Goitein, *A Mediterranean Society*, vol. 1, *Economic Foundations* (Berkeley, Los Angeles, and London: University of California Press, 1967), p. 97.
4. *ibid.*, p. 202.
5. Philip. D. Curtin, *Cross-Cultural Trade in World History* (Cambridge: Cambridge University Press, 1984), pp. 104–5.
6. *ibid.*
7. Lombard, *op. cit.*, pp. 119, 129, 135.
8. H. van Werveke, "The Rise of the Towns," in *The Cambridge History of Europe*, vol. III, eds. M. M. Postan, E. E. Rich, and Edward Miller (Cambridge: Cambridge University Press, 1971), pp. 38–39.
9. Goitein, *op. cit.*, p. 252.
10. *ibid.*, pp. 79, 152.
11. *ibid.*, pp. 95–97.
12. Richard W. Bullet, *Islam: The View from the Edge* (New York: Columbia University Press, 1994), p. 131.
13. Lombard, *op. cit.*, pp. 154–56.
14. Lapidus, *op. cit.*, p. 346.
15. Hitti, *op. cit.*, pp. 214–15.
16. T. Bianquis, "Egypt from the Arab Conquest until the end of the Fatimid State," in *General History of Africa*, vol. III, *Africa from the Seventh to the Eleventh Century*, ed. M. El Fasi (Heinemann, Calif.: UNESCO, 1988), pp. 180–87.
17. Hitti, *op. cit.*, p. 220.
18. Max Rodenbeck, *Cairo: The City Victorious* (London: Picador, 1998), pp. 102–3.
19. Hitti, *op. cit.*, p. 247.
20. Geoffrey Barraclough, ed., *The Times Atlas of World History* (London: Times Books, 1978), pp. 134–35, 138–39, 172–73.
21. Curtin, *op. cit.*, p. 107.
22. *ibid.*

FOUR: THE PRACTICE OF SLAVERY

1. *Encylopaedia of Islam*, new ed., vol. 1, A–B, for the entry "ABD" (Leiden: E. J. Brill, 1960), p. 25.
2. *ibid.*, p. 26.

3. I. P. Petruchevsky, *Islam in Iran*, trans. Hubert Evans (London: The Athlone Press, 1985), p. 158.

4. The Koran, trans. Arberry, *op. cit.*, p. 356.

5. *Encyclopaedia of Islam, op. cit.*, p. 26.

6. *ibid.*

7. H. R. Palmer, *The Bornu Sahara and Sudan* (London, 1936), p. 218.

8. John Lewis Burckhardt, *Travels in Nubia*, 2nd ed. (London: John Murray, 1822), p. 328.

9. John Hunwick, "Black Africans in the Mediterranean World: Introduction to a Neglected Aspect of the African Diaspora," in *The Human Commodity: Perspectives of the Trans-Saharan Slave Trade*, ed. Elizabeth Savage (London: Frank Cass, 1992), pp. 12–13.

10. Marshall G. S. Hodgson, *The Expansion of Islam in the Middle Periods*, vol. II of *The Venture of Islam* (Chicago and London: University of Chicago Press, 1974), p. 141.

11. Cited in Hunwick, *op. cit.*, p. 21.

12. Ibn Ḥawqal, *Opus Geographicum*, ed. J. H. Kramers (Leiden, 1939), p. 110. Lombard, *op. cit.*, provides on p. 197 a map that places a castration center close to Cordoba.

13. *Ibn Battuta: Travels in Asia and Africa, 1325–1354* (London: Routledge & Kegan Paul, 1984), p. 336.

14. Oscar Lenz, *Timbouctou. Voyage au Maroc au Sahara et au Soudan*, vol. I (Paris, 1881), p. 395.

15. Bernard Lewis, *Race and Slavery in the Middle East* (New York and Oxford: Oxford University Press, 1990), p. 59.

16. Hodgson, *op. cit.*, p. 145.

17. *ibid.*, pp. 145–46.

18. According to the tenth-century historian al-Masʿūdī, *Les prairies d'or*, vol. VIII (Paris, 1861–77), p. 58.

19. E. A. Belyaev, *Arabs, Islam and the Caliphate in the Early Middle Ages* (New York and London: Pall Mall, 1969), pp. 240–47.

20. Nehemia Levtzion, "The Western Maghrib and Sudan," in *The Cambridge History of Africa*, vol. 3, ed. Roland Oliver (Cambridge: Cambridge University Press, 1977), p. 447.

21. Daniel Pipes, *Slave Soldiers and Islam: The Genesis of a Military System* (New Haven and London: Yale University Press, 1981), pp. 62–68 and *passim*.

22. *ibid.*, pp. 6–9.

23. Lewis, *op. cit.*, p. 25.

24. *ibid.*, p. 37.

25. *ibid.*, p. 41.

26. *ibid.*

27. Fārūqī and Fārūqī, *op. cit.*, p. 191.

28. Lewis, *op. cit.*, p. 28.

29. *ibid.*, p. 29.

30. I. Hrbek, in *General History of Africa*, vol. III, *op. cit.*, p. 30.

31. Cited in St. Clair Drake, *Black Folk Here and There*, vol. 2 (Los Angeles: University of California, Center for Afro-American Studies, 1990), pp. 56–57. The relevant passage probably comes from Galen's *Commentary on Hippocrates' Airs, Waters, and Places*, which is not extant in the original Greek. Knowledge of the passage itself comes from Mas'ūdī's *Murūj al-Dhahab wa Ma'ādin al-Jawhar*, edited and translated into French by Charles Pellat (Paris, 1962), p. 69.

32. Cited in E.I.J. Rosenthal, *Political Thought in Medieval Islam* (Cambridge: Cambridge University Press, 1958), pp. 154–55.

33. Sā'id al-Andalusī, *Tabaqāt al Umam*, ed. L. Cheiko (Beirut, 1912), p. 9; cited by Lewis, *op. cit.*, pp. 47–48.

34. Ibn Khaldūn, *The Muqaddimah*, trans. F Rosenthal, vol. I (New York: Pantheon, 1958), p. 301.

35. Cited by J. O. Hunwick, "Black Africans in the Islamic World: An Understudied Dimension of the Black Diaspora," *Tarikh*, vol. 5, no. 4 (1978), p. 27.

36. John Lewis Burckhardt, *Travels in Arabia*, vol. I London (1829), pp. 340–42.

37. *ibid.*, p. 429.

38. Burckhardt, *Travels in Nubia, op. cit.*, pp. 278–79.

39. John Laffin, *The Arabs as Master Slavers* (Englewood, N.J.: SBS Publishing, 1982), p. 17.

40. Burckhardt, *Travels in Arabia*, vol. I, *op. cit.*, p. 290.

41. *ibid.*, vol. II, pp. 186–89.

42. Lewis, *op. cit.*, p. 65.

43. H. J. Fisher, "The eastern Maghrib and the central Sudan," in *The Cambridge History of Africa*, ed. Oliver, *op. cit.*, p. 269.

44. See Hunwick, in *The Human Commodity*, ed. Savage, *op. cit.*, p. 35, note 63, for the various sources.

45. *ibid.*, p. 20.

46. Ralph A. Austen, "The Trans-Saharan Slave Trade: A Tentative Census," in *The Uncommon Market: Essays in the Economic History of the Atlantic Slave Trade*, eds. H. A. Gemery and J. S. Hogendorn (New York: Academic Press, 1979), pp. 66–68.

47. Paul E. Lovejoy, *Transformations in Slavery* (Cambridge: Cambridge University Press, 1983), p. 24.

48. *ibid.*, p. 60.

49. *ibid.*, p. 137.

50. Paul E. Lovejoy, "The Impact of the Atlantic Slave Trade on Africa: A Review of the Literature," in *Journal of African History* 30 (1989), p. 358.

51. Raymond Mauvy, *Les Siècles obscurs de l'Afrique Noire* (Paris: Fayard, 1970), cited in *The African Slave Trade from the Fifteenth to the Nineteenth Century* (Paris: UNESCO, 1979), pp. 169–70, 173.

52. Basil Davidson, "Slaves or Captives? Some Notes on Fantasy and Fact," in *Key Issues in the Afro-American Experience*, vol. I, eds. Nathan I. Huggins, Martin Kilson, and Daniel M. Fox (San Diego and New York: Harcourt Brace Jovanovich, 1977), p. 58.

53. *ibid.*, p. 59.

54. *ibid.*

55. Goitein, *op. cit.*, p. 147.

56. Bernard Lewis, "The Invading Crescent," in *The Dawn of African History*, ed. Roland Oliver (Oxford: Oxford University Press, 1961), p. 34.

57. Thomas F. Glick, *Islamic and Christian Spain in the Early Middle Ages* (New Jersey: Princeton University Press, 1979), p. 130.

58. Daniel J. Schroeter, "Slave Markets and Slavery in Moroccan Urban Society," in *The Human Commodity*, ed. Savage, *op. cit.*, pp. 194–95.

59. *ibid.*, p. 193.

60. Edmondo Amicis, *Morocco: Its People and Places* (London, Paris, and New York, 1882), p. 308.

61. Pinon, cited in André Raymond and Gaston Wiet, *Les Marches du Caire* (Cairo: IFADC 1979), p. 225.

62. Antonius Gonzales, *Hierusalemsche Reyse* (Cairo: IFADC 19, 1977), p. 110.

63. W. G. Browne, *Travels in Africa, Egypt and Syria* (London, 1799), p. 298.

64. Foreign Office 84/815 20/1/50.

65. Allan G. B. Fisher and Humphrey J. Fisher, *Slavery and Muslim Society in Africa* (New York: Doubleday, 1971), p. 12, citing Abou Obeid el-Bakri, *Description de 'lAfrique septentrionale*, trans. MacGuckin de Slane (1857, reprinted 1965), p. 317.

66. James Richardson, *Travels in the great desert of Sahara, in the years 1845 and 1846*, vol. I (London, 1848), p. 63.

67. Lovejoy, *Transformations in Slavery, op. cit.*, p. 151.

68. *ibid.*

69. H. J. Fisher, *op. cit.*, p. 270.

70. Lewis, *op. cit.*, p. 84.

71. Austen in *The Human Commodity*, ed. Savage, *op. cit.*, pp. 232–34.

72. Hourst, *Mission hydrographique du Niger*, 1896, cited in Fisher and Fisher, *op. cit.*, p. 93.

73. Gustav Nachtigal, *Sahara und Sudan, Ergebnisse sechsjähriger Reisen in Afrika*, vol. i (Berlin, 1879); vol. ii (Berlin, 1881); vol. iii, (Leipzig 1889). Fisher and Fisher, *op. cit.*, p. 4, ascribe to Nachtigal's book the genesis of their own, and it is their translated citations that are used here and in Chapter 9.

74. Nachtigal, vol. ii, pp. 652–53.

75. *ibid.*, p. 752.

76. *ibid.*, vol. i, pp. 228–29, 368.

77. H. Barth, *Travels and discoveries in north and central Africa*, vol. 2 (London, 1857–58), pp. 143–44.

78. D. Denham and H. Clapperton, *Narrative of travels and discoveries in northern and central Africa in the years 1822, 1823 and 1824* (London, 1826), p. 49.

79. H. Clapperton, *Journal of a second expedition into the interior of Africa with the Journal of Richard Lander from Kano to the seacoast* (London, 1829), p. 292.

80. Joseph Thomson, *To the central African lakes and back*, vol. ii, (1881), pp. 73–74.

81. Heinrich Minutoli, *Reise zum Tempel des Jupiter Ammon . . . 1820 und 1821* (Berlin, 1824), pp. 201–2.

82. Ettore Rossi, *Storia di Tripoli e della Tripolitania* (Rome: Istituto per l' oriente, 1968), p. 316.
83. Lovejoy, *Transformations in Slavery, op. cit.*, p. 317, citing Edmond B. Martin and T.C.I. Ryan, *Kenya Historical Review* 5 (1977), p. 79, on the Indian Ocean trade.
84. *Kitab al-Istiqsa'*, vol. 5 (Casablanca, 1955), pp. 131–34, cited by Hunwick in *Tarikh, op. cit.*, pp. 37ff.

FIVE: THE FARTHER REACHES
1. Cited by Olivia Remie Constable, *Trade and Traders in Muslim Spain* (Cambridge: Cambridge University Press, 1994), p. 6.
2. Joseph Needham, *Science and Civilisation in China*, vol. IV: 3 (Cambridge: Cambridge University Press, 1971), p. 517.
3. Y. Talib, "The African Diaspora in Asia," in *General History of Africa*, vol. III: *Africa from the Seventh to the Eleventh Century*, ed. M. El Fasi, *op. cit.*, pp. 731–32.
4. Entitled *Ping-chou k'otan* and cited in "Geographical Notes on Some Commodities Involved in the Sung Maritime Trade," *Journal of the Malayan Branch of the Royal Asiatic Society* 32, no. 2 (1961), p. 54.
5. Illustrated in Runoko Rashidi, ed., *African Presence in Early Asia* (New Brunswick, N.J.: Transaction Publishers, 1995), p. 141.
6. Cited by Bethwell A. Ogot, "Population movements between East Africa, the Horn of Africa and the neighbouring countries," in *The African Slave Trade from the Fifteenth to the Nineteenth Century* (Paris: UNESCO, 1985), p. 176.
7. Curtin, *op. cit.*, p. 127.
8. Needham, *op. cit.*, vol. III (1959), pp. 556–58.
9. Gervase Mathew, "The Land of Zanj," in *The Dawn of African History*, ed. Roland Oliver, *op. cit.*, p. 50.
10. *ibid.*, p. 51.
11. Needham, *op. cit.*, vol. IV: 3, p. 462.
12. *Ibn Battuta: Travels in Asia and Africa, op. cit.*, pp. 229–30.
13. Hunwick, *Tarikh, op. cit.*, p. 32.
14. The details that follow are drawn from Joseph E. Harris, "Malik Ambar: African Regent-Minister in India," in *African Presence in Early Asia*, ed. Rashidi, *op. cit.*, pp. 146–52; and from *The Oxford History of India* (Oxford: Oxford University Press, 1961), pp. 281–302.
15. Cited by D. R. Seth, "The Life and Times of Malik Ambar," in *Islamic Culture: An English Quarterly* 31 (Hyderabad, January 1957), p. 155.
16. Omar Khalidi, "Research Note: The Case of the Habashis of the Dakan," in *African Presence in Early Asia*, ed. Rashidi, *op. cit.*, pp. 153–54.
17. Irwin, *op. cit.*, p. 245.
18. M. Talki, citing sources, in "The Independence of the Maghrib," in *General History of Africa*, vol. III, ed. M. El Fasi, *op. cit.*, pp. 248–49.
19. *ibid.*, p. 269.
20. Cited by Constable, *op. cit.*, p. 22.
21. E. Lévi-Provençal, *Histoire de l'Espagne musulmane*, vol. 3: (Paris and Leiden: Brill, 1950–53), p. 172.

22. Glick, *op. cit.*, pp. 113–14.

23. *ibid.*, p. 116.

24. Hitti, *op. cit.*, p. 169.

25. Cited in Constable, *op. cit.*, pp. 205–6.

26. *ibid.*, p. 206.

27. Glick, *op. cit.*, pp. 200–1; Irwin, *op. cit.*, p. 246.

28. Glick, *op. cit.*, p. 80.

29. Constable, *op. cit.*, p. 80.

30. Peter C. Scales, *The Fall of the Caliphate of Cordoba* (Leiden and New York: Brill, 1994), p. 75, citing Ibrāhīm b. al-Qāsim al-Kātib al-Qayrawānī.

31. Constable, *op. cit.*, p. 8.

32. J. O'Callaghan, *A History of Medieval Spain* (Ithaca: Cornell University Press, 1975), p. 286.

33. Levtzion, in *The Cambridge History of Africa*, vol. 3, ed. Oliver, *op. cit.*, p. 348.

34. Glick, *op. cit.*, pp. 34–35.

35. *Ibn Battuta: Travels in Asia and Africa, op. cit.*, pp. 314–17.

36. Irwin, *op. cit.*, p. 308.

SIX: INTO BLACK AFRICA

1. Cited in Levtzion, in *The Cambridge History of Africa*, vol. 3, ed. Oliver, *op. cit.*, p. 349.

2. Richard Jobson, *The Golden Trade, or a Discovery of the River Gambia* (1623, reprint London, 1932), p. 106.

3. Roland Oliver and J. D. Fage, *A Short History of Africa* (Harmondsworth, England: Penguin Books, 1962), pp. 85–90.

4. Fisher, in *The Cambridge History of Africa*, vol. 3, ed. Oliver, *op. cit.*, p. 261.

5. *ibid.*, p. 262.

6. J. F. Schon, *Magana Hausa: native literature, or proverbs, tales, fables and historical fragments in the Hausa language, to which is added a translation in English* (London, 1885), p. 52.

7. Ivan Hrbek, "Egypt, Nubia and the Eastern Deserts," in *The Cambridge History of Africa*, vol. 3, ed. Oliver, *op. cit.*, p. 70.

8. Hubert Gerbeau, "The slave trade in the Indian Ocean," in *The African slave trade from the fifteenth to the nineteenth century, op. cit.*, pp. 189–90.

9. Taddesse Tamrat, "Ethiopia, the Red Sea and the Horn," in *The Cambridge History of Africa*, vol. 3, ed. Oliver, *op. cit.*, p. 139.

10. Cited in *ibid.*

11. H. Neville Chittick, "The East Coast, Madagascar and the Indian Ocean," in *The Cambridge History of Africa*, vol. 3, ed. Oliver, *op. cit.*, pp. 188–94.

12. Curtin, *op. cit.*, p. 122.

13. Cited in Randall L. Pouwels, *Horn and Crescent: Cultural Change and Traditional Islam on the East African Coast 800–1900* (Cambridge and New York: Cambridge University Press, 1987), p. 29.

14. Chittick, *op. cit.*, p. 217.

15. *Ibn Battuta: Travels in Asia and Africa, op. cit.*, pp. 112–13.

16. Pouwels, *op. cit.*, p. 53.

17. *ibid.*, pp. 93–94.

18. *ibid.*, p. 78.

19. Richard F. Burton, *Zanzibar: City, Island, and Coast,* vol. 1 (London, 1872), p. 262.

20. The account of Michael W. Shepard in 1844, cited in Norman R. Bennett and George Brooks, *New England Merchants in Africa* (Boston: Boston University Press, 1965), p. 263.

21. Mathew, "The Land of Zanj," in *The Dawn of African History,* ed. Oliver, *op. cit.,* p. 48.

22. Chittick, *op. cit.*, p. 216.

SEVEN: THE OTTOMAN EMPIRE

1. Cited in Andrew Wheatcroft, *The Ottomans* (London: Penguin Books, 1995), p. 23.

2. Cited in Bernard Lewis, *Istanbul and the Civilization of the Ottoman Empire* (Norman, Okla.: University of Oklahoma Press, 1963), p. 27.

3. Halil İnalcik with Donald Quataert, eds., *An Economic and Social History of the Ottoman Empire, 1300–1914* (New York and Cambridge: Cambridge University Press, 1994), pp. 453–54.

4. Leslie P. Peirce, *The Imperial Harem* (New York and Oxford: Oxford University Press, 1993), p. 22.

5. *ibid.*, p. 72.

6. *ibid.*, pp. 99–100, citing *Tarih-I Perçevi,* 2 vols. (Istanbul, 1864–67), vol. 2, pp. 360–61.

7. İnalcik with Quataert, *op. cit.*, p. 285.

8. *ibid.*, p. 597.

9. *ibid.*, p. 729.

10. *ibid.*, p. 598.

11. *ibid.*, pp. 541–42.

12. *ibid.*, p. 716.

13. Lewis, *Race and Slavery in the Middle East, op. cit.,* pp. 80–82.

14. Alan Fisher, in *Macmillan Encyclopedia of World Slavery,* eds. Paul Finkelman and Joseph C. Miller (New York: Macmillan, 1998), p. 663.

15. For a comprehensive study of this, see Mishna Glenny, *The Balkans, 1804–1999* (London: Granta Books, 1999).

EIGHT: THE "HERETIC" STATE: IRAN

1. Y. Armajani, *The Saffavids—A Study in Iranian Nationalism,* a paper delivered at the International Congress of Orientalists, Moscow, 1960, *Congress Papers,* vol. 2, 1963, p. 169.

2. Hitti, *op. cit.*, p. 109.

3. *Encyclopaedia Britannica,* 14th ed., 1937, vol. 17, entry on Persia by Sir Percy Sykes, p. 591.

4. Joseph Harris, *The African Presence in Asia: Consequences of the East African Slave Trade* (Evanston, Ill.: Northwestern University Press, 1971).

5. *ibid.*, p. 77, citing E. Bastani-Parizi, *Tarikh-e-Kerman* (Tehran, 1961), pp. 307, 476.

6. Hunwick, *Tarikh, op. cit.,* p. 25.

7. *ibid.*, p. 33.

8. Thomas M. Ricks, *Slaves and Slave Trading in Shi'i Iran, 1500–1900*, a paper presented at the annual meeting of the American Historical Association, Cincinnati, 1988. I am most grateful to Professor Ricks for having made a copy available to me.

9. *ibid.*, p. 3, citing Adnan Mazara'i, *Tarikh-i Iqtisadi va Ijtima'i-yi Iran va Iraniyan az Aghaz ta Safaviyyih* (Tehran, 1348/1969), p. 314.

10. *ibid.*, citing J. Aubin, *Deux Sayyids de Bam au XVe siècle* (Wiesbaden, 1956), pp. 92, 94.

11. *ibid.*, p. 11, citing Muḥammad Hashim Asaf, *Rustam al-Tavarikh*, ed. Muḥammad Mushiri (Tehran, 1348/1969), pp. 106–7.

12. *ibid.*, citing Mirza Muḥammad Khalil Mara'shi Safavi, *Majmu' al-Tavarikh*, ed. Abbas Iqbal (Tehran, 1327/1948), p. 38.

13. Harris, *op. cit.*, pp. 77–78.

14. *Encyclopaedia of Islam*, *op. cit.*, p. 33.

15. *ibid.*, p. 36.

16. Lady Mary Eleanor Sheil, *Glimpses of Life and Manners in Persia* (London, 1856), pp. 243–45.

17. Harris, *op. cit.*, p. 118.

18. *ibid.*, p. 119.

19. Robert W. Olson, *The Siege of Mosul and Ottoman-Persian Relations, 1718–1743* (Bloomington: Indiana University Press, 1975), p. 106.

20. Charles Issawi, ed., *The Economic History of Iran 1800–1914* (Chicago: University of Chicago Press, 1971), pp. 125–26, citing dispatches in 1842, FO 84/426.

21. *ibid.*, p. 126.

22. John Barrett Kelly, *Britain and the Persian Gulf* (London: Oxford University Press, 1968), p. 602.

23. Lewis, *Race and Slavery in the Middle East*, *op. cit.*, p. 81.

24. Hicks, *op. cit.*, p. 13.

25. *ibid.*, p. 14.

26. *ibid.*, p. 15.

27. *ibid.*, pp. 15–16, citing John D. Gurney, "A Qajar Household and Its Estates," in *Iranian Studies* 16, nos. 3–4 (1983), pp. 137–76.

28. *ibid.*, p. 15, citing Mirza Husayn Khan, "Tachvildar-i Isfahan," in *Jughrafiya-yi Isfahan*, ed. Manuchihr Satudeh (Tehran, 1342/1963), p. 122.

29. *Anti-Slavery Reporter*, 4th series, vol. 18, no. 1, 1898.

30. Henri de Monfried, *Pearls, Arms and Hashish* (New York, 1936), pp. 115–16.

31. Issawi, *op. cit.*, p. 38, citing *Proshloe i nastoyashchee Seistana*.

32. *The Encyclopaedia of Islam*, *op. cit.*, p. 38.

33. *ibid.*, p. 36.

34. Ricks, in *Macmillan Encyclopedia of World Slavery*, *op. cit.*, p. 611.

NINE: THE LIBYAN CONNECTION

1. Herodotus, Book IV, 183, in *The Histories*, ed. Rieu (Harmondsworth, England: Penguin Books, 1954) p. 304.

2. Robert W. July, *A History of the African People*, 4th ed. (Prospect Heights, Ill.: Waveland Press, 1992), p. 35.

3. *Ibn Battuta: Travels in Asia and Africa*, *op. cit.*, p. 337.

4. *ibid.*, p. 338.
5. Magali Morsy, *North Africa 1800–1900* (London and New York: Longman, 1984) p. 53.
6. *ibid.*, p. 59.
7. G. F. Lyon, *A Narrative of Travels in Northern Africa in the Years 1818, 1819 and 1820* (New Impression of 1821 edition, London: Frank Cass, 1966), p. 4.
8. *ibid.*, p. 90.
9. *ibid.*, p. 99.
10. *ibid.*, p. 109.
11. *ibid.*, p. 112.
12. *ibid.*, p. 120.
13. *ibid.*, pp. 121–22.
14. *ibid.*, pp. 200–1.
15. *ibid.*, pp. 280–81.
16. *ibid.*, p. 280.
17. *ibid.*, p. 288.
18. *ibid.*, p. 343.
19. Morsy, *op. cit.*, p. 63.
20. *ibid.*, pp. 129–31.
21. *ibid.*, p. 277.
22. The rate in 1900 was £1 = $4.872; £200,000 in 1900 would be equivalent in value to £10.8 million in February 2000, or—at an exchange rate of £1 = $1.6—to $17.3 million.
23. Curtin, *op. cit.*, p. 53.
24. Henri Duveyrier, *La Confrèrie musulmane de Sidi Mohammed Ben Ali Es Senousie* (Paris: Société de Géographie, 1884), pp. 21–22.
25. John Wright, "The Wadai-Benghazi Slave Route," in *The Human Commodity*, ed. Savage, *op. cit.*, p. 179.
26. Silva White, *From Sphinx to Oracle: Through the Libyan Desert to the Oasis of Jupiter Ammon* (London, 1899), p. 157.
27. A. A. Boahen, *Britain, the Sahara, and the Western Sudan, 1788–1861* (Oxford: Oxford University Press, 1964), p. 186.
28. Nachtigal, *op. cit.*, vol. iii, p. 266.
29. *ibid.*, vol. i, p. 64.
30. *ibid.*, pp. 253–54.
31. *ibid.*, p. 133.
32. *ibid.*, vol. ii, p. 15.
33. *ibid.*, vol. iii, pp. 3–4.
34. *ibid.*, vol. i, p. 133.
35. *ibid.*, p. 701.
36. Austen, in *The Human Commodity*, ed. Savage, *op. cit.*, p. 222.
37. *ibid.*, p. 227.
38. *ibid.*, p. 229.
39. Jamil M. Abun-Nasr, *A History of the Maghrib* (Cambridge: Cambridge University Press, 1971), p. 305.

40. Austen, *op. cit.*, citing British Parliamentary Papers, 1893/94, 85, p. 245.
41. Morsy, *op. cit.*, p. 276.
42. Rosita Forbes, *The Secret of the Sahara: Kufara* (London, 1921), pp. 205–6.
43. Hassanein Bey, *The Lost Oases* (London, 1925), p. 179.
44. Knud Holmboe, *Desert Encounter: An Adventurous Journey through Italian Africa* (London, 1936), p. 188. The exchange rate in 1930 was £1 = $4.862.

TEN: THE TERRIBLE CENTURY
1. V. Maurizi, *History of Seyyid Said* (London, 1819), p. 29.
2. R. W. Beachey, *The Slave Trade of Eastern Africa* (London: Rex Collings, 1976), pp. 48–49, citing *Selections from the Records of the Bombay Government*, 633, no. XXIV, new series (Bombay, 1856).
3. John Iliffe, *A Modern History of Tanganyika* (Cambridge: Cambridge University Press, 1979), p. 42.
4. R. Coupland, *The Exploitation of East Africa, 1856–1890* (London: Faber and Faber, 1939), p. 5.
5. Beachey, *op. cit.*, p. 60.
6. Captain Colomb, R.N., *Slave-Catching in the Indian Ocean* (London, 1873), pp. 395–96.
7. *ibid.*, p. 374.
8. Beachey, *op. cit.*, pp. 122–25.
9. Curtin, *op. cit.*, pp. 235–40.
10. British Sessional Papers, House of Commons: Correspondence relating to the Slave Trade on the East African coast, LXXII, no. 68, January 31, 1866.
11. Beachey, *op. cit.*, p. 132.
12. *ibid.*, p. 135, citing Romolo Gassi, *Seven Years in the Sudan* (London, 1892).
13. British Sessional Papers, *op. cit.*, LXXVIII, no. 57, April 2, 1889.
14. *Anti-Slavery Reporter*, 4th series, vol. 7, November–December 1887.
15. Beachey, *op. cit.*, p. 145.
16. Information provided by Christopher Fyfe.
17. *Anti-Slavery Reporter*, vol. 5, February 1884.
18. De Monfried, *op. cit.*, pp. 106–15.
19. *Anti-Slavery Reporter*, vol. 21, no. 2, May 14, 1878.
20. British Sessional Papers, *op. cit.*, LXI, no. 88, 1870.
21. *Anti-Slavery Reporter*, vol. 20, no. 9, March 1881.
22. A. B. Wylde, *'83 to '87 in the Soudan*, vol. 2 (London, 1888), p. 257.
23. Coupland, *op. cit.*, pp. 165–66.
24. 1871 Committee, 116. Brigadier W. M. Coghlan.
25. A. J. Swann, *Fighting the Slave Hunters in Central Africa* (London, 1910), p. 62.
26. Beachey, *op. cit.*, p. 187, citing Père Guilleme, whose account was contained in Cardinal Lavigerie, *Slavery in Africa* (Boston, 1888).
27. H. M. Stanley, "Slavery and the Slave Trade," *Harpers New Monthly Magazine*, March 1893, p. 622.
28. A. J. Swann, *op. cit.*, p. 48.
29. 1871 Committee, C. Vivian, Q. 25.

30. *ibid.*, Q. 938.

31. David Livingstone, *Narrative of an Expedition to the Zambesi and its Tributaries* (London, 1865), p. 392.

32. Coupland, *op. cit.*, pp. 146–47.

33. 1871 Committee, Vivian, Q. 37, 99–104.

34. Captain G. L. Sulivan, *Dhow Chasing in Zanzibar Waters* (London, 1873), pp. 168–69.

35. *Church Missionary Intelligencer*, April 1893.

36. W. A. Chanler, *Through Jungle and Desert* (London, 1896), p. 214.

37. Beachey, *op. cit.*, p. 259.

38. M. Hiskett, "The Nineteenth-Century Jihads in West Africa," in *The Cambridge History of Africa*, vol. 5, ed. John E. Flint (Cambridge: Cambridge University Press 1976), pp. 138–39.

39. E. W. Bovill, ed., *Missions to the Niger*, vol. III (Cambridge: Cambridge University Press, 1966), p. 420.

40. H. Clapperton, *Journey of a Second Expedition into the Interior of Africa from the Bight of Benin to Soccatoo* (London: Frank Cass, 1966), p. 171.

41. Bovill, *op. cit.*, p. 360.

42. Abdullahi Mahadi, "The Aftermath of the *Jihād* in the Central Sudan as a Major Factor in the Volume of the Trans-Saharan Slave Trade in the Nineteenth Century," in *The Human Commodity*, ed. Savage, *op. cit.*, p. 111.

43. Bovill, *op. cit.*, vol. II, pp. 548–50.

44. Cited in Morsy, *op. cit.*, p. 59.

45. Mahadi, *op. cit.*, pp. 118–19, p. 127, note 51.

46. Nachtigal, *op. cit.*, vol. ii, p. 103.

47. Mahadi, *op. cit.*, pp. 121–22.

48. H. Barth, *Travels and Discoveries in North and Central Africa*, vol. II (London: Frank Cass, 1965), p. 556.

49. Mahadi, *op. cit.*, p. 124.

50. Nachtigal, *op. cit.*, vol. ii, p. 21.

51. Mahadi, *op. cit.*, p. 125.

52. Martin A. Klein, "The Slave Trade in the Western Sudan during the Nineteenth Century," in *The Human Commodity*, ed. Savage, *op. cit.*, pp. 41–43.

53. A. E. Atmore, "Africa on the Eve of Partition," in *The Cambridge History of Africa*, vol. 6 (1985), eds. Roland Oliver and G. N. Sanderson, *op. cit.*, p. 15.

54. Klein, *op. cit.*, p. 48.

55. El Hajj Abd Salam Shabeeny, *An Account of Timbuctoo and Housa: territories in the interior of Africa*, ed. and trans. J. G. Jackson (London, 1820), p. 21.

56. E. Ann McDougall, "Salt, Saharans, and the Trans-Saharan Slave Trade: Nineteenth Century Developments," in *The Human Commodity*, ed. Savage, *op. cit.*, p. 63.

57. *ibid.*, p. 67.

58. *ibid.*, pp. 76–70.

ELEVEN: COLONIAL TRANSLATIONS

1. F. Lugard, *Instructions to political and other officers, on subjects chiefly political and administrative* (London: Waterlow, 1906), p. 136.

2. J. S. Hogendorn and Paul E. Lovejoy, "The Reform of Slavery in Early Colonial Northern Nigeria," in *The End of Slavery in Africa*, eds. Suzanne Miers and Richard Roberts (Madison and London: University of Wisconsin Press, 1988), p. 396.

3. See *ibid.*, pp. 400–7, for details.

4. G. Deherme, *L'Afrique occidentale française: action politique, action économique, action sociale* (Paris: Bloud, 1908), p. 366.

5. Richard Roberts, "The End of Slavery in the French Soudan, 1905–1914," in *The End of Slavery in Africa*, eds. Miers and Roberts, *op. cit.*, p. 285.

6. *ibid.*, p. 288.

7. Census data cited by Klein, *op. cit.*, p. 47. Klein adds qualifications: "There were also sometimes changes in the borders of cercles. There was a tendency in all areas to show an increase as administrators became more familiar with their districts." Yet the extent and incidence of the cited increases suggest the character and scale of the migrations.

8. Roberts, *op. cit.*, pp. 294–302.

9. E. Ann McDougall, "A Topsy-Turvy World: Slaves and Freed Slaves in the Mauritanian Adrar, 1910–1950," in *The End of Slavery in Africa*, eds. Miers and Roberts, *op. cit.*, p. 364.

10. *ibid.*, pp. 364–65.

11. *ibid.*, p. 368.

12. *ibid.*, p. 378, citing various writings and interviews.

13. *ibid.*, pp. 380–82.

14. Lee V. Cassanelli, "The Ending of Slavery in Italian Somalia: Liberty and the Control of Labour," in *The End of Slavery in Africa*, eds. *op. cit.*, Miers and Roberts, pp. 309–10.

15. M. Colucci, *Principi di diritto consuetudinario della Somalia italiana meridionale* (Florence: La Voce, 1924), p. 82.

16. Cassanelli, *op. cit.*, p. 324.

17. Oral recollections from interviews conducted as late as 1970 and cited in *ibid.*, p. 327.

18. Sinclair to Long, April 11, 1917, Colonial Office, 618/17, Public Records Office, London.

19. Frederick Cooper, *From Slaves to Squatters* (New Haven and London: Yale University Press, 1980), p. 112.

20. *ibid.*, p. 120, footnote.

21. *ibid.*, p. 146.

22. A. J. Hughes, *East Africa* (Harmondsworth, England: Penguin Books, 1969), p. 92.

23. Northey to Milner, September 11, 1919, Colonial Office, 533/213.

24. Cooper, *op. cit.*, p. 237.

25. Hughes, *op. cit.*, p. 133.

26. Cooper, *op. cit.*, p. 293.

27. *ibid.*, p. 286.

TWELVE: SURVIVALS OF SLAVERY

1. *Anti-Slavery Reporter,* June 1960, citing report No. 75 of the French Union Session, 1955–56.
2. *ibid.*
3. John Laffin, *The Arabs as Master Slavers, op. cit.,* p. 4.
4. *ibid.,* p. 66, citing James Morris, *The Market of Seleukia* (London: Faber and Faber, 1957).
5. *Al-Ahram,* January 27, 1961.
6. *Al-Goumhouriya,* March 2, 1962.
7. Laffin, *op. cit.,* pp. 69–70.
8. *ibid.,* p. 70.
9. Anti-Slavery Society memorandum of May 18, 1970.
10. Laffin, *op. cit.,* p. 7.
11. *ibid.,* p. 73.
12. Alan Whittaker, "Seven Years in Slavery," *Anti-Slavery Reporter,* 1990, pp. 20–28.
13. The World Bank, Washington, D.C.
14. *Mauritania's Campaign of Terror* (New York and Washington, D.C.: Human Rights Watch, April 1994), p. 1.
15. John Mercer, *Slavery in Mauritania Today* (London: Anti-Slavery Society, 1982), p. 1.
16. Stanley Meisler, "U.N. Agency Assails Sudan, Mauritania on Slavery," *Los Angeles Times,* March 9, 1993.
17. Kevin Bales, *Disposable People* (Berkeley and London: University of California Press, 1999), p. 81.
18. *Mauritania's Campaign of Terror, op. cit.,* p. 84.
19. *ibid.,* p. 85, citing interview in Senegal, May–June 1990.
20. Michelle Faul, "Slavery Abolished in Mauritania but Continues Nonetheless," Associated Press, April 4, 1992.
21. Elinor Burkett, "God Created Me to Be a Slave," *The New York Times Magazine,* October 12, 1997, p. 58.
22. Bales, *op. cit.,* p. 87.
23. Burkett, *op. cit.*
24. *Mauritania's Campaign of Terror, op. cit.,* p. 84.
25. *ibid.*
26. Bales, *op. cit.,* p. 99.
27. *ibid.,* p. 87.
28. Mercer, *op. cit.,* p. 8.
29. *Mauritania's Campaign of Terror, op. cit.,* p. 49.
30. Mark Doyle, "Blood Brothers," *Africa Report,* July–August 1989, p. 16. Doyle personally counted 38 Dakar dead in the central mortuary there.
31. *Mauritania's Campaign of Terror, op. cit.,* p. 26, citing an interview in Dakar, May 14, 1990.
32. In a press release on April 5, 1991, Amnesty International estimated the number of those arrested at 3,000. The annual U. S. Department of State's *Country Reports on*

Human Rights Practices for 1991 estimated that there had been "possibly as many as 3,000 arrests." Some Mauritanian exiles put the number at 5,000.

33. *Mauritania's Campaign of Terror, op. cit.*, pp. 74–75.
34. *Anti-Slavery Reporter*, March 1998, p. 3.
35. The *World Bank Atlas, 1997*, gives a population figure of 26.7 million for the year 1995.
36. *Sudan's Invisible Citizens* (London: African Rights, February 1995), p. 7.
37. Richard P. C. Brown, *Public Debt and Private Wealth, Capital Flight and the IMF in Sudan* (London: Macmillan, 1992), pp. 216ff.
38. *Sudan's Invisible Citizens, op. cit.*, p. 10.
39. David Hurst, *The Guardian*, May 27, 1997.
40. *The Tears of Orphans* (London: Amnesty International Publications, 1995), p. 1.
41. *ibid.*, p. 9.
42. John Vidal, "Great Hunger Bites Sudan's Rebel Tribes," *The Guardian*, September 16, 1998.
43. The locations are listed in *Sudan's Invisible Citizens, op. cit.*, pp. 17–18.
44. *Children of Sudan: Slaves, Street Children and Child Soldiers* (New York and Washington, D.C.: Human Rights Watch Africa, 1985), pp. 20–23.
45. *ibid.*, p. 37, citing Ushari Aḥmad Maḥmud and Suleyman Ali Baldo, *Human Rights Abuses in the Sudan, 1987*.
46. *ibid.*, pp. 40–41, citing sources.
47. Peter Verney, *Slavery in Sudan*, Anti-Slavery International, London, May 1997, p. 23.
48. *ibid.*, p. 5.
49. *ibid.*
50. A. M. Rosenthal, *The New York Times*, April 23, 1999.
51. AP Geneva, reported in *The Guardian*, December 23, 1999.
52. Jennifer Parmelee, "Sudan razes homes, relocates thousands," *The Washington Post*, March 7, 1992.
53. *Sudan's Invisible Citizens, op. cit.*, p. 32.
54. *The Tears of Orphans, op. cit.*, pp. 40–41.
55. UN Doc. E/CN.4/1994/48.
56. *The Tears of Orphans, op. cit.*, p. 111.
57. Mark Huband, *op. cit.*, p. 158.

EPILOGUE: AMERICA'S BLACK MUSLIM BACKLASH

1. Michael A. Gomez, "Muslims in Early America," *Journal of Southern History* 60, no. 4 (November 1994), p. 686.
2. Gilles Kepel, *Allah in the West: Islamic Movements in America and Europe*, trans. Susan Milner (Cambridge: Polity Press, 1997), p. 21.
3. *ibid.*, pp. 21–22.
4. *ibid.*, pp. 16–17, citing mainly Erdmann Doane Benyon, "The Voodoo Cult among Negro Migrants in Detroit," *The American Journal of Sociology*, May 1938, pp. 894–907.

5. Malu Hasa, *Elijah Muhammad: Religious Leader* (New York: 1991), p. 45.
6. Elijah Muhammad, *Message to the Blackman*, new edition (Chicago, undated), pp. 45–46.
7. Malcolm X (with Alex Haley), *The Autobiography of Malcolm X* (New York: Grove, 1973), p. 38.
8. Estimates extend from 100,000 to 250,000, Kepel, *op. cit.*, p. 242, note 8.
9. Peter Goldman, *The Death and Life of Malcolm X* (Urbana: University of Illinois, 1979), p. 6.
10. *Malcolm X Speaks*, ed. George Breitman (New York: Pioneer Publishers, 1965), p. 13.
11. Jonathan Kaufman, *Broken Alliance* (New York: Charles Scribner's Sons, 1988) pp. 75–76.
12. *Malcolm X: Speeches at Harvard*, ed. Archie Epps (New York: Paragon House, 1991), p. 9.
13. Bruce Perry, *Malcolm* (Barrytown, N.Y.: Station Hill Press, 1992), p. 338.
14. "Malcolm Rejects Racist Doctrine," *The New York Times*, October 4, 1964.
15. Arthur J. Magida, *Prophet of Rage: A Life of Louis Farrakhan and His Nation*, (New York: Basic Books, HarperCollins, 1996), p. 32, citing an interview with Farrakhan, August 5, 1993. Magida's book, written with Farrakhan's cooperation, is the source for most of the biography and many of the opinions expressed by Farrakhan cited in this chapter.
16. Karl Evanzz, *The Judas Factor* (New York: Thunder's Mouth Press, 1992), p. 321.
17. *The New York Times*, October 19, 1976.
18. *ibid.*, March 19, 1978.
19. Magida, *op. cit.*, pp. 130–31.
20. *ibid.*, p. 133.
21. The author already encountered these accusations from American blacks in the late 1950s.
22. Magida, *op. cit.*, p. 137, citing C. Eric Lincoln, *The Black Muslims in America* (Queens, N.Y.: Kayode Publications, 1991), pp. 175–77.
23. *ibid.*, p. 141.
24. *ibid.*, pp. 174–76.
25. *ibid.*, p. 179.
26. *ibid.*, pp. 186–87.
27. *ibid.*, p. 200.
28. Clarence Page, *Baltimore Sun*, February 22, 1996.
29. Goitein, *op. cit.*, p. 140. The opinion expressed by Neustadt is cited by Goitein in note 70 on p. 435, and is from Neustadt's article in Hebrew, "Economic Life of the Jews in Egypt during the Middle Ages," *Zion* 2 (1937), pp. 225–26. The one "possible exception" mentioned by Goitein refers to a document which records of a merchant that "he arrived back in Egypt and sold the slavegirls. Because of the defectiveness of the text, it is impossible to say whether this was a Muslim or a Jew." This, too, is part of note 70 in Goitein, p. 435.
30. *ibid.*, p. 211.

31. See Ronald Segal, *The Black Diaspora* (New York: Farrar, Straus & Giroux, 1995), pp. 18–27, and *passim*.

32. Henry Louis Gates, Jr., "Black Demagogues and Pseudo-Scholars," *The New York Times*, July 20, 1992.

33. An impression gained by the author not only from a visit to such a school in Chicago but from interviews with non-Muslim black activists in Detroit and other cities during his researches for *The Black Diaspora*.

34. Kepel, *op. cit.*, p. 9.

35. Andrew Hacker, *Two Nations* (New York: Charles Scribner's Sons, 1992), pp. 197, 227.

36. Elliot Currie, *Reckoning* (New York: Hill and Wang, 1993), pp. 124–25.

37. Hacker, *op. cit.*, p. 180.

38. *ibid.*, footnote on p. 191.

39. *ibid.*, pp. 189–90.

40. Julian Borger, "Black youths face rough justice in US," *The Guardian*, April 27, 2000.

41. Karen Armstrong, *The Battle for God: Fundamentalism in Judaism, Christianity and Islam* (London: HarperCollins, 2000), p. 366.

PERMISSIONS

INDEX

'Abbas, al-, 120, 150
'Abbas I, Shah, 120
'Abbasid dynasty, 22, 77, 120
Abboud, General Ibrahim, 214
'Abd al-Rahman I, 77
'Abd al-Rahman II, 80
'Abd al-Rahman III, 24, 39, 82
Abdallah, Salim b., 101
Abdin, Al Tayib Zain al, 222
Abraham, 17
'Abū Bakr, 11, 20
Abu-Nasr, Jamil M., 142
Abyssinians, 50–51
Afdal, al-, 24
African Liberation Forces of Mauritania
    (FLAM), 209
African Presence in Asia, The (Harris), 121
Africanus, Leo, 93
Afro-Arabs, 49, 61, 150, 157, 160, 161,
    173
Afro-Shirazi Party (ASP), 196–97
Aghlabid dynasty, 53
agriculture, 81, 89, 91, 166; in French
    colonies, 186; in Ottoman Empire, 106;

paid employment in, 180; in Somalia,
    189; Swahili, 99; see also plantation la-
    bor
Ahmadnagar, Sultanate of, 73, 74
Ahmad Shah, 73
Ahmed I, Ottoman Emperor, 110, 112–
    13
AIDS, 235
Akbar, Mughal Emperor, 33, 74
'Alawid dynasty, 54–55
Albanians, 54
Alexander the Great, 17
Algeria, 62, 137
'Alí, 21, 22, 29, 119
'Alí, Muhammad, 54
'Ali, Muhammad (Ottoman Viceroy of
    Egypt), 150
'Ali, Sonni, 91
'Alí, Sultan, 139–40
'Ali ibn Nāfi, Abū'l-Hasian, 80
Al-Ma'mūn, 28
Almohad Empire, 54, 85–87
Almoravid dynasty, 54, 84–86, 89, 91
Ambar, Malik, 73–76

Amnesty International, 216, 217
Amr ibn al-'As, 21
'Anbar, Siddi, 76
Andalusī, Sāid al-, 48
Anglo-Egyptian Convention (1877),
    152
anti-Semitism, 234–39
Anti-Slavery Reporter, 154–56
Anti-Slavery Society, 126–27, 202, 203,
    205, 219
apartheid, 221, 223
Arabia, 13–17, 20, 61, 70, 95, 125–26,
    153; Iran and, 125–26; Mamluk rule
    of, 31; military slaves in, 150; pilgrim-
    ages to, 122; plantation labor in, 44;
    Sanūnsī order in, 138; Whahhabi
    movement in, 162; Zanj rebellion in,
    42–45; *see also* Saudi Arabia
Arabic language, 120, 164, 208
Arabs, 5, 34, 122, 135, 149, 166; Awlad
    Sülayman tribe of, 137; Bedouin, 130;
    in black Africa, 93–96, 98–100; in
    British colonies, 192, 195–97; in
    China, 69; color prejudice of, 46–47;
    in French colonies, 199; in India, 75,
    76; in Libya, 136, 139; Omani, 61, 101,
    145–47; Persian resistance to, 119–20;
    preoccupation with honor of, 39–40;
    slave raids by, 37; in Spain, 77, 83, 86;
    in Sudan, 154, 214, 216, 218; *see also*
    Afro-Arabs
Arabs, The (Hitti), 120
Armenians, 28, 125
Armstrong, Karen, 241
Aryans, Indian, 124
Asian Art Museum (San Francisco), 69
assimilation, social, 61–62
Atlantic Trade, 3, 4, 49, 57, 61, 88, 145,
    241; Ottoman Empire and, 106; Sudan
    as catchment area for, 171
Austen, Ralph, 55, 57, 60, 141–42
Austria, 33; Ottoman Empire and, 116
Awf, 'Abd al-Rahman bin, 35
Awlad Sülayman Arab tribe, 137

Ayyūbid dynasty, 54, 94
Azerbaijan, 28
Azhar, al-, University of, 29
Azizieh, 155

Bade people, 167
Baggara tribe, 154, 219
Baghirmi, 41; Sultanate of, 167–68
Bagirmi, 63
Bahadar, Sultan, 73
Bahmani dynasty, 72–74
Baker, Samuel, 151
Balali, 225
Bales, Kevin, 206, 207
Balkans, 32, 54, 117
Bambara, 165
Bantu language, 97
Baptists, 10
Barbak Shah, Sultan Rukn al-Din, 72
Barbar, Land of, 96
Bari people, 153
Barth, Heinrich, 63
Bashir, Omar Hasan al-, 222
Bashir, wazir of Bornu, 63
Battle for God, The (Armstrong), 241
Battūtā, Ibn, 41, 72, 87–88, 91, 94, 99,
    130
Baybars, 31, 32
Bedouin, 32, 130, 135
Bello, Muhammad, 164
Benadir Company, 187
Benyamine, El Hassan Ould, 206
Berat, Sultanate of, 73–74
Berbers, 23, 29, 30, 37, 62, 122, 130;
    "black," 95; Ibāqī, 93; in Spain, 77, 82,
    83, 85, 86
Bey, Hussanein, 143
Bible, 6, 225, 227, 228
Bidar, Sultanate of, 73–74
Bijapur, Sultanate of, 73–74
Bint m'Bareck, Salkha, 205
Biró, Gaspar, 221
birth rate, 62

Black Muslims, *see* Nation of Islam
bonded labor, 205
Borger, Julian, 240–41
Bornaway, Hadji Aly el, 37–38
Bornu, 37, 41, 63, 91, 94, 137, 151, 165–70
Brahmins, 75
Brazil, 7, 10
Britain, 10, 59, 101, 202; African colonies of, 137, 171, 178–80, 188, 190–97; India Raj, 34, 76, 162; Libya and, 132–37, 140; nineteenth-century slave trade opposed by, 125–26, 141, 145, 147–57, 159–62; Ottoman Empire and, 116; Persia and, 122–23, 125–27; in War of 1812, 225
Buchanan, John, 161
Buganda, 160
Bulgars, 48
Bunyoro, 160
Burckhardt, John Lewis, 37–38, 50–53
Burma, 70
Burton, Richard, 101
Busaidi dynasty, 101
Butlan, Ibn, 38
Byzantine Empire, 16–17, 23, 30–32, 103, 109

capitalism, development of, 4, 104, 106
castration, 40, 80, 95, 109, 170–71
Catholics, 5, 156
Chan Ju-kua, 69
Chêng Ho, 70
China, 25, 67–71, 81, 98, 102
Chingiz Khan, 73, 74
Chittick, Neville, 101
chivalry, Christian code of, 39
Christians, 3, 5, 9, 20, 25–26, 239, 241; African kingdoms of, 94–96; black, 10, 225, 226, 228, 232; castration performed by, 40; code of chivalry of, 39; Crusades of, 30; and empire of Mali, 91; enslavement of, 125, 154;

Ethiopian, 14, 96, 100; identification of slavery with blackness by, 49; Muḥammad and, 15, 17; Muslim alliances with, 33; opposition to slave trade of, 6–7, 10; original sin and, 19; Ottoman Empire and, 103–4, 108–9, 131; Qarmatism and, 29; in Spain, 67, 77, 78, 81, 83–88; Sudanese, 214, 218
Christian Solidarity International (CSI), 220
Chu Fu, 71
Chu Yu, 69, 71
Circassians, 54, 149
civil rights movement, 229–30
clove plantations, 146, 191–92
coffee, transit trade in, 104
Cold War, 197
Colomb, Captain, 148–49
color prejudice, 8, 9, 46–49, 123–24
Colucci, M., 188
Columbus, Christopher, 88
Comer, Lord, 153
Companions, 46
concubines, 4, 24, 38–39, 49–51, 55, 60, 100; in British colonies, 179, 180; eunuchs as, 41; in French colonies, 187; Nubian, 94; in Ottoman Empire, 109–11, 113; in Spain, 80
Congressional Black Caucus, 235
Cooper, Frederick, 191, 194–96
Copts, 28
cotton, 104
crime: in British-controlled Zanzibar, 191; in United States, 239–41
Crone, Patricia, 16, 17
Crusades, 30–31, 104
Currie, Elliot, 239–40
Curtin, Philip, 34, 98, 139

dallāl (slave broker), 38
Danaqli, 152
Darfur, Sultanate of, 151
Davidson, Basil, 57

Deccan party, 73
Denmark, 33
Depression, 195
dervish movement, 188
Dinka people, 218, 219
djariyas (slave wives), 78
Djatts, 28
domestic slaves, 38, 39, 42, 57–58, 100,
    176; in British colonies, 180; in Egypt,
    60, 94, 150, 152; in Spain, 80
Doyle, Mark, 211
Drew, Timothy, 225–26
Dudmurra, Sultan, 140
Dutch, 33
Duveyrier, Henri, 139

East African slave trade, 55, 56, 61
East India Company, 34
Ebery, Brahim Ould, 213
Egypt, 20, 21, 23, 44, 46, 52, 60–62, 150–
    52; Ayyūbid dynasty, 54; Britain and,
    147, 153, 155; castration in, 40; Cru-
    sades in, 31; Fatimid dynasty in, *see* Fa-
    timids; importation of "Nubian" slaves
    to, 94–95; Mamluk dynasty in, 31–32,
    37, 52, 54; military slaves in, 53–54;
    Nasserist, 201; Oromo slaves in, 154; in
    Ottoman Empire, 32, 103, 104, 114;
    plantation labor in, 44; slave market in,
    59; trade routes to, 92–93, 98, 131,
    138, 149–50; Tūlūnid dynasty in, 54;
    wealth in, 24
Elizabeth II, Queen of England, 199
emancipation, 35–37
Encyclopaedia of Islam, 122, 127
England, 34, 75
Ethiopia, 17, 46, 48, 95, 125, 129; Chris-
    tians in, 14, 96, 100; Italian invasion of,
    189; slaves from, 16, 50, 71–73, 123–
    26, 152, 154–55, 202
eunuchs, 39–41, 52–53, 62, 94, 95, 156,
    170; in China, 70; in India, 72; in
    Libya, 133; in Ottoman Empire, 109,

111–14; in Persia, 120–21, 127; in
    Spain, 80

Fadlallah, Rabih, 151
Faqīh, Ibn al-, 67
Fard, Wallace, 226–27, 233
Farrakhan, Louis, 231–37, 241
Fascists, 189
Faso, Mohamed El, 212
Fāṭima, 21, 29
Fatimids, 22, 29, 30, 39, 51, 53, 54, 57,
    94, 95
Federal Bureau of Investigation (FBI),
    226, 231
Fettah Khan, 75
Fezzan, Sultanate of, 131–38
Firuz, Sultan, 72–73
Fisher, H. J., 61, 93
Fodio, Abdullahi dan, 164
Fodio, Usmān dan, 164–66
Forbes, Rosita, 143
France, 77, 101; African colonies of, 62,
    137, 141, 151, 154, 166, 171, 173, 175,
    180–85, 199, 209; Ottoman Empire
    and, 33, 116
Frank, Louis, 62
fratricide, 110
Frescobaldi, Leonardo, 32
From Slaves to Squatters (Cooper), 196
Fruit of Islam, 229, 232
Fulani, 162, 164–65, 168, 169
fundamentalism, 11
Futa people, 174

Galen, 48
Gambia, 92, 174
Gao, 92–93
Garvey, Marcus, 228, 231
Gates, Henry Louis, Jr., 238
Georgians, 125, 149
Germany: African colonies of, 162; Nazi,
    9, 239; Ottoman Empire and, 116

Ghana, 89, 92
Giriama, 194, 196
Glenny, Misha, 122
Glick, Thomas, 58, 78
global economy, bonded labor in, 205
Goitein, E. S., 57
Goitein, S. D., 237–38
Golconda, Sultanate of, 73–74
gold, 23–25, 42, 81–82, 89, 90, 92, 93, 98
Gomez, Michael, 225
Gonzales, Antonius, 59
Gordon, Charles, 152
Greeks, ancient, 95, 129; homosexuality among, 41–42
Guild of the Teachers and Students of the University of al-Azhar, 29
Guinea, 173

Habshis, 71–76
Hacker, Andrew, 240
hadīth (Prophet's sayings), 17–18, 35
hajj (pilgrimage), 18
Hakam II, al-, 24
Halpulaar people, 213
Hammody of Atar, 186–87
Hanafi Muslims, 233
Hapsburgs, 33
Haram, Sheikh el, 53
harems, 24, 39, 153, 156; eunuchs as guards of, 39–41; in Ottoman Empire, 109, 111, 112; in Persia, 120, 121
Harrieff, Hasan, 231
Harris, Joseph, 121–24
Hasan, Abd'l-Muzzafar, 99
Hasan, al-, 21
Hausaland, 164, 167
Hawqal, Ibn, 58, 78, 80
Heikal, Muḥammad, 200
Herodotus, 129
hijra (migration), 15
Hindus, 33, 75, 76
Hippalos, 95

Hitler, Adolf, 235
Hitti, Philip K., 32, 78, 120
Hodgson, Marshall G. S., 40–42
Holocaust, 9, 234, 239
homosexuality, 41–42
Hor, El, 208
Hubbard, Mark, 19
Humanism, 19, 20
Human Rights Watch/Africa, 204
Hungary, Ottoman conquest of, 32, 33
Husayn, 119

Ibāḍī Berbers, 93
Ibn Saud, King of Saudi Arabia, 201
İbrāhīm the Debauched, 113
Ibrahim Shah, 72
Idrīsī, al-, 50, 51, 89, 96, 97
Ifriqiya, 53
Ikshidid dynasty, 52
Ilorin, emirate of, 165
imams (leaders of Islam), 29, 77
India, 61, 67, 70–76, 95, 102; British Raj in, 34, 76, 162; color prejudice in, 124; merchants from, in East Africa, 146, 159, 196; Mughal rule of, 33, 34, 72–76
Indonesia, 34
industrial revolution, 4, 104, 106
infant mortality, 62
Inquisition, 88, 100
International Labor Organization, 205
Iran: color prejudice in, 123–24; see also Persia
Iraq, 20, 21, 80–81; court manners in, 80–81; eunuchs in, 41; messianism in, 28; Mongol invasion of, 30; in Ottoman Empire, 103, 125; wealth in, 24; Zanj rebellion in, 42–44, 93, 102, 121
iron, 97
Irwin, Robert, 88
Ismā'il, 'Alawid, 55
Isma'īlī strain of Shi'a, 29

Italy: conquest of Libya by, 142–43; control of Somalia by, 187–90; silk industry in, 106

Ja'aliyyīn, 150–51
Jahangir, Mughal Emperor, 74, 75
Jalil, 'Abd al-, 137, 138
Jamāl, Shaykh, 116
Jennifer (slave), 203
Jews, 6, 9, 20, 21, 26, 51, 57, 241; castration performed by, 40; Christian attacks on, 30; demonized by Nation of Islam, 234–39; Muḥammad and, 15, 17; in Ottoman Empire, 104; in Qarmat movement, 29; in Spain, 40, 78, 80, 81, 84, 86, 88
jihads (holy wars), 20, 100, 164–67, 173
Johnson, Lyndon, 239
Johnson, Robert, 92
Johnston, Harry, 161
Justice Department, U.S., 240

Ka'ba, 14
Kababash tribe, 154
Kadjars, 122
Kafus, Abu'l-Misk, 52
Kamara, Cheich Saad Bouth, 213
Kānamī, Muḥammad al-Amīn, 165, 167, 168
Kanem, 93–94
Kedourie, Elie, 11
Kelly, John Barrett, 125
Kemal, Mustafa, 34
Kennedy, John F., 230
Kenya, 160, 190, 192, 195
Kepel, Gilles, 226
Khadafi, Muammar, 237
Khadijah, 14
Khaldūn, Ibn, 49
Khamis, Ismail, 217
Kharidjism, 77
Khartoumers, 151

Khusraw, Nasir-I, 54
King, Martin Luther, Jr., 229, 230, 236
Kinta, 175–76
Kiswahili language, 97
Koran, 5, 6, 10, 17–20, 35–36, 40, 93, 115, 120, 134, 160, 164, 184, 203, 226, 239, 241
Kösem, Valide Sultan, 113–14

Laffin, John, 52, 199–200, 202
Laing, Alexander Gordon, 168
Lander, Richard, 64
Lapidus, Ira, 20
Lebanon, 203–4
Lévi-Provençal, E., 78
Levtzion, Nehemia, 44, 86
Lewis, Bernard, 46, 62
Libya, 64, 129–43, 200
Li Hsi-Hsiung, 70
Livingstone, David, 148, 159
Lombard, Maurice, 24, 29
Long Wars, 33
Louis XIV, King of France, 112
Lovejoy, Paul, 56, 57
Lugard, Lord, 178
Lyon, Captain G. F., 132–36

Ma Ba, 173
Maghrib, 29
Maghribi Caliphate, 85
Mahadi, Abdullahi, 167, 171
Mahdi, 28
Mahmud II, Ottoman Emperor, 116
Majid, 147
Malcolm X, 228–32, 235
Mali, empire of, 91
Malik, 'Abdul, 120
Malinda, 70
Mamluk dynasty, 31, 37, 52, 54, 94
Mande clans, 91
Mani, Muḥammad, 93
Mansūr, al-, 54

Mansur, al-Zubair Rahma, 151
manumission, 61, 142
marabouts, 173
Maraka people, 174
Marathas, 75
Marzouk, 201
Mascarene Islands, 61
Masmuda tribes, 85
Masonic movement, 29
Mas'ūdī, al-, 48, 69, 96–97
Mathew, Gervase, 102
matrilineal inheritance, 98
Mau-Mau rebellion, 195
Mauritania, 11, 174, 175; French rule in, 183–87; persistence of slavery in, 204–13, 222
Mauritanian Human Rights Association, 213
Mauvy, Raymond, 57, 59–60
Mbarak, Mohamed ould, 205
Mbaye, Fāṭima, 213
McDougall, Ann, 176, 186
McMurdo, Captain, 153
Meccan Trade and the Rise of Islam (Crone), 16
medicine, ancient, 48
Mehdi, Sheikh Muḥammad, 200–201
Mehmed II (the Conqueror), Ottoman Emperor, 103, 104, 108, 112, 115
Mehmed III, Ottoman Emperor, 112
Mehmed IV, Ottoman Emperor, 113
Menelik, King of Ethiopia, 155
Mesopotamia, Lower, 28
Messianism, 28
Messoud, Boubacar Ould, 206, 213
Methodists, 10
Mijikenda, 194
military slaves, 4, 45–46, 53–55, 166; in Egypt, 150; in India, 74–75; Nubian, 94–95; in Ottoman Empire, 54, 110, 115; in Spain, 80
Miller, A., 127
Million Man March, 236
Ming dynasty, 70

miscegenation, 7, 83
Mlozi, 161–62
Mogadishu, 70; Sultanate of, 96
Mongols, 30–32
Montgomery bus boycott, 229
Moors, 173–75, 183, 185–86
Morocco, 25, 61, 86, 92, 131, 175, 183; castration in, 41; military slaves in, 54–55; plantation labor in, 44; slave market in, 58–59
Morris, James, 200
Morsy, Magali, 130
Mossi people, 174
Moustapha, 205–7
Mu'āwiya al-Marwānī, 'Abu Bakr Muḥammad b., 81
Mu'āwiyah, 21
Mu'izz, 53
Mu'um, 'Abd al-, 85
Mubarak Shah, 72
Mughal Empire, 33, 34, 72–76
Muḥammad (Songhai emperor), 91
Muḥammad, Aḥmad b., 165–66
Muḥammad, 'Alī ibn, 43, 44
Muhammad, Elijah, 227–34
Muhammad, Khallid Abdul, 235–36
Muḥammad, Prophet, 11, 13–20, 29, 35, 40, 46, 64, 71, 98, 120, 138, 165, 169
Muhammad, Wallace, 233
muhtasib (policing official), 38
Mukani, Muḥammed al-, 132, 134, 135, 137
mukātaba (contract between owner and slave), 36
Murad IV, Ottoman Emperor, 113
Musa, Mansa, 91
Muscat, Sultanate of, 125, 202
musicians, slave, 38
Muslim Mosque, Inc., 231
Mustafa, Ottoman Emperor, 112
Mustafa Agha, 112–13
Mustanṣir, al-, 51
Muwaffaq, 43, 44

Nachtigal, Gustav, 63, 140, 141, 170
Nasiri, Ahmad ibn Khalid al-, 65
Nasirid dynasty, 87
Nasser, Gamal Abdel, 200, 201
National Association for the Advancement
  of Colored People (NAACP), 234
National Black United Fund, 234
National Council on Crime and Delin-
  quency, 240
National Democratic Alliance of Sudan,
  222
National Islamic Front (NIF), 216, 218,
  219
Nation of Islam, 225–41
Nazism, 9, 239
Needham, Joseph, 67
Neustadt, David, 238
Ngoni, 161
Nigeria, 178–80
Nkonde, 161–62
Nuba people, 216–19, 221
Nubia, 37–38; Afro-Arabs in, 150; Egyp-
  tian conquest of, 150; gold mines of,
  23, 42; Mamluk rule of, 31; slaves from,
  49–52, 94–95, 123, 124
Numeiri (President of Sudan), 214
Nyerere, Julius, 197

Oman, 17, 61, 101, 145–47, 202
Omdurman, Battle of, 153
Organization of Afro-American Unity,
  231
Oromo, 154
Osman I, 103
Ottoman Empire, 32–34, 103–17, 162,
  171; charitable foundations in, 6, 108;
  economy of, 104–8; Libya and, 131,
  132, 137–42; military slaves in, 54, 110,
  115; nineteenth-century British opposition to slave trade in, 150, 152, 155;
  Persia and, 120, 125; rulers of,
  108–14
Oyo empire, 165

Page, Clarence, 237
Palestine, 25
Party Kingdoms, 83–84
Pasha, Yūsuf, 167–68
Peçevi, Ibrahim, 112
Pehlevi Shahs, 34
Peirce, Leslie, 110
Pemba, 60, 70, 97, 162, 197; British rule
  of, 190, 196; plantation labor on, 45,
  192; slaves exported to China from, 69,
  70
Pentecostalism, 10
Periplus of the Erythraean Sea, The, 95
Persia, 5, 21, 25, 61, 119–27, 155; Chi-
  nese trade with, 70; color prejudice in,
  47–48; homosexuality in, 42; India
  and, 75; Qajar dynasty in, 34; Safavid
  dynasty in, 32–34, 120, 122; Samanid
  dynasty in, 120; Sassanid Empire, 17,
  23, 24, 119
Petherick, J., 150
Pipes, Daniel, 45
plague, 32, 62
plantation labor, 3, 4, 42, 44, 49, 60, 100,
  174, 179; in Egypt, 152; in Ottoman
  Empire, 106; in Zanzibar, 191–92
Poitiers, Battle of, 77
Portuguese, 33–34, 70, 75, 99–101;
  African colonies of, 162
Pouwels, Randall, 100
primogeniture, 6
prostitution, 186, 207
Protestants, 5
Protocols of the Elders of Zion, 235

Qajar dynasty, 34
Qarāmānlī, Ahmad, 132
Qarāmānlī, 'Alī, 137
Qarāmānlī, Muḥammad, 137
Qarāmānlī, Yūsuf, 132, 137
Qaranful, 72
Qarmat movement, 28, 29
Qāsim al-Qarawī, Ibrāhīm b. al-, 80

Qatar, 199
Qu'rān. See Koran
Quraysh tribe, 14–16

Rabāh, Bilāl ibn, 46
Rabāh, Nusayb ibn, 47
racism, 6–11, 64–65, 228; Black Muslims and, 231, 234–37, 239
Ramadan, fast of, 18
Ransom, Oliver, 202
Rashīd, Hārūn al-, 24, 28, 97
Red Sea coast slave trade, 55, 56
Revolt of the Naked, 28
Ricks, Thomas, 121, 126, 127
Roman Empire, 48, 103
Rosenthal, A. M., 220
Rouej, Naji ould, 205
Russia, 116

Sa'dians, 54
Safavid dynasty, 32–34, 120, 122
Said, Nasires, 201
Sa'id, Shaykh, 73
Sa'id, 'Umar b., 166
Said ibn Sultan, Sayyid, 101, 146–47
Salāhuddīn (Saladin), 30, 31
salāt (ritual prayer), 18
Saljuq Turks, 30
Samanid dynasty, 120
Samori, 173–75
Sanūsī, Muhammad bin 'Alī al-, 138, 142
Sanūsī order, 139, 143
Saqatī, al-, 38
Sarwar, Malik, 72
Sassanid Persian Empire, 17, 23, 24, 119
Saudi Arabia, 199–203
Schroeter, Daniel, 59
Science and Civilization in China (Needham), 67
segregation, 8
Segu, 174, 175
Sekkin, 'Abū, 63

Senate, U.S., 235
Senegal, 173, 174, 186, 209, 211–12
shahādah, 18
Shambu, 73
Shari'a (Islamic law), 84, 217
Sharif, Sultan Muhammad al-, 139
Sheil, Mary Eleanor, 122–24, 127
Shi'a Muslims, 21, 22, 28, 33, 34, 73, 119, 120, 122
Siam, 70
Siddis, 71–72, 74, 76
Sierra Leone, 203
Sikasso, 173, 175
silk industry, 104, 106
Slavery Convention (1926), 218
Slavs, 48, 54
smallpox, 64
Società agricola italo-somala (SAIS), 189
Sofala, Land of, 96
Sokoto Caliphate, 168, 178
Somalia, 96, 100, 187–90; slaves from, 202
Songhai Empire, 91–93
SOS-Slaves, 206, 213
South Africa, 221, 223
Spain, 131; Inquisition in, 100; Islamic, 22, 25, 38, 39, 45, 48, 51, 57, 58, 67, 76–88, 202; Jews in, 40, 104
Stanley, H. M., 157
State Department, U.S., 237
Sudan, 11, 29, 30, 44, 57, 65, 152–53, 174; Atlantic Trade and, 171; British control of, 153–54; Egyptian conquest of, 150; French, 180–83; gold mines of, 23; jihads in, 164–67, 173; persistence of slavery in, 213–22; slaves exported from, 94, 131; see also Bornu; Hausaland
Sudan People's Liberation Army (SPLA), 216, 218
Sudan People's Liberation Movement, 222
Sufism, 85
sugar plantations and refineries, 104, 152

Suhaym, 47
Suleiman I, Ottoman Emperor, 111
Süleyman Agha, 113–14
Sultan, Yaʻqūb, 121
Sultan Ḥusayn, Shah, 121
Sundiata, 89, 91
Sung dynasty, 69, 70
sunnah (collection of Prophet's sayings), 17, 36
Sunni Muslims, 21, 30, 33, 73, 119, 120
Supreme Court, U.S., 240
Suwaida, Ishraq as-, 51
Swahili, 70, 97–100, 192, 194
Swann, A. J., 156, 157
Syria, 13, 16, 21, 23, 37, 77; Crusades in, 31; Mamluk rule of, 29; in Ottoman Empire, 32, 33, 103; Umayyad dynasty in, 97

T'ang dynasty, 25, 69
Tadjakan, 175
Talki, M., 78
Tamil states, 73
Tanganyika, 146
Tanzania, 197
taríqah (Islamic orders), 188
Tāshfīn, Ibn, 84, 85
Tāshfīn, Yūsuf b., 54
Teda people, 129
Theodore, Emperor of Ethiopia, 154
Thomson, Joseph, 64
Thousand and One Nights, 40
Tippu Tip, 157
Tobu people, 129
trans-Saharan slave trade, 55–56, 129–31, 139–42, 167–68
Tripolitania, 131
Tuareg, 130–33, 138, 166, 168, 173, 175, 176
Tucker, Bishop, 160
Tucolor, 162
Tughi, Muḥammad b., 52
Tukulor people, 166

Ṭūlūn, Aḥmad b., 53–54
Tūmart, Muḥammad b., 85
Tunisia, 53, 62
Turabi, Hassan al-, 216, 222
Turhan, Valide Sultan, 113–14
Turkey, 34; secularization of, 117
Turkmanchai, Treaty of (1828), 125
Turkmens, 125
Turks, 29, 30, 54, 73; *see also* Ottoman Empire

Uganda, 152, 160
Ukraine, 115
ʻUmar, 20, 21
Umayyads, 21, 22, 77, 81, 97, 120
umma (community of Muslims), 154
Union of Democratic Forces (UFD), 212
United Nations, 199, 203; Commission on Human Rights, 221–22; Working Group on Contemporary Forms of Slavery, 219
Universal Declaration of Human Rights, 199, 222
Universal Negro Improvement Association, 228
Universities Mission to Central Africa, 159
Urban II, Pope, 30
urbanization, 25–26; in Spain, 78
Uthmān, 17
Uthmān ibn Idrīs, King of Bornu, 37
Uzbeks, 125

Valide Sultan, 109, 111, 113
Vandals, 76
Vidal, John, 217

Wadai, Sultanate of, 139
wageni (foreigners), 100
Waller, Horace, 159
Waq-Waq, Land of, 96

War of 1812, 225
War on Poverty, 239
washenzi (barbarians), 100
Wazzan es Zayyati, al-Hasan ben Muḥam-
   mad el, 93
Whah-habi movement, 162
white slaves, 49, 149; eunuchs, 52; in Ot-
   toman Empire, 108–9, 112; in Spain,
   78, 80
white supremacy, 8
Wilberforce, Lord, 202
wine, drinking of, 81
World Bank Atlas, 204
World Community of al-Islam in the
   West, 233
World War I, 9, 117, 182, 194
World War II, 186, 189, 195
Wylde, A. B., 153, 156

Ya'qūb, 120
Ya'qūbī, al-, 93
Yahya, Sherif Ghaleb, 51

Yemen, 16, 17, 61, 98; in Ottoman Em-
   pire, 103, 104
Yezdigird, King of Persia, 119
Yoruba, 165

Zahiri, Khalil al-, 31–32
zakāt (almsgiving), 18
Zanj, 42–45, 47, 49, 60, 93, 99, 102, 121;
   Land of, 96–97
Zanzibar, 60, 96, 97, 101, 146–49, 159,
   162; British control of, 190–92, 195–
   97; plantation labor on, 45; slaves from,
   122, 123, 125, 126; Sultanate of, 61
Zanzibar National Party (ZNP), 196–97
Zeila, 96
Zimbabwe, 98
Zinder, emirate of, 169–70
Zirids, 53
Ziryāb, 80–81
Zoroastrians, 20, 47
Zotts, 28
Zubayr, Rabih al-, 173